T0207469

Communications in Computer and Information Science 1523

More information about this series at https://link.springer.com/bookseries/7899

Giancarlo Succi · Paolo Ciancarini ·
Artem Kruglov (Eds.)

Frontiers in Software Engineering

First International Conference, ICFSE 2021
Innopolis, Russia, June 17–18, 2021
Revised Selected Papers

 Springer

Editors
Giancarlo Succi ⓘ
Innopolis University
Innopolis, Russia

Paolo Ciancarini ⓘ
University of Bologna
Bologna, Italy

Artem Kruglov ⓘ
Innopolis University
Innopolis, Russia

ISSN 1865-0929   ISSN 1865-0937 (electronic)
Communications in Computer and Information Science
ISBN 978-3-030-93134-6   ISBN 978-3-030-93135-3   (eBook)
https://doi.org/10.1007/978-3-030-93135-3

This Springer imprint is published by the registered company Springer Nature Switzerland AG
The registered company address is: Gewerbestrasse 11, 6330 Cham, Switzerland

Preface

This volume contains the papers presented at the International Conference on Frontiers in Software Engineering (ICFSE) held during June 17–18, 2021, in Innopolis, Russia.

All of the submitted research papers went through a rigorous peer-review process. Each paper was reviewed by three members of the Program Committee. Only 13 were accepted as short papers with an acceptance rate of 35%.

These days, it's hard to overestimate the importance of the IT industry: software, smart devices, computers, and networks - we interact with them nonstop. Certain areas of IT are very widely covered both in the scientific community and in industry. It is all the more surprising that software engineering, the methodological basis of software development, is not well covered, and only a few scientific conferences around the world are devoted to this topic.

The International Conference on Frontiers in Software Engineering is intended to remedy this situation and provide a platform, mostly for young scientists and industry representatives, to highlight new and relevant ideas and concepts in this field. The conference covers such topics as software engineering tools and environments, empirical software engineering, model-driven and domain-specific engineering, human factors and social aspects of software engineering, cooperative, distributed, and global software engineering, component-based software engineering, software metrics, and software engineering for green and sustainable technologies.

We hope that you will find the ICFSE 2021 post-proceedings useful for your professional and academic activities. Finally, we would like to thank all the people who contributed to ICFSE 2021 including the authors, the sponsors, the reviewers, the volunteers, and the chairs.

November 2021

Giancarlo Succi
Paolo Ciancarini
Artem Kruglov

Organization

Program Committee Chairs

Giancarlo Succi	Innopolis University, Russia
Paolo Ciancarini	University of Bologna, Italy

Organizing Committee Chair

Artem Kruglov	Innopolis University, Russia

Program Committee

Tony Wasserman	Carnegie Mellon University, USA
Vladimir Ivanov	Innopolis University, Russia
Ioannis Stamelos	Aristotle University of Thessaloniki, Greece
Andrey Sadovykh	Innopolis University, Russia
Luigi Benedicenti	University of Regina, Canada
Daniel Russo	Columbia University, USA
Alessandro Golkar	Skoltech, Russia
Panos Fitsilis	University of Thessaly, Greece
Letizia Jaccheri	Norwegian University of Science and Technology, Norway
Leonid Dorosinsky	Ural Federal University, Russia

Contents

Institutional Commitment and Leadership as Prerequisites for Successful Comprehensive Internationalization

Iouri Kotorov[1], Yuliya Krasylnykova[1], Petr Zhdanov[2], Manuel Mazzara[2(✉)],
Hamna Aslam[2], Elmira Akhmetgaraeva[2], Maria Naumcheva[2],
and Joseph Alexander Brown[2]

[1] Karelia University of Applied Sciences, Joensuu, North Karelia, Finland
[2] Innopolis University, Innopolis, Republic of Tatarstan, Russian Federation
m.mazzara@innopolis.ru

Abstract. Internationalization of higher education institutions in the twenty-first century is commonly regarded as a process that is essential for the development of a wide range of activities and engagements. Nowadays, a growing number of leaders of higher education institutions do not question the need of internationalization, but instead are actively looking for the ways of how to engage in it. Becoming an increasingly important phenomenon in higher education, the internationalization is though often practiced as an incremental adjustment to the current international activities of a university. However, a considerable body of evidence suggests that it is critical for the higher education institutions to develop a systematic approach to internationalization. Emerging in research as a powerful tool to international advancement of a higher education institution, the internationalization has attracted considerable attention. This paper seeks to explore the institutional practices of internationalization in higher education within the framework of 'comprehensive internationalization' proposed by the Center for Internationalization and Global Engagement (CIGE). The present paper has a dual purpose, firstly, to explore and build upon previous findings in this area to advance the discussion around such an important topic as internationalization and, secondly, to inform the actions of higher education leaders as well as other stakeholders on building international activities to further the university's mission and objectives and make a positive social impact.

Keywords: Internationalization · Higher education · Globalization

1 Introduction

Internationalization as an answer to accelerating globalization has received an increased attention in the twenty-first century, especially among researchers and practitioners of higher education. The two terms of 'internationalization' and 'globalization' are certainly linked, but should not be used interchangeably. The

G. Succi et al. (Eds.): ICFSE 2021, CCIS 1523, pp. 1–11, 2021.
https://doi.org/10.1007/978-3-030-93135-3_1

former, in particular in higher education, is considered as a process that 'involves increasing the range of international activities within universities and between universities and other educational institutions and the numbers of international students and academic staff' [1], while the latter generally represents the trends of the increasing international interdependence and growth of cross-border activities. The globalization thus urges universities across the world to re-invent themselves and to introduce transformative institutional changes that would serve as a 'foundation for a balanced and integrated university experience at the interface of global and local exposure' [2]. The transformative institutional changes that the internationalization brings, are often conceived as a means to gain a competitive advantage on international markets and also to internationalize current practices and strategies of a university [1].

The definition of internationalization as such remains being a subject of significant debate despite the growing number of publications dedicated to it. The most often cited and arguably the most encompassing definition of internationalization in higher education is suggested by Knight [3] who describes the internationalization as:

"the process of integrating an international, intercultural or global dimension into the purpose, functions or delivery of post-secondary education".

Although Knight's definition demonstrates the procedural and integrative nature of internationalization, it remains fairly vague in further description. One of the most practically-oriented definitions though might be formulated by Center for Internationalization and Global Engagement (CIGE) [4] that argues that the internationalization is:

"a strategic, coordinated process that seeks to align and integrate international policies, programs, and initiatives, and positions colleges and universities as more globally oriented and internationally connected institutions. This process requires a clear commitment by top-level institutional leaders, meaningfully impacts the curriculum and a broad range of stakeholders, and results in deep and ongoing incorporation of international perspectives and activities throughout the institution".

Additionally to integration, the other essential requirements of internationalization are mentioned as to be aligning in its nature and leadership-driven, if a university has the objective to introduce a meaningful change. To represent the 'comprehensive' process of integration of policies, programs, and initiatives, CIGE [4] also proposed a model for the implementation of 'comprehensive internationalization' at higher education institutions. The model depicts internationalization as a double arrow linking six pillars that collectively form a 'comprehensive internationalization' approach: (1) articulated institutional commitment, (2) administrative leadership, structure, and staffing; (3) curriculum, co-curriculum and learning outcomes; (4) faculty policies and practices; (5) student mobility; (6) collaboration and partnerships. The interconnectedness of individual pillars through the 'comprehensive internationalization' demonstrates the idea that progress or lack of it in one area can have a positive or negative impact on the others [1]. Although the system of six pillars brings clarity to the overall process of the implementation of internationalization, it should not be understood as a model for the standardization of higher education institutions. Instead, universities are encouraged to use the internationalization to differentiate themselves, promote cultural diversity, including promotion of their own culture, as well as to foster intercultural understanding, respect, and tolerance among peoples' [5]. The curricula, policies and practices in a particular university of a particular country might require a specifically adjusted internationalization approach taking into account the culture and socio-economic conditions [6].

As the purpose of this paper is to explore the practices of internationalization within the systematic approach, the practically-oriented breakdown of 'comprehensive internationalization' proposed by CIGE will be beneficial to categorize the possible internationalization practices. A limitation of this approach is that certain internationalization practices are intertwined between several of pillars and thus could arguably belong to each of them. Such cases will be discussed individually and their primary inclusion criteria will be noted. The internationalization practices discussed in this paper represent measures, policies, programs, and activities that develop and guide internationalization efforts and facilitate internationalization progress of higher education institutions. Despite its exploratory nature, the purpose of the present paper is to build upon previous findings and to advance the discussion around the internationalization and thus to assist higher education leaders, practitioners, and other relevant stakeholders to further their missions and more effectively achieve their objectives of internationalization.

2 Articulated Institutional Commitment

Higher education institutions across the world are in a period of significant transformation. The accelerating globalization and the emergence of global markets urge universities to become increasingly internationally competitive, in particular, in providing quality education, attracting talented students and researchers, and securing funding of their operations and projects. The competitiveness that previously was a driving force primarily for private sector nowadays shifts even the public sector towards managerialism [7]. Although the use of business-like principles and practices in higher education can undoubtedly bring the efficiency and the effectiveness, such transformation of higher education institutions and their adaptation to the new international realities requires comprehensive strategical, structural and cultural institutional adjustments [8]. This section will mostly discuss the strategical aspect of institutional adjustments to globalization while the structural and cultural aspects of it will be examined further in the text.

In higher education, internationalization is often discussed as a process that is fundamental to the successful adaptation to globalization. As Maringe and Gibbs [9] argue, the higher education institutions that successfully adapted the internationalization demonstrate: (1) an articulated institutional commitment with well-defined strategies and objectives; (2) an expanding scope and scale of international student and staff exchange programs; (3) a strong position on the international student recruitment market; (4) practices of international educational services export; (5) integration of international aspects into curriculum and pedagogical approaches; (6) development of internationally focused research; and (7) development of joint research and other higher education initiatives with international and global organizations. Considering these characteristics of a successfully internationalized university, it can be concluded that the internationalization does not only assist in the integration of international or intercultural aspects into the educational and research activities but also helps to establish the business-like principles and practices such as strategy development or services export, and scale them internationally.

The first and foremost decision when introducing internationalization at the higher education institutions must be taken regarding the key internationalization strategic choices. As the internationalization can be referred to as:

"an ongoing, future-oriented, multidimensional, interdisciplinary, leadership-driven vision that involves many stakeholders working to change the internal dynamics of an institution to respond and adapt appropriately to an increasingly diverse, globally focused, ever-changing external environment [10],"

it becomes clear that the role of the leadership of a university and its vision are central to the strategy development process. Although strategies are formal institutional documents, they do not have a single format. Most certainly the strategies include mission statements and the objectives formulated based on the vision of the leadership of a university. Besides the central direction of development, the strategies as one of the tools that managerialism brought to higher education, are supposed to guide the planning, target-setting, implementation and control processes of their activities [11]. In other words, the strategies, especially the overall institutional strategies, have to identify the mission statement of a university, its objectives, the social, cultural, political and economic environment in which the university operates, the target markets of students and staff and the ways to reach them as well as the assessment procedures to evaluate the progress. The fact that all three principal functions of universities, including education, research and knowledge transfer, offer global prospects, obligates the universities to include international aspects into their strategies [12]. The invasive nature of internationalization only proves the critical importance of it for the higher education institution as a whole and suggests the prioritization of it as the inability of achieving the desired state of international affairs of the university may 'throw the whole system into jeopardy' [13]. The emphasis on internationalization typically is either incorporated in the overall institutional strategy or articulated in a separately developed formal internationalization strategy. If published separately, its close alignment with the overall institutional strategy has to be considered. Ideally, the internationalization strategy must only strengthen the institutional strategy.

The strategizing process of higher education institutions becomes though even more challenging in the globalized environment of the twenty-first century. The global markets of students and staff bring new aspects for the universities to consider while articulating the strategies. With the growing national and cultural diversity of international students, faculty members, and staff on campus, the first and the foremost aspect to be considered might be the ethics or the course of actions, values, beliefs, and understandings in the multicultural environment that the strategy encourages. Regarding the encouragement of the academic and administrative staff, the notion of responsibilization in higher education is often discussed that suggests that there must be a system established at the university that would specify and impose what is expected of each employee and recognize and reward responsible and successful behavior [14]. The new ethical multiculturalism or what might be referred to as 'international mindedness' is one of the practices to be expected and rewarded for in the twenty-first century as well as to be promoted among individuals, cultures, and societies, especially on campus [15]. The dynamic nature of international student enrollment and exchange as well as the dynamic nature of international research and collaboration only bring another layer of challenges and support the institutional initiatives aimed at the regular contextual analysis and revision of the institutional and internationalization strategies.

Additionally to strategizing, the managerialism and internationalization in higher education also transformed financial management. As internationalization as a comprehensive process might require significant level of commitment and investments, the largest part of funding typically is covered by the internal resources of a higher education institution. The emergence of global markets though allowed universities to gain the access to various new external sources of income and funding such as international student fees, international research organizations, international non-government organizations, and others. Considering the risks of internal investments and the emergence of international funding, as it is argued by Taylor [11], human resources with new skills of higher education and internationalization administration are required, especially equipped with international marketing, business planning, and risk management skills. These skills will help to efficiently distribute the resources, recover the internal investments, grow the external income sources, and attract the external funding. Even though the current trends might radically challenge modern universities in adaptation to the new international realities, they are also able to reward those that respond with an entrepreneurial spirit with the access to the new forms of cross-border activities and international income and funding sources.

The overall progress of institutional internationalization as a rule is monitored by the higher education institutions using internal data collection, but also can be assessed based on the world university rankings. The rankings are generally the listings of universities ranked according to several estimates, including international outlook and internationalization of education, research and knowledge transfer. In terms of internationalization, the evaluation criteria of rating agencies often include number of international students, number of international staff, and reputation among international researchers and employers. The rankings are constructed and published by the independent rating agencies such as ShanghaiRanking Consultancy (ARWU), Times Higher Education, QS Quacquarelli Symonds and others, the recent emergence of which is often explained by the four main drivers: (1) transition to knowledge-intensive economies; (2) demographic pressures and the global pursuit of talent; (3) criticality of higher education to the economy and society; and (4) informed student choice and consumerist attitudes towards higher education [16]. It can even be argued that the rankings have significantly contributed to the establishment of the international market of higher education of the twenty-first century. It is worth noting that the rating agencies provide mostly the quantitative data and their rankings processes, evaluations and methods are barely transparent and accountable [17]. Therefore, it is highly recommended for the universities to also internally collect and analyze quantitative and qualitative data such as the integration of internationalization into the university's culture, its motto and campus life; influence of internationalization of campus life on its members and societies; quality of teaching and learning of global skills cultural awareness, and the sense of global responsibility; and improvement of university's academic partnerships and research activities. The evident difference between the data that is collected by the rating agencies and the data to be collected internally raises the point of the importance to strategically define the progress criteria that will not merely serve the improvement of the ranking position but will be beneficial for the qualitative improvements of a higher education institution with the development of its internationalization. Although the internationalization has already become an essential and vital aspect of higher education, it still might be a time-consuming, resource-demanding, and fairly long process for certain universities. Furthermore, considering the fact that the rating agencies publish in their listings only the limited number of the top universities large number of which have a history of tens of years, it could be rational for the universities not to change the institution's strategy and mission to comply with the ranking criteria and to put their long-term focus on the qualitative improvements that the internationalization can bring.

3   Administrative Leadership, Structure, and Staffing

The relatively recent phenomena of globalization and the global markets represent nowadays a new global environment in which the universities of the twenty-first century operate. The fact that universities are now exposed to the international competition not merely poses the threats but simultaneously offers new opportunities, especially for the innovative and forward-thinking universities. The internationalization of higher education, as it has been discussed in the previous section, is a key strategy adopted by universities as a response to the influence of accelerating globalization and the emergence of global markets, the implementation of which requires the university-wide integration. As the strategy and structure of the university have long been considered as fundamental variables of organizational change and innovation, it is reasonable to suggest that the internationalization also requires adjustments to the university's structure [8]. The institutional structural adjustments might involve development of new leadership forms and offices, development of new hiring policies and training programs for administrative and academic staff, and changes in the organizational culture [18].

The wide scope of international activities that a university in the twenty-first century might be engaged in and the complexity of the internationalization as a process from the managerial perspective require strong university leadership, accountable organizational structure, and professional staff. Even though the forms of leadership and the organizational structures of higher education institutions may differ depending on the particular institutional strategy, its objectives, and organizational culture, the key elements of organizational arrangements of the universities since the intensification of the international competition, as argued by Foskett [12], are common: (1) the president, chancellor, rector, or as it is sometimes called the director of a university has a well-articulated strategic vision of the development of the university and recognizes the vital role of internationalization for the overall institutional development; (2) there is a senior member of institutional leadership, typically holding a position of vice-president, vice chancellor or vice-rector, that is responsible for the internationalization and international activities; (3) the university has an international office or international relations office established for the coordination and implementation of the internationalization strategy. The three necessary structural characteristics of the internationally engaged universities above all demonstrate the internationalization's administratively intensive nature.

The top leadership of a university as a management body consists of the president, chancellor, rector, or director of the university and its deputies or senior members of leadership that may hold the positions of vice-presidents, vice-chancellors, vice-rectors depending on the particular university structure. Although the presidents are generally considered to be the top catalysts for the internationalization of higher education institutions, the other administrative staff are playing the key roles [1]. The international office of a university that is directly involved into coordination of the internationalization reports in such structure to the vice-president, vice-chancellor or vice-rector for internationalization. As the American College President Study's research demonstrates that more than half of the responding presidents of higher education institutions do not have any type of international experience or training [1], the second element of the university leadership structure of internationally engaged universities which is the senior member of leadership who is responsible for internationalization is often the key driver of internationalization in the university. The lack of international perspective only hampers the presidents from the complete understanding of the international aspects of higher education and the position of vice-president, vice chancellor or vice-rector for internationalization who has a well-articulated vision of what its means to be an internationally engaged university becomes essential for the development and management of the internationalization strategy. The appointed senior member of leadership as the primary driver of internationalization must report directly to the president and be actively involved into the discussion of the institutional strategy, especially its international aspects, manage the linkages and partnerships of the university, and represent the university on the global arena [1]. The position of senior member of leadership for internationalization as such is most likely becoming a necessary feature and common practice of the higher education in the twenty-first century.

The effective integration of the internationalization of a university is typically coordinated by a single office [1]. Therefore, the last but certainly not least element of the organizational arrangements of the globally engaged universities after the recognition of the institutional internationalization as a key strategic activity by the president of the university and the appointment of the senior member of leadership for internationalization is the establishment of international office that could act as a central unit of internationalization and international activities. The administrative staff of the international office plays a key role in the institutional internationalization as its functions may include negotiation of partnerships, maintenance of the global networks, and development of mobility and joint-research programs. The operations of the international office are coordinated by the head of the office. The subordinate coordinators of the international office might either be assigned to the faculties of the university or work as the university-wide coordinators depending on how integrated the faculties and departments are. The integrated universities provide strong formal interconnectedness between university management and the university's faculties and thus provide a centralized decision-making process, while in the non-integrated universities the faculties represent autonomous legal bodies with their own decision-making authority [19]. Independently from the degree of the integration of the faculties, international offices must have good links with all other departments, faculties, and services of a university to fully realize their tasks and the overall institutional internationalization.

Discussing the three elements of the structural arrangements of the internationally - oriented universities and the overall integration of the internationalization, it is critical to point out the factors that might significantly influence the university internationalization. One of the factors that has been gaining an increased attention in the academic literature over the last two decades is the organizational culture. Unlike the strategy and its objectives, that due to the international prospects of teaching, research, and knowledge transfer, have to incorporate international aspects and thus might only encourage internationalization, the organizational culture depending on its attributes can either hinder or facilitate the process of internationalization. Developed as a result of the high frequency of social interactions, the organizational culture, particularly in the university, represents the values, beliefs and attitudes of everyone associated with it, including institutional top leadership, board members, academic and administrative staff, and students [8]. Based on the typology of Sporn [20], organizational cultures can be characterized by two attributes: (1) weak or strong; (2) internally focused or externally focused. Although the weak and internally focused organizational culture with its characteristic internal disintegration of units and focus on bureaucracy can be effective in certain environments, such culture will not provide a significant contribution and rather hinder the process of the comprehensive university-wide internationalization. The typology implies that the strong and externally focused organizational culture is more likely to provide support to the management to adapt to the dynamic external environment. Shared values, meanings, understandings, commitment to entrepreneurship, and flexibility of the strong and externally focused culture can certainly help to integrate the internationalization effectively [8].

All three elements of the organizational arrangements of the internationally-oriented universities also depend on the professionalism of the academic and administrative staff. The overall professionalization of higher education and its internationalization as an intrinsic aspect of higher education is one of the recent trends in the university management of the twenty-first century. The emergence of such organizations as the American Council on Education's Center for Internationalization and Global Engagement in the United States of America and the European Association for International Education in Europe only supports the importance of internationalization and the need of universities for the expertise, research, networking, collaboration and additional resources in this area [11]. International literacy becomes a high priority in higher education [8]. The international literacy of the academic and administrative staff of the university as well as its overall internationalization can be easily examined looking at the mission statement, strategic plan, job descriptions of the top leadership and other information that can be found on the website of the university. Also, the universities of the twenty-first century realize the need to establish globally focused development programs for the academic and administrative staff not necessarily working in the international offices but employed in the enabling offices such as admissions, education, student affairs offices, housing [1]. Experts with the professional experience of international activities, especially in the educational sector, are actively sought after by the globally engaged universities as only the formalized structures with professionals associated with it can guarantee accountability and quality assurance in the internationalization of higher education.

4 Conclusions

Globalization is dramatically reshaping political and economic boundaries, increasing the exchange flow of almost everything - especially in education. Institutions of higher education that remain incapable of operating effectively within the framework of globalization, will be at a disadvantage more than ever before. Thus, internationalization should be seen as a necessity rather than a requirement.

Internationalization of higher education institutions in the twenty-first century is definitely a time-consuming, resource-demanding, and fairly long process. As a result, institutional commitment and administrative leadership become pivotal as they lay the foundation on which other components of internationalization will be then based.

It is worth pointing out that comprehensive internationalization is driven by the mission, values, and motivations of these institutions. However, the final goal of comprehensive internationalization is not to prescribe a specific model or standard, but by recognizing a diversity of approaches, to allow each institution to choose its own path, which is consistent with its mission, values, programs, and resources.

At present, just a few institutions have made the systemic commitment to comprehensive internationalization. What differentiates these institutions is that they usually have a broad, deep, and long-standing framework of views and commitment at all levels including administration, teaching and research staff, and students, while others start comprehensive internationalization virtually from scratch quite often having very little or no experience in international matters or just having the student and staff mobility.

Recognizing the ever-changing global environment, higher education institutions should strategize to make sustainable and systemic changes to their structure, processes and activities to let comprehensive internationalization be successful. And, this could be one of the possible directions for future research.

References

1. Robson, S.: Internationalization: a transformative agenda for higher education? Teach. Teach. **17**(6), 619–630 (2011)
2. Cross, M., Mhlanga, E., Ojo, E.: Emerging concept of internationalisation in South African higher education: conversations on local and global exposure at the university of the Witwatersrand (wits). J. Stud. Int. Educ. **15**(1), 75–92 (2011)
3. Knight, J.: Updated definition of internationalization. Int. High. Educ. (33) (2003)
4. Helms, R.M., Brajkovic, L.: Mapping internationalization on us campuses. American Council on Education, Washington, DC (2017)
5. International Association of Universities. Towards a century of cooperation: internationalization of higher education (1998)
6. Becker, R.F.J.: International branch campuses: markets and strategies. Observatory on Borderless Higher Education (2009)
7. Chan, D., Lo, W.: Running universities as enterprises: university governance changes in Hong Kong. Asia Pac. J. Educ. **27**(3), 305–322 (2007)
8. Bartell, M.: Internationalization of universities: a university culture-based framework. High. Educ. **45**(1), 43–70 (2003)
9. Maringe, F., Foskett, N.: Globalization and Internationalization in Higher Education: Theoretical, Strategic and Management Perspectives. A&C Black (2012)
10. Ellingboe, B.J.: Divisional strategies to internationalize a campus portrait: results, resistance, and recommendations from a case study at a us university. Reform. High. Educ. Curric.: Int. Campus **1998**, 198–228 (1998)
11. Taylor, J.: The management of internationalization in higher education. Glob. Int. High. Educ.: Theor. Strategic Manag. Perspect. 97–107 (2010)
12. Foskett, N.: Global markets, national challenges, local strategies: the strategic challenge of internationalization. Glob. Int. High. Educ.: Theor. Strategic Manag. Perspect. 35–50 (2010)
13. Gross, E.: Universities as organizations: a research approach. Am. Sociol. Rev. 518–544 (1968)
14. Amsler, M., Shore, C.: Responsibilisation and leadership in the neoliberal university: a New Zealand perspective. Discourse Stud. Cult. Polit. Educ. **38**(1), 123–137 (2017)

15. Maringe, F.: The meanings of globalization and internationalization in he: findings from a world survey. Glob. Int. High. Educ.: Theor. Strategic Manag. Perspect. **1**, 17–34 (2010)
16. Hazelkorn, E.: Rankings and the Reshaping of Higher Education: The Battle for World-Class Excellence. Springer, Heidelberg (2015)
17. Hammarfelt, B., De Rijcke, S., Wouters, P.: From eminent men to excellent universities: university rankings as calculative devices. Minerva **55**(4), 391–411 (2017)
18. Rumbley, L.E.: Internationalization in the universities of Spain: changes and challenges at four institutions. Glob. Int. High. Educ.: Theor. Strategic Manag. Perspect. **207** (2010)
19. Draskic, V., et al.: Organising successful student mobility. A guide for mobility officers. King Baudouin Foundation (2014)
20. Sporn, B.: Managing university culture: an analysis of the relationship between institutional culture and management approaches. High. Educ. **32**(1), 41–61 (1996)

Software Engineering as an Alchemical Process: Establishing a Philosophy of the Discipline

Manuel Mazzara$^{(\boxtimes)}$ ⓘ, Mirko Farinaⓘ, Adéla Krylováⓘ, Elizaveta Semenova, and Mosab Mohamed

Innopolis University, Universitetskaya 1, Innopolis, Russian Federation
m.mazzara@innopolis.ru

Abstract. Far from being a bizarre pastime, alchemy played a crucially important role in the history of science, being supported and promoted by leading political and scientific figures (such as Rudolf II, Jābir ibn Hayyān, Gerard of Cremona, Adelard of Bath, Roger Bacon, Paracelsus, and even Newton). To understand alchemy, however, one has to approach it from both a material and a spiritual (perhaps philosophical) perspective. On the one hand, alchemists wanted to transform, or better transmute, materials (such as lead into gold). On the other hand, though, alchemists were also aiming at transforming qualities and aspects of themselves. In this paper, we show that Computer Science, and in particular Software Engineering, can be partly understood as alchemical processes. We thus draw analogies and specify points of contact between these two, prima facie, distinct and very distant worlds. In doing so, we also formulate and discuss a number of important questions regarding the nature and metaphysics of computation, that can be of interests to many researchers in computer science.

Keywords: Software engineering · Software Process · Alchemy · Artificial Intelligence · Artificial intuition

1 Introduction

Despite fantastic achievements attained in software engineering in recent decades, it can be argued that meta-theoretical reflections on the role and status of the discipline are somewhat lagging behind. Probably, most illustrative in this respect, is the debate started by Knuth and colleagues back in the 1970s on the understanding of programming as an art rather than as a mere science or formalised engineering practice [47,84]. Knuth famously argued that attempts to place programming on the scale of an evolutionary progression from artisanal practice to formalised process, tend to ignore some of the key (and most crucial) aspects of this rather unique type of human activity. Knuth argued, computer science ought to be understood as a form of art, progressing and embracing a

© Springer Nature Switzerland AG 2021
G. Succi et al. (Eds.): ICFSE 2021, CCIS 1523, pp. 12–31, 2021.
https://doi.org/10.1007/978-3-030-93135-3_2

variety of techniques and methods that are alternative but also quintessentially complementary to those traditionally deployed by scientific disciplines [48].

Knuth further defended this intuition [49] and famously argued for the existence of a sense 'of software aesthetics' among computer scientists [46].

Knuth's ideas became very influential in computer science. For example [11], following Knuth, claimed that software should be considered as an artistic medium. More recently, [24] explored the interrelations and profitable relationships between art and aesthetics, demonstrating that they can both coalesce to boost and enhance creativity and productivity among software developers [25].

As the recent evolution of programming demonstrates, we can say that Knuth's ideas were largely correct in as much as computer science and software engineering have not been reduced to a mere set of formalised practices [21,70].

Under the scope of software engineering, programming is often seen as a low-level activity. This viewpoint must shift if we are to more clearly depict programs as models, while textual programs are relegated to the role of assembly language-a necessary but low-level construct. Programming is a very creative experience. Important discoveries can be made by coincidence or even through misunderstanding during the programming process. The programming language itself is designed to be used in a specific way (grammar and terms, syntax), but what it expresses has not been fixed, giving the programmer a lot of flexibility in using it. Programming is a never-ending process of discovery, and enlisting the help of others to construct a program for you leaves out a lot of the creative aspects that are crucial to the work's ultimate aesthetic and even substance [25].

However, existing debates on the conceptualization of programming as an art have been mostly concerned (as we have shown above) with drawing a series of parallels between the practice of programming and the aesthetic appreciation of certain forms of art [21,70]. In this contribution we want to extend these results and explore the ramification of this debate in the broader field of philosophy of software engineering, by drawing original parallels between programming and the historical practice of alchemy. Specifically, we argue that alchemy -seen by many historians of science [73] as a precursory practice to a number of scientific disciplines (such as chemistry) [66]- can provide insights on the current state of the evolution of software engineering. In addition, we propose that alchemy can also help us understanding the special status of software engineering as an experimental, constructive practice where the creation of artefacts is deeply entangled with the processes of explicit and implicit mental modelling, profoundly affecting the experimenter himself.

In Sect. 2 and 3 we start off our journey by discussing Software Engineering and Alchemy as two mutually complementing practices, which - we argue- are closer than one would *prima facie* think. In Sect. 4, we propose a preliminary analysis focused on the status and relevance of metatheoretical reflections in Computer Science and call for the need of more philosophy in the discipline. Section 5 discusses and establishes a series of more practical parallels between alchemy and the practise of software engineering. Further analogies are briefly summarised in Sect. 6 before drawing a set of preliminary yet important conclusions Sect. 7.

2 History of Alchemy: A Brief Overview

To understand alchemy as a discipline, it is necessary to understand the etymology of the word *"alchemy"*. The term came to the English language via Arabic, Greek, and medieval Latin. The word consists of two parts *"al"* ("the") and *"kīmiyā"* ("art of transmuting metal"). Indeed, transformations of metals played a key role in the alchemy practise.

It can be argued that alchemy as a discipline was born out of philosophical thinking. In the 7th century B.C. Thales of Miletus begun seeking the *arche*; the underlying physical yet divine basis of everything, which he identified with the water. Other early philosophers (such as Empedocles, Heraclitus, Anaximander, Anaximenes of Miletus) continued Thales' quest for the *arche* and produced a number of accounts of the universe that significantly shaped Post-Socratic philosophy. Suffice it to say that both Plato and Aristotle developed their unitary cosmologies on the basis of this early pre-socratic reflections [56]. From these early cosmologies people subsequently derived the first basic chemical rules, for example: the idea that *Water* could be turned or transformed into *Earth* if the *Wet* element was extracted and the *Dry* element promptly added thereafter. One of Aristotle's successor Theophrastus developed several formulas for producing artificial stones; for example he realised that from red cinnabar one could make quicksilver (metal mercury). [44] These primitive and rather elementary rules constituted the backbone of early alchemical experiments, at least until the Renaissance.

Nevertheless, it is worth noting that Keyser [44] argues that the beginning of proper Alchemy can be traced back many decades before Theophrastus, to Democritus, who argued for the existence of a "magical" perspective in things. Democritus gave "recipes" for the transformation of copper into silver. The practise of gaining precious metals out of cheap ones continued throughout the years and new techniques arose. Alchemists created plenty of different recipes for creating precious metals, the motivation behind this effort is evident - precious metals were widely used as fiat currencies.

Between 180 and 280 A. D. Mediterranean culture underwent a cultural transformation. Early alchemical practises were also "transformed from a scientific (if erroneous) search for transmutation into a mystical search for personal transformation" [44]. Hence, the transformation of cheap materials into precious ones became a metaphor for a *transformation of one's soul*. As Keyser [44] brilliantly noticed: "In any event the transformation happened: what had begun as an experimental science founded on the best scientific thought of the age - Aristotle's four-element theory-became a search for personal transformation".

After a long break, Alchemy reappeared in Europe after Robert of Chester translated an important book from Arabic to Latin. The book's title was: The Book of the Composition of Alchemy (Liber de compositione alchemiae): translated in 1144. This was the first book on alchemy to become available in Europe.

[64]. Throughout the middle ages Alchemy was deeply influenced by Christianity. Matus [57] argued that: "in the 13th century alchemical authors sought theological justification for their work"; for example, they believed that knowledge about the process of gold purification, may be beneficial to learn how to purify the human soul. Moreover, alchemists started using Christian metaphors and symbols for their recipes [57].

During the Late Middle Ages, scholars continued believing that the transmutation of metals was really possible. This idea was popular also during the Renaissance because -at that time- there was not clear distinction between 'science' and 'magic' [36]. However, with the advent of the scientific revolution, the belief in Alchemy gradually lost its strength [56] (which does not mean that nobody continued in this practise, Newton's occult studies were a notable exception). However, as the distinction between 'science' and 'magic' begun to more clearly emerge alchemy begun to be considered as an obscure discipline, as a 'pseudo-science'. Alchemists though were still employed by the elite to try to develop the *elixir of life*, the *panacea* for all diseases. Thus, alchemists begun to produce chemical substances and medicines, mostly for the wealthiest [69].

3   Software Engineering and Alchemy

Software Engineering, we believe, shares with alchemy much more - in terms of underlying principles, processes, and even methods (and more on this below), than the layperson might, prima facie, be inclined to think. In fact, although these two disciplines seem antithetic to the untrained eye, we shall argue that they are not so diametrically opposed.

On the one hand, we are generally led to believe that scientific, field-oriented, disciplines (such as software engineering) uniquely originate and ultimately find their epistemological justification in the usage of formalised languages, characterised by procedures invariably stemming from logic and mathematics, as a consequence and application of the eternal desire to rationalize and mechanize thinking ("Calculemus!" [30,53]. Such an understanding perhaps found its apical point in the early years of the 20th century, with attempts to reduce arithmetic to logic [28] or -more generally- to formalise mathematics [3,38]). However, [31], showed the inherent limitations of such an approach, demonstrating that formal axiomatic systems are not always capable of modelling basic arithmetical formulas.

On the other hand, alchemy -and more generally everything escaping rationality or related to esoterism; that is, not adhering to fully-fledged scientific methodologies- tends to be demonised or considered as sub-optimal knowledge, by-product of a pre-scientific image of the world. Many scientists as well as philosophers [9,22,23,52] found significant epistemological merits in such esoteric practices. Nevertheless, it is not the purpose of this manuscript to delve in this topic.

What is important in the economy of this paper is to note that there is a strong tendency in western societies, at least, to sharply separate the sciences from the humanities, or more generally from other (normative or axiological) approaches to knowledge that do not necessarily rely on standard scientific assumptions or methodologies. As [85] aptly noticed "the intellectual life of the whole of western society" has become split into "two cultures" and this division is a major handicap to both in solving the world's problems.

This tendency usually attributes an ontological and even an epistemological superiority (or primacy) to the natural sciences over the humanities [51]. In brief, for proponents of such a naturalist stance [5], science provides the only legitimate epistemic authority needed for those (experts) who can master it, and this authority is due to its naturalistic character. See [33] for important criticism of this idea.

Software engineering and alchemy then, on such an understanding, would indeed appear to occupy diametrically opposite conceptual spaces and any attempt to make them closer would, perhaps, appear to be useless or even blaspheme.

Yet, we believe that bringing together these two disciplines, and indeed drawing analogies and specifying points of contact between them, may be particularly helpful for those interested in understanding their relations from the descriptive, meta-theoretical perspective, of the philosophy of software engineering [32,68].

Of course, we are not interested in making claims about commensurability between these disciplines. In other words, we do not want to argue that software engineering can be turned into a form of alchemy. Rather, we propose a more modest argument, which claims that in its current state software engineering is not fully describable in mere scientific terms, and that its 'artistic' or non scientific components should be valued and better appreciated.

In that respect, the historical parallel between the perception of alchemical practices and the perceptions of bleeding-edge technologies in contemporary society provides crucial terms for comparisons. For example, [45], draws such a parallel between the politics underlying the development of alchemy during the Middle Ages [69] and contemporary political responses to biotechnology (such as [2,86]), largely defined by the mistrust and information asymmetries between experimenters and the general public [37]. On a similar vein, one could compare the same kind of responses in some of the most interesting areas of software development (such as artificial intelligence and blockchain -[7]) where these ideas are occasionally met with open hostility by policymakers.

During the Middle Ages, in Europe, much of the criticism against alchemy revolved around the controversial issue of mankind's power and potential control over the natural world, which -to some extent- threatened the church's authority and its plan for world dominance [45].

Similarly, growing political criticism against the development of AI, is -often-framed as a threat to what is permissible to humans, in terms of manipulation of the 'natural state'. However, fundamentally, much of the debate matters, because it goes into the core issue of who has the authority to define the 'natural state' of affairs in any given society. No less interesting are the parallels with various criticism of blockchain technology [67], which is normally but not solely used, as a foundation for the implementation of cryptocurrencies [61], digital asset designed to work as a medium of exchange for services in place of fiat money. Central to the growing political and religious hostility towards alchemy during the Middle Ages, was the well-founded fear that alchemists could potentially debase fiat money, by using artificial gold to counterfeit it [60,64]. This resulted in the papal bull titled: 'Spondent quas non exhibent', issued by the Pope John XXII, against alchemists in 1317. In fact, as [45] points out the bull was directed expressly against alchemists, who used their chrysopoetic expertise for counterfeiting, rather than against alchemy as a science. One can easily see a parallel here with recent regulatory attempts taking place in various countries - aimed at reducing the adoption of Bitcoin and various other cryptocurrencies. At the time of writing, countries such Algeria, Egypt and Morrocco (in Africa), Bolivia (in South America), and Nepal (in Asia have) have a total ban on Bitcoin (and related crypto instruments). There are indeed different grounds and reasons for such decisions: some of these are religious, some ideological, some financial and pragmatic, other are simply concerned with issues related to legal legacy. For example, In Egypt, Dar al-Ifta, the primary Islamic legislator, has issued a religious decree classifying commercial transactions in bitcoin as *haram* (prohibited under Islamic law) [15]. India also plans to introduce a law to ban private cryptocurrencies (such as Bitcoin), in order to provide a framework for the creation of an official digital currency. In many other countries, however, cryptocurrencies remain unregulated.

4   The Philosophy of Software Engineering

This paper, however, does not intend to describe and study the many complex normative and axiological issues underlying the perception or application of software engineering experiments in society, quite the opposite. It attempts to analyse and explore the meta-theoretical considerations regarding the status of the discipline. This attempt can be seen not only as a much needed theoretical clarification of the humanist aspects underlying the practice of both software engineers and developers, but also as a foundation for further profitable future reflections and speculations. As noted by [32], currently there are, at least, three major competing paradigms in the philosophy of software engineering. The first one is the so-called *'formalist'* approach, which typically emphasises the strong logical and mathematical structure (or base) of software engineering. Such a paradigm calls and actively advocates for the adoption of quantitative mathematical methods for software quality assurance, such as theorem-proving and model-checking [13,29]. The second paradigm is the so-called *'engineering'* approach, which emphasises the *constructivity* of software engineering[1], along the lines of rigorous production schemes and workflow models, as implemented and directly used in many mechanical factories [62]. Finally, according to [32], the

---

[1] Its nature of being made of *constructive procedures*, i.e. procedures which can be carried out, as opposed to non-constructive procedures, those that can be specified but not carried out.

third paradigm characterising current approaches to the philosophy of software engineering, the so-called *'humanist'* approach, emphasises the social dimension and collaborative interactions observed during the process of software development, as well as analysing the broader implications of software engineering in the wider society.

Information scientists [89], often inspired by positivist thinking [6,14], may consider themselves as fully rational agents, creatures utterly in command of their emotions, capable of ignoring the movements of the unconscious and/or dominating (perhaps deliberately) reason. In brief, they sometimes consider themselves as being in possession of the ability to go beyond mankind's rational limitations, by adopting formal languages and proceduralized techniques, which are inspired by stringent logical thinking [10]. One could therefore consider the average computer scientist as firmly belonging to this neopositivist group [50,81]. Many information scientists would perhaps be honored to be listed among such ranks. We tend to disagree with this interpretation nonetheless.

As [32] argues, we believe, that the humanist approach above-mentioned is of particular interest because it allows us to overcome any reductionist (positivist or neopositivist) interpretation of programming as a mere, highly formalizable, procedural technique. Such an approach in fact allows us to address and possibly resolve the paradox of software engineering seen as a mere branch of traditional computer science. This paradox notably emerges from the observation that traditionally understood scientific inquiries, are involved in discovering regularities and laws of cause-effect, concerning natural phenomena. However, one cannot always identify such laws in the practice of computer scientists. This, as [32] successfully shows, raises the dilemma of how to bridge the category gap from ontology ("discovering facts") to deontology ("how projects should be run best"), without committing the notorious naturalist fallacy [71]. In truth, this problem is also closely related to the unique status of experiments in computer science, setting them apart from the experimentation typically conducted in the natural sciences [80].

To reiterate, the humanist approach allows us to overcome some of the problems described above, concerning attempts to constrain or limit software engineering within the boundaries of formalised mathematical/logical practices [12]. [32] warns about the futility of any attempt to confine best practices in software engineering in the constraints of technological standards, developed in the imitation of empirically supported 'laboratory' scientific standards. Not only this approach, [32] argues, ignores the wider reach and scope of software engineering, in which we often have to deal with larger projects, various human or corporate stakeholders, legal and financial constraints [17]. It also gives rise to various myths concerning the alleged insularity of software engineering as a practice [76].

There are thus good reasons to resist this view, hence to try to expand our understanding of the role of software engineering in the direction suggested by the humanist approach [17]. This, however, does not amount saying that the scientific or engineering components of programming fade (or ought fading) into the background, quite the opposite. In this paper, we do not aim to challenge the engineering paradigm, postulating that software engineering indeed constitutes a 'science'; rather, we challenge the assumption that all key aspects of software engineering can be grasped and fully interpreted or summarised by or within the boundaries of this narrow paradigm. In other words, we agree with [47] when he claims that a better analysis and comprehension of the artistic elements (the artisanal components) underlying software engineering is instrumental and paramount to the understanding of the unique character of this practice.

These key elements or components of programming can be discovered with the help of some concepts found in the literature dedicated to the practice of alchemy. In the following section, we analyse some of such concepts and explain their significance and relevance for a proper understanding of software engineering as well as for the development of future methodologies and best practices.

5   Software Process as a Frame

In this section, we discuss and establish a series of parallels between alchemy and the practise of software engineering. In particular, such parallels are drawn with respect to three of the most important phases underlying the software development process. These are: i. requirements and elicitation, ii. compilation,and iii. verification. As shown in Fig. 1, these correspond to three main alchemic steps (which we metaphorically label as **nigredo, albedo**, and **rubedo**)

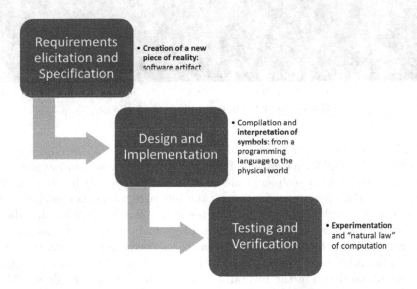

Fig. 1. Alchemic Process of Software Engineering

5.1   Creation of a New Reality: Software Requirements

We argue that the processes and activities underlying the development and production of a software can be said to be analogous to those of carried out by alchemists, in underground laboratories or garages[2] (see Fig. 2).

Fig. 2. Alchemic underground lab in Prague

The first phase of any software development process involves, at least, two steps: elicitation and formalization. These initial steps are human-intense, meaning that humans are the recipients and are therefore also highly involved in them. In this stage, the software engineer typically interacts with other intelligent biological actors, in order to create a new artefact, a software artefact, that did not exist before. As every human artifact, in order to be realised, needs somehow to be conceived in the mind of its creator, the software artifact has to be visualized in the mind of its maker. This is thus the phase were such an artifact is alchemically produced in the mental universe of the Software Engineer. This is a fully creative phase. While successive phases, such as specification or testing, can be automated (partially or in full), requirements elicitation and formalization cannot exist or prescind from humans and from the creative interaction that

---

[2] https://www.fastcompany.com/90270226/the-origins-of-silicon-valleys-garage-myth.

is established in relation with them. In other words, humans are the repositories of the need that any given software ought be satisfying. Here is also where the rhetorical abilities of the Software Engineer comes to play a role, since it is often her credibility and persuasiveness that determine the success of a project since its very early stages. Aristotle's Rhetoric, the ancient Greek treatise on the art of persuasion (dating from the 4th century BCE) is still the best reference for what concerns the description of rhetorical abilities required by an individual. Roughly speaking, three are the means of persuasion that an orator must use and rely on, according to Aristotle. Those grounded on credibility (*ethos*), those entrenched in the emotions and psychology of the audience (*pathos*), and those that can be found in patterns of reasoning (*logos*) [4]. A good Software Engineer should be trained to such rhetorical abilities and should be fully aware of their use; indeed this is increasingly part of the curriculum of any top engineering school [75].

5.2 Materialization of Symbols: Compilation

The root word for "magic" derives from the Greek term *"magoi"*, referring to a Median tribe in Persia and their religion, Zoroastrianism. The word "magic" should be here intended as the application of man's inner will in order to achieve outer results. Magic, in this sense, is an act of man-made creation. Over the centuries many of the ideas that were once confined into magical theory and practice have been then isolated and reformulated in different fields of study. Magic and science have more in common then what first meet the eyes, they both realized that, provided the fact that correct laws are discovered, man can somehow influence the natural world. Magic consists of signs, rituals and formulas that, through the actions of the magician, can create realities and meaning out of "meaningless" (syntactic) signs. It should not be difficult to individuate the analogies with Software Engineering.

Software engineers typically construct a 'model' of a software system before that software system itself comes into existence [32]. Thus, when developing a product (either a software or a technological artifacts), it is common practice to write something similar to a user' manual, outlining a blueprint and a clear plan for ensuring the satisfactory construction of the product. A functional specification (otherwise called a requirements specification) therefore is formulated to describe the intended behavior of an item that needs to be produced [40]. Mental concepts operationalised as abstract data types become materialised as computer hardware or software [55]. The development process then generate a concrete model. A model is an inert representation of a software that the magician (Software Engineer) through a ritual (Software Process) and an instrument (Compiler) can bring into life (Execution).

Beyond modelization, further analogies can be found. Signs and their interpretation and manipulation represent another astonishing parallel between two these apparently distant disciplines and practices. A (syntactic) sign is a static object void of meaning in itself, which is only activated (interpreted) by the action of an external (intelligent) entity (the individual) to whom the core potential of interpretation belongs. This is, we claim, exactly the function of a compiler, or interpreter. Signs (or programs) by themselves do not have a meaning, and the behavior is determined by the compiler (the intelligent agent) [82,83].

The role of *interpretation* and, more generally of *compilation*, is the construction an *isomorphism between a structure of complex signs (a computer program) and a binary structure of truth-values representing thresholds of clearly identifiable electrical voltage*. The extraordinary role of interpretation is to operate a *concretion* from an archetypal world, *the abstract world of the logos of a programming language*, to a physical form, consisting of electrical signals of which by themselves lack of semantics [1].

Alchimists influenced by kabbalists also conceived the *Tree of Life* as the medium through which the subconscious gets access to archetypes and higher meanings, which would not otherwise be communicable in writing to humans (see Fig. 3). Another important point to mention is that meditation with focus on specific symbols in a widespread alchemic practice. According to Jung, two components are indispensable in order to embark on alchemical work: *meditatio*[3] and *imaginatio*[4]:

"The place or the medium of realization is neither mind nor matter, but that intermediate realm of subtle reality which can be adequately only expressed by the symbol. The symbol is neither abstract nor concrete, neither rational nor irrational, neither real or unreal. It is always both." [42].

5.3   'Experimental-ness': Software Verification and Testing

In the natural sciences, it is a requirement that the experimenter is only an external observer of the phenomenon to be explained. However, experimental procedure de facto are never completely neutral and are affected by bias of different nature [] or, in the case of quantum mechanics actual impossibility for the observer of not altering the result of the experiment itself []. In the same way, during the phases of specification, design and implementation, the programmer is actively involved in the process (often a computation) that leads to the production of the software artifacts and cannot be considered an outsider with respect to the phenomenon (i.e., an artifact) that has been created. Experimental work in computer science thus tell us more about the people that have done the job, than the way the world is [80].

The parallel between the two disciplines is therefore established and can be reinforced looking at things at another level; i.e. experimentation happens at the moment of testing or, more in general at the time of software verification. In the classic waterfall model, testing and verification are the last steps required before deployment and maintenance [8]. Even in more modern approaches (such as agile methodologies [27]), verification is still present as a crucial step [54].

---

[3] "The name of an Internal Talk of one person with another who is invisible, as in the invocation of the Deity, or communion with one's self, or with one's good angel".

[4] "It is the Star in Man, the Celestial or Supercelestial Body".

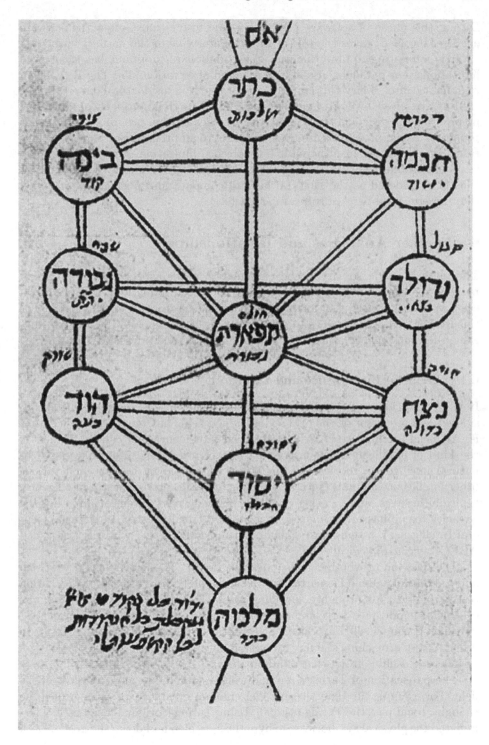

Fig. 3. Tree of life, Illustration from Brockhaus and Efron Jewish Encyclopedia, 1906–1913 (Creative Common license)

During this phase of software production, the tester (most often the software engineer involved) takes the role of experimenter, like in the natural sciences.

It is interesting to note that the static analysis of programs has theoretical limitations that parallel those of experimental observation [35]. The Rice Theorem, named after Henry Gordon Rice who proved it in his doctoral dissertation of 1951 at Syracuse University, states that for any non-trivial property of programs, no program can decide in the general case whether another program exhibits that property. Trivial properties are those applying to all programs or none [74]. This result establishes an insurmountable theoretical limitation of software verification, and therefore speaks about its 'Experimental-ness'. The Rice theorem can thus be considered as the "natural law" of computation, posing limits also on the 'Experimental-ness' of software artifacts.

6   Further Analogies and Relationships

The analysis made so far can be extended to other aspects of computation; namely to artificial intelligence and even to software production processes. However, we do not consider an analysis in those fields a priority for this paper. For this reason, we only introduce the discussion of these important factors here and leave their full-scale treatment for future, more detailed, investigations.

6.1   Artificial Intelligence and Intuition

In this subsection we nevertheless specify in which sense alchemy might be considered as a precursor of one of the most hyped fields in Computer Science; that is, Artificial Intelligence (AI) [34]. Artificial intelligence [58] can be defined as the kind of intelligence demonstrated by machines. AI is often juxtaposed to natural intelligence; the kind of intelligence displayed by humans and various other intelligence animals (such as primates, dolphins etc.). Natural intelligence, typically involves, among other qualities, consciousness, intentionality, and the capacity to emphasize. *Strong AI*, which is also labelled as AGI (Artificial General Intelligence), attempts to emulate natural intelligence, which is also called ABI (*Artificial Biological Intelligence*).

The question of whether *"machines can think?"* is one that has a very rich and long history. René Descartes, for instance, prefigured aspects of the Turing test in his [18]. Yet, roughly speaking, we can say that this question became of crucial importance for computer science only after the publication of [88], in which Turing itself introduced his "Imitation Game" (or Turing Test), in order to test a machine's ability to exhibit intelligent behaviour equivalent to, or indistinguishable from, that of a human.

The publication of Turing's seminal work, sparked enormous interest in the field. For example, in 1966, Joseph Weizenbaum created a program which, he thought, could pass the Turing test [90]. Using Turing's original insights, [63] formulated the physical symbol system hypothesis, which laid down the groundwork for the development of the computational theory of mind [26]; a very influential paradigm in linguistic, philosophy, and cognitive science. Devastating critiques, however, quickly followed, highlighting the insurmountable difficulties (both technical/mathematical - [59] and philosophical - [82] and [19]) underlying the possible development of a strong AI [20], thereby opening up to modern approaches to the problem (such as those based on connectionism [77] and [72]. In recent years, Ali Rahimi, a prominent researcher in AI at Google, presented Machine Learning (ML) algorithms as a "form of alchemy". Despite the informal use of the term, his point is meaningful: computers now can learn through trial and error and researchers do not exactly know the reason behind some algorithms working and some others not, and there are no rigorous criteria for choosing one AI architecture over another [39].

However, we see AI as a much broader discipline than only ML, and in the same way it was intended by its precursors, way before statistical methods and big data become relevant. AI is about mechanization of thinking with meta-reflection about machine consciousness and intuition [78]. In particular, Artificial Intuition is the theoretical capacity of an artificial software to function similarly to human consciousness, specifically in the capacity of human consciousness known as intuition. We believe that the work of Carl Jung can function as a point of connection to help us specify the analogy between alchemy and AI. In Carl Jung's concept of *synchronicity*, the concept of *"intuitive intelligence"* is described as something like a capacity that transcends ordinary-level functioning to a point where information is understood with a greater depth than is available in more simple rationally-thinking entities[43].

In Jung's view the symbols of Paracelsian alchemy, and those underlying alchemical literature in general (see, for example Fig. 4), are a veiled reference to the evolution of the individual psyche, i.e. that dialectical process of 'individuation' in which consciousness is confronted with the forces of the unconscious mind [79]. Jung's believed that alchemical symbolism expresses psychological processes:

"I had long been aware that alchemy is not only the mother of chemistry, but is also the forerunner of our modern psychology of the unconscious. Thus Paracelsus appears as a pioneer not only of chemical medicine but of empirical psychology and psychotherapy." [41].

In the search for alchemical origin of Artificial Intelligence and Intuition, Jung offers interesting insights. With alchemical symbols expressing psychological processes, therefore relating thinking processes and symbolism to a deeper level than what a parser based on context-free grammars can do, and being able to see a fil rouge connecting *synchronicity* and intuition, Jung seems to suggest that purely algorithmic based analyses of data (no matter how large) may not be able to give rise to what we understand as *intelligence*, and even less so as *intuition*. In this sense, Machine Learning may be not be suitable tool to reach Artificial Intuition. Just as alchemy is a quest for creating a universal truth, so is our intuition.

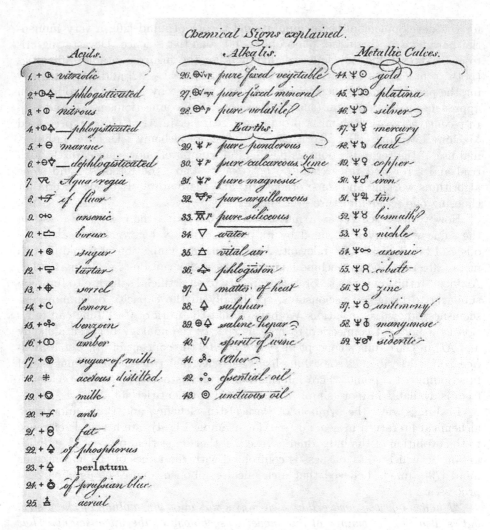

Fig. 4. Alchemical symbols in Torbern Bergman's 1775 Dissertation on Elective Affinities (Creative Common license)

6.2   Asymmetry of Knowledge Distribution

In alchemy *occultus* is used to identify powers or qualities that escaped sensory perception [65]. In Software Engineering this often corresponds to non-existence of credible evidence regarding the effects of method and tools [76]. What types of investigations may be methodologically admitted as 'empirical studies' if software engineering at large does not (and cannot) happen in the closed environment of a well-controlled physics laboratory? [32]. A second meaning of occultus in alchemy is - a branch of knowledge that needs to be kept from others (Newman, 2009), as shown through our discussion of the Tree of Life above. Proprietary software and software security attempt to do the same, often with significant ethical and social implications [17,87].

6.3   Metaphysics of Computation

In theoretical computer science it is known that the cardinality of the set of computer programs is numerable, while the cardinality of functions from natural numbers into natural numbers is not numerable [16]. This means that we have less programs that functions defining problems, less algorithmic answers and mathematically definable problems. If not every conceivable problem can be expressed in algorithmic terms, should this be considered like the existence of transcendent truths that both the conscious and the unconscious mind would never been able to reach? Even accepting compilation as an alchemic process, this fundamental limitation of computation put us in front of the absence of prima materia to be transformed. We do not have actual first matter to put together and to transform to reach certain trascendental truths, to achieve some superior understanding.

7   Conclusions

Any investigation, regardless of the discipline under question, acquires a greater value, both philosophical and ethical, when it moves towards the understanding of truth. At that point, necessarily it has to move towards the semantics of the sign (whatever nature it has), its interpretation and the connection between syntax and semantics, which means between the sign and the representation of truth, with all the limitations that great minds of the past have outlined around the issue. The debate around true and false is certainly as old as humanity, and the issue has been addressed by all disciplines, modern and ancient, from linguistics to mathematics and physics to alchemy.

In modern times, the work of Gödel is the *Summa Mathematica* of a process of understanding of linguistic and mathematical paradoxes, which spanned over millennia. Gödel has shown - together with Cantor, Turing and other great minds - that mathematical truth does not exist, and any model having as objective to formally represent reality is doomed to fail. The circle of Copenhagen and the interpretation of quantum mechanics have further disillusioned and distanced us from an anthropocentric view. We understand how not even the physical reality can be captured by our fallible senses.

Computer Science, as an illustrious daughter of logic - for its theoretical foundations - and of physics - for some of its founding fathers and for the definition of entropic nature of the information bit - is concerned with defining complex meanings according to a logic based on two values of truth, although deprived of any epistemological and cognitive value.

While an epistemology and philosophy of Computer Science does exist, Software Engineering as a human-intensive sub-discipline, and with important practical applications, is still behind in developing adequate meta-reflections, often relegated as a sub-product of "programming". In this paper we started posing the foundations of an epistemology of Software Engineering, that will certainly require future steps to get established.

References

1. Abelson, H., Sussman, G.J.: Structure and Interpretation of Computer Programs. The MIT Press, Cambridge (1996)
2. Aerni, P., Rieder, P.: Public policy responses to biotechnology. In: BIOTECHNOLOGY-Volume XIII: Fundamentals in Biotechnology, vol. 13, p. 47 (2009)
3. An, W., Russell, B.: Principia mathematica. Cambridge (1910)
4. Aristotle: Ars Rhetorica. Oxford UP, Oxford (1959)
5. Atkins, P.: Science as truth. Hist. Hum. Sci. 8(2), 97–102 (1995)
6. Ayer, A.J.: Logical Positivism, vol. 2. Simon and Schuster (1959)
7. Beckers, S.: AAAI: an argument against artificial intelligence. In: Müller, V.C. (ed.) PT-AI 2017. SAPERE, vol. 44, pp. 235–247. Springer, Cham (2018). https://doi. org/10.1007/978-3-319-96448-5_25
8. Benington, H.D.: Production of large computer programs. Ann. Hist. Comput. 5(4), 350–361 (1983)
9. Berto, F.: There's Something About Gödel: The Complete Guide to the Incompleteness Theorem. Wiley, Hoboken (2011)
10. Blumberg, A.E., Feigl, H.: Logical positivism. J. Philos. 28(11), 281–296 (1931)
11. Bond, G.W.: Software as art. Commun. ACM 48(8), 118–124 (2005)
12. Broy, M.: Mathematics of software engineering. In: Möller, B. (ed.) MPC 1995. LNCS, vol. 947, pp. 18–48. Springer, Heidelberg (1995). https://doi.org/10.1007/ 3-540-60117-1_3
13. Clarke, E.M., Grumberg, O., Peled, D.A.: Model Checking. MIT Press, Cambridge (1999)
14. Comte, A.: A General View of Positivism. Reeves & Turner (1880)
15. Global Legal Research Directorate, The Law Library of Congress: Regulation of cryptocurrency around the world (2018). https://www.loc.gov/law/help/ cryptocurrency/cryptocurrency-world-survey.pdf. Accessed 26 Feb 2020
16. Davis, M.: Computability and Unsolvability. Dover Publications (1958)
17. DeMarco, T.: Software engineering: an idea whose time has come and gone? IEEE Softw. 26(4), 96 (2009)
18. Descartes, R.: A Discourse on the Method. OUP Oxford (2006/1637)
19. Dreyfus, H.: What computers can't do (1976)
20. Dreyfus, H.L., Hubert, L., et al.: What Computers Still Can't Do: A Critique of Artificial Reason. MIT Press, Cambridge (1992)
21. Edmonds, E.: The art of programming or programs as art. Front. Artif. Intell. Appl. 161, 119 (2007)
22. Feyerabend, P.: Killing Time: The Autobiography of Paul Feyerabend. University of Chicago Press, Chicago (1996)
23. Feyerabend, P., et al.: Against Method. Verso (1993)
24. Fishwick, O.P., Malina, R., Sommerer, C., Bertelsen, W., Fishwick, P.: Aesthetic computing "manifesto" (2003)
25. Fishwick, P.A.: Aesthetic Computing. MIT Press, Cambridge (2008)

26. Fodor, J.A.: The Language of Thought, vol. 5. Harvard University Press, Cambridge (1975)
27. Fowler, M., Highsmith, J., et al.: The agile manifesto. Softw. Dev. **9**(8), 28–35 (2001)
28. Frege, G.: Begriffsschrift, a Formula Language, Modeled Upon that of Arithmetic, for Pure Thought. Frege and Gödel, Two Fundamental Texts in Mathematical Logic, translated into English by S. Bauer-Mengelberg. Harvard University Press, Cambridge (1879)
29. Gallier, J.H.: Logic for Computer Science: Foundations of Automatic Theorem Proving. Harper & Row Publishers, Inc. (1985)
30. Garber, D.: Descartes, mechanics, and the mechanical philosophy. Midwest Stud. Philos. **26**, 185–204 (2002)
31. Gödel, K.: Über formal unentscheidbare sätze der principia mathematica und verwandter systeme i. Monatshefte für mathematik und physik **38**(1), 173–198 (1931)
32. Gruner, S.: Problems for a philosophy of software engineering. Minds Mach. **21**(2), 275–299 (2011). https://doi.org/10.1007/s11023-011-9234-2
33. Haack, S.: Scientism and its discontents. In: Proceedings of the Agnes Cuming Lectures in Philosophy, University College Dublin School of Philosophy, Dublin, Ireland 22 (2016)
34. Haugeland, J.: Artificial Intelligence: The Very Idea. MIT Press, Cambridge (1989)
35. Heisenberg, W.: Uber den anschaulichen Inhalt der quantentheoretischen Kinematik und Mechanik. Z. Phys. **43**, 172–198 (1927)
36. Henry, J.: Magic and science in the sixteenth and seventeenth centuries. In: Olby, R.C., Cantor, G.N., Christie, J.R.R., Hodge, M.J.S. (eds.) Companion to the History of Modern Science, pp. 583–596. Routledge (1990)
37. Herring, R., Paarlberg, R.: The political economy of biotechnology. Annu. Rev. Resour. Econ. **8**, 397–416 (2016)
38. Hilbert, D.: The grounding of elementary number theory. In: From Kant to Hilbert: A Source Book in the Foundations of Mathematics, vol. 2, pp. 1157–1165 (1931)
39. Hutson, M.: Has artificial intelligence become alchemy? Science **360**(6388), 478 (2018)
40. IEEE: IEEE recommended practice for software requirements specifications (1998). http://ieeexplore.ieee.org/xpls/abs_all.jsp?arnumber=720574
41. Jung, C.G.: Alchemical Studies. Princeton University Press, Princeton (1967)
42. Jung, C.G.: Psychology and Alchemy. Princeton University Press, Princeton (1968)
43. Jung, C.G.: Psychological Types, Collected Works. Princeton University Press, Princeton (1971)
44. Keyser, P.T.: Alchemy in the ancient world: from science to magic. Illinois Class. Stud. **15**(2), 353–378 (1990). http://www.jstor.org/stable/23064297
45. Kirkham, G.: Is biotechnology the new alchemy? Stud. Hist. Philos. Sci. Part A **40**(1), 70–80 (2009). https://doi.org/10.1016/j.shpsa.2008.12.004. https://linkinghub.elsevier.com/retrieve/pii/S0039368108001131
46. Knuth, D.: The art of programming. ITNow **53**(4) (2011)
47. Knuth, D.E.: Computer programming as an art. Commun. ACM **17**(12), 667–673 (1974)
48. Knuth, D.E.: Literate programming. Comput. J. **27**(2), 97–111 (1984)
49. Knuth, D.E.: The Art of Computer Programming, vol. 3. Pearson Education, London (1997)
50. Kraft, V.: The Vienna Circle: The Origins of Neo-Positivism. Open Road Media (2015)

51. Ladyman, J., et al.: Every Thing Must Go: Metaphysics Naturalized. Oxford University Press on Demand (2007)
52. Lakatos, I., Feyerabend, P.: For and Against Method: Including Lakatos's Lectures on Scientific Method and the Lakatos-Feyerabend Correspondence. University of Chicago Press (1999)
53. Wilhelm von Leibniz, G.: The Art of Discovery (1685)
54. Li, N., Guo, J., Lei, J., Li, Y., Rao, C., Cao, Y.: XP Workshops, p. 18. ACM
55. Liskov, B., Zilles, S.: Programming with abstract data types. In: Proceedings of the ACM SIGPLAN Symposium on Very High Level Languages, pp. 50–59. Association for Computing Machinery, New York (1974)
56. Martin, C.: Alchemy and the renaissance commentary tradition on meteorologica IV. Ambix **51**(3), 245–262 (2004). https://doi.org/10.1179/amb.2004.51.3.245
57. Matus, Z.A.: Alchemy and Christianity in the middle ages. Hist. Compass **10**(12), 934–945 (2012). https://doi.org/10.1111/hic3.12013. https://onlinelibrary.wiley.com/doi/abs/10.1111/hic3.12013
58. McCarthy, J.: What is Artificial Intelligence? (1998)
59. Minsky, M., Papert, S.: An Introduction to Computational Geometry. Cambridge TIASS, HIT (1969)
60. Mottana, A.: Counterfeiting gems in the 16th century: Giovan Battista Della Porta on Glass 'Gem'making. J. Gemmol. **35**(7), 652 (2017)
61. Mukhopadhyay, U., Skjellum, A., Hambolu, O., Oakley, J., Yu, L., Brooks, R.: A brief survey of cryptocurrency systems. In: 2016 14th Annual Conference on Privacy, Security and Trust (PST), pp. 745–752. IEEE (2016)
62. Naur, P., Randell, B.: Software Engineering: Report of a Conference Sponsored by the NATO Science Committee, Garmisch, Germany, 7–11 October 1968, Brussels, Scientific Affairs Division, NATO (1969)
63. Newell, A., Simon, H.A., et al.: Human Problem Solving, vol. 104. Prentice-Hall, Englewood Cliffs (1972)
64. Newman, W.: Technology and alchemical debate in the late middle ages. Isis **80**(3), 423–445 (1989)
65. Newman, W.R.: Brian Vickers on alchemy and the occult: a response. Perspect. Sci. **17**(4), 482–506 (2009)
66. Newman, W.R., Principe, L.M.: Alchemy vs. chemistry: the etymological origins of a historiographic mistake1. Early Sci. Med. **3**(1), 32–65 (1998)
67. Nofer, M., Gomber, P., Hinz, O., Schiereck, D.: Blockchain. Bus. Inf. Syst. Eng. **59**(3), 183–187 (2017)
68. Northover, M., Kourie, D.G., Boake, A., Gruner, S., Northover, A.: Towards a philosophy of software development: 40 years after the birth of software engineering. J. Gen. Philos. Sci. **39**(1), 85–113 (2008)
69. Nummedal, T.: Alchemy and Authority in the Holy Roman Empire. University of Chicago Press, Chicago (2008)
70. Pyshkin, E.: In the right order of brush strokes: a sketch of a software philosophy retrospective. SpringerPlus **3**(1) (2014). https://doi.org/10.1186/2193-1801-3-186. https://springerplus.springeropen.com/articles/10.1186/2193-1801-3-186
71. Qingshan, Y.: The naturalist fallacy: from Moore to Husserl. Philos. Res. **2** (2008)
72. Ramsey, W., Rumelhart, D.E., Stich, S.P.: Philosophy and Connectionist Theory. Psychology Press (2013)
73. Read, J., Sawyer, F.H.: Prelude to Chemistry: An Outline of Alchemy, its Literature and Relationships. G. Bell (1936)
74. Rice, H.G.: Classes of recursively enumerable sets and their decision problems. Trans. Am. Math. Soc. **74**, 358–366 (1953)

75. Robinson, J.A.: Engineering thinking and rhetoric. J. Eng. Educ. **87**(3), 227–229 (1998). https://doi.org/10.1002/j.2168-9830.1998.tb00347.x
76. Rombach, D., Seelisch, F.: Formalisms in Software Engineering: Myths Versus Empirical Facts, Balancing Agility and Formalism in Software Engineering: Second IFIP TC 2 Central and East European Conference on Software Engineering Techniques, CEE-SET 2007, Poznan, Poland, 10–12 October 2007, Revised Selected Papers (2008)
77. Rumelhart, D.E., Hinton, G.E., McClelland, J.L., et al.: A general framework for parallel distributed processing. In: Parallel Distributed Processing: Explorations in the Microstructure of Cognition, vol. 1, no. 45–76, p. 26 (1986)
78. Russell, S.J., Norvig, P.: Artificial Intelligence: A Modern Approach, 3rd edn. Pearson, London (2009)
79. Sauder-MacGuire, A.: Jung, Carl Gustav, and Alchemy. In: Leeming, D.A., Madden, K., Marlan, S. (eds.) Encyclopedia of Psychology and Religion. Springer, Boston (2010). https://doi.org/10.1007/978-0-387-71802-6_362
80. Schiaffonati, V., Verdicchio, M.: Computing and experiments: a methodological view on the debate on the scientific nature of computing. Philos. Technol. **27**(3), 359–376 (2014). https://doi.org/10.1007/s13347-013-0126-7
81. Schlick, M.: Moritz schlick. Philos. Pap. **2**, 1925–1936 (1979)
82. Searle, J.R.: The Chinese room revisited. Behav. Brain Sci. **5**(2), 345–348 (1982)
83. Searle, J.R.: Is the brain's mind a computer program? Sci. Am. **262**(1), 25–31 (1990)
84. Sedelow, S.Y.: The computer in the humanities and fine arts. ACM Comput. Surv. (CSUR) **2**(2), 89–110 (1970)
85. Snow, C.P.: The Two Cultures. Cambridge University Press, Cambridge (2012)
86. Thacker, E.: The Global Genome: Biotechnology, Politics, and Culture. MIT Press, Cambridge (2006)
87. Turilli, M.: Ethics and the practice of software design, pp. 171–183. IOS Press (2008)
88. Turing, A.M.: Computing machinery and intelligence. Mind **59**(236), 433–460 (1950)
89. Vickery, A., Vickery, B.C.: Information Science in Theory and Practice. Walter de Gruyter (2005)
90. Weizenbaum, J.: Computer Power and Human Reason: From Judgment to Calculation (1976)

AI Empowered DevSecOps Security
for Next Generation Development

Bhawna Yadav[1], Gaurav Choudhary[2], Shishir Kumar Shandilya[1],
and Nicola Dragoni[2(✉)]

[1] School of Computer Science and Engineering (SCSE), VIT Bhopal University,
Bhopal, India
`bhawna.yadav2018@vitbhopal.ac.in`
[2] DTU Compute, Technical University of Denmark, 2800 Kgs., Lyngby, Denmark
`ndra@dtu.dk`

Abstract. In DevSecOps, development phase advancement goes
through various effective solutions, but efficient bug detection, reliability,
accurate reports, and user-friendly solution are still lacking. The existing
tools raising a false alarm and somewhere no alarm at all at potential
threats are no rare sight. Still, there has been no advancement towards
a practical solution that could solve the issue mentioned above. In this
paper, we have developed a state-of-the-art approach to the problem
by leveraging artificial intelligence, enabling us to facilitate the analysis
detection and generate more advanced reporting. In particular, we have
integrated Machine Learning with DevSecOps to minimize false error
rates. The proposed approach determines debugging errors in less time.
Moreover, it provides beginner-friendly analysis for developers to accomplish
by our precisely tailored machine learning models trained on the
data-set derived from SEI CERT Standard.

Keywords: Software development · Machine learning · Security ·
DevSecOps

1 Introduction

Development, Security, and Operations, i.e., DevSecOps, ensures the security
integration at each phase of Software Development Lifecycle (SDLC), from the
initial requirements to design integration, implementation, testing, deployment,
and software delivery. [15]. The emerging new technologies are enhancing the
productivity of the companies using procedure/methods of DevOps, but less
attention is paid to security. In 2016, total 64,000 incidents and 2,300 security
breaches were reported [9]. In 2019, 7.9 billion data records got exposed, and by
2020, the security breaches got increased by 273% over last year (2019) [24]. Thus
protecting confidential information as well as personal data is highly important
nowadays.

The way development organizations approach security has seen a natural and
necessary evolution represented by DevSecOps. In earlier days, security features

© Springer Nature Switzerland AG 2021
G. Succi et al. (Eds.): ICFSE 2021, CCIS 1523, pp. 32–46, 2021.
https://doi.org/10.1007/978-3-030-93135-3_3

were considered at the end of the development attended by different teams, and the independent quality assurance (QA) team tested them by validations and verifications. As per current market requirements, it can be handled initially by adopting Agile and DevOps practices. This team should focus on the minimization of software development cycles by considering security at the initial phase [15].

Agile and DevOps processes and tools seamlessly integrate application and infrastructure by DevSecOps. Considering security earlier at the stages makes it simpler to fix as they emerge when they are more accessible and less expensive. Development, safety, and IT operations teams have it as a shared responsibility rather than the sole responsibility of a security silo. The DevSecOps motto enables "software, safer, sooner" without slowing the software development cycle by automating the delivery of secure software [15].

1.1 Problem Statement and Our Contribution

Every year more than 10,000 vulnerabilities are found across the software used by organizations and individuals, costing them a massive toll on resources and reputation [7]. Most of the vulnerabilities even go undetected long after the production, especially during the covid times when companies rushed their products without proper QA cycles. The recent trends saw the most vulnerable software causing alone 2.1 Billion dollars to the IT industry [7]. When software development techniques such as development, operations, and security are integrated into the SDLC lifecycle, DevSecOps, it takes full advantage of responsive development and agile models from the beginning. This step does drift the security aspect from a single isolated team to the entire development team, though the issue of outdated security software remains at its place. This results in false or no alarm at all, leaving the potential threats in plain sight, yet no significant measures have been taken to solve them. Existing solutions emphasize automation and user reliability, whereas accuracy in bug detection, low false alarms, and security aspects are not fully touched.

In this paper we propose an approach that provides three main contributions:

- Integrating Machine Learning with DevSecOps to minimize false error rates.
- Determine debugging errors in less time with ML.
- Beginner-friendly analysis for developers.

The rest of the paper is organized as follows. Section 2 reviews state-of-the-art DevSecOps solutions and models. Section 3 provides the necessary background of DevSecOps and traditional software development. Section 4 describes the approach proposed in this paper. Finally, Sect. 5 sums up conclusions and future works.

2   Related Works

Carter and Kim [3] depicted the drawbacks of the security phase in the development. They suggested that the DevSecOps implementation can only be done if the security team arranges tools and required knowledge and the DevOps team executes them. A development team can take up security in a much easier manner compared to the reverse scenario. Gamification of bug findings has seen an awe-inspiring result that the companies can adopt if taken up professionally. Involving the security team on board brings a lot of confidence and reliability for the customers.

Casale et al. [4] presented detailed synopsis about Software Engineering's current issues and future challenges for Services and Applications (SESA). In the SDLC life cycle, designing and developing a new software engineering app-roach is challenging. So, the stage changes from one method to another process are considered crucial. Cloud-based services and tools are being planned for rapid software prototyping to boost productivity and reduce software develop-ment costs, taking big data into account for a high computational requirement. The authors also presented an overview of the research topics in the software engineering area, highlighting the challenges in medium terms.

Casola et al. [5] presented SLA (Service Level Agreements) methodology to unify security in Development Operations through Design Security approach to assist in risk management life-cycle (Risk analysis and automated Security assessment phase) for a cloud application.

Diaz et al. [6] focuses on the difficulties in DevOps with the increase of the IoT system integrates and its complexity. They have proposed a self cyberse-curity event monitoring system to enhance security practices in the DevOps environment as an enabler to introduce the security practices in the DevOps environment for IoT-based Systems.

The'Fast and Continuous Feedback provides the fast detection of problems and suggestions to fix them from Ops to Dev' approach. The system focuses on obtaining fast and continuous feedback from operation to development at earlier stages of the development life cycle to find security issues and bugs at a fast rate to anticipate security problems and attack patterns. Kumar et al. [10] showed that user data security and privacy assurance gets lower priority. Integrating security to DevOps would save resources and be institutionalized as DevSecOps with practical considerations for a given business context to facilitate the adop-tion. The authors have presented the ADOC model for the business measures profiting by OSS over the cloud. The proposed ADOC model depends on the pro-posed consistent security calculated system, incorporating improvement, secu-rity, and activity exercises through computerization of safety controls utilizing OSS over the cloud just as between working OSS apparatuses for automatiza-tion of the proposed security controls in the ADOC work process. Its generalized reception empowers organizations to convey time-to-showcase security-prepared applications and administrations with speed and economic deftness in a finan-cially savvy way.

Laukkanen et al. [11] showed deployment challenges (from the continuous deployment of applications to automatically deployed as a product with eleven limitation factors) and provided solutions related to system designs, integration, Testing, Release, Human and organizational Resource. Luz et al. [12] presented

Table 1. The state of the artworks for the DevSecOps solutions and models. P1: Definition's, P2: Tools and Procedures, P3: Transitional and Future Challenges, P4: Cloud, P5: IOT, P6: Security Control Methods/Solutions P7: Artificial Intelligence

Authors	P1	P2	P3	P4	P5	P6	P7
Diaz et al. [6]	Yes	–	Yes	–	Yes	Yes	–
Casale et al. [4]	Yes	–	Yes	–	–	–	–
Carter and Kim. [3]	Yes	–	Yes	–	–	Yes	–
Kumar et al. [10]	Yes	Yes 1	Yes	Yes	–	Yes	–
Mohan et al. [14]	Yes	Yes	Yes	–	–	Yes	–
Casola et al. [5]	Yes	–	–	Yes	–	–	–
Luz et al. [12]	–	Yes	Yes	–	–	Yes	–
Shahin et al. [23]	Yes	Yes	Yes	–	–	Yes	–
Laukkanen et al. [11]	–	–	Yes	–	–	Yes	–
Rahul et al. [19]	–	Yes	–	–	–	Yes	–

the detailed scenarios of DevOps adoption, theory-related successful DevOps adoption in companies, a model depicting workflow for DevOps adoption, and a case study. The actual complex scenarios are being explained about the roles of the category during DevOps adoption.

Rahul et al. [19] demonstrated the DevSecOps using open-source tools which can be freely downloaded and used to exhibit information. To run the regular course of coordination and testing for information security requires more assets and time separately. The issue got defeated through execution and joining of safety as a feature of the pipeline cycle and consequently can accomplish quicker reaction time, fight against threats, and establish a safe climate and more secured framework. Shahin et al. [23] discussed a broad scope of difficulties that require progressed future exploration work for non-interrupt joining, proposed delivery, and deployment approaches, tools, and security measures. The state of the artworks for the DevSecOps solutions and models is shown in Table 1.

3 Background

DevSecOps is a cultural shift in the product business that intends to heat security into the quick delivery cycles that require future application improvement and organization, called the DevOps development. Accepting this shift-left attitude expects associations to overcome any barrier that usually exists among improvement and security groups to where large numbers of the security measures are computerized and dealt with by the advancement development team and groups itself [19].

3.1   Developement

Development Teams consistently work on developing state-of-art software applications for internal usage of the corporation, serving any specific purpose, API-based bridges for the legacy system and the new innovative service block that intends to be added to it and sometimes leveraging the open-source contribution streamlining the source code. A Generalized illustration of DevSecOps is shown in Fig. 1.

The fashion of development has seen a vital shift in recent years. Focus from the traditional sequential, waterfall-style process has transformed to rely more on agility and responsive models, which could benefit the developers by prioritizing the improvement regularly. Not considering the operations and security while the development of new applications or features and developers working in isolation could potentially raise operational issues or security vulnerabilities, which would take a heavy toll on the resources of the organization, making it a setback for the entire team [21].

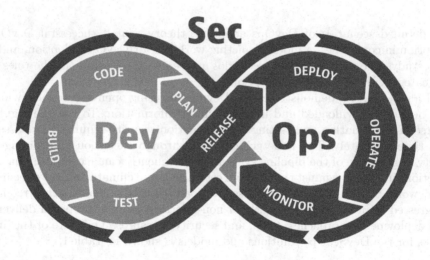

Fig. 1. A Generalized illustration of DevSecOps [13].

3.2   Operations

Operations terms to the complete process of managing and maintaining the software components throughout its delivery and use of the life cycle, including program performance, debugging, post-update testing and changes, and software upgrade release. As the necessity of running the development cycle and operation principles parallelly arose, the popularity of DevOps increased on the same hand as this was the key to achieve the desired outcome.

An isolated post-development operation is a much simpler and precise way to detect and address the potential flaws, but this comes with its own cost as it requires the entire development team to re-iterate and work on the problems before they could move forward with the development, which would intricate the whole process flow instead of simplifying it. Whereas integrating the operations principle into the development cycle would save a lot of resources for the company making it much more efficient and preferable [21].

3.3 Security

Now, as the companies and the developers are aware of the benefits of integrating the DevOps model into the system, the following crucial requirements of the security perimeter for the new software applications need to be streamlined. Traditionally application security was considered after the development is completed for the application.

But this posed many issues; firstly, the vulnerabilities were not to be detected until it is deployed, missing the run-time context as the vulnerabilities that would only be exposed under specific run time, making it more dangerous. Secondly, the cause for this was the static vulnerability scan, the traditional security method applied by security teams working in isolation with the other departments. This also made the entire process slow down. By integrating security as a unified process along with the development and operations (Called the DevSecOps) from the very initial designs to the due course implementation, organizations can efficiently maintain and align the three most crucial elements of software creation and shipment [21].

3.4 DevSecOps and Traditional Software Development

Earlier, Developers mostly had enough time for the production code to go through the security-testing and quality assurance procedures, even though the separate specialized teams were contracted internally or externally in a big way. As the developers from the tech giants were used to publishing the updated versions of their application basically every few months or even sometimes years, demonstrating how the developers from the tech giants kind of were used to issue the updated versions of their application every pretty few months or even sometimes years, or so they thought [19].

However, the past decade has chiefly witnessed the monolithic applications being broken down into generally much smaller elements that function independently. This was very kind of more result of the rise in public clouds, containers, and the microservice model being used more widely in a fairly significant way. But this alteration in the development process has explicitly impacted the frequency of rolling releases and agile development practices. The currently available tools and technology essentially have also made it possible to automate the process making the innovation by an organization faster, making it possible for them to maintain competency in the market. This alteration in the development process has explicitly impacted the frequency of rolling releases and agile development practices. At the same time, the changes and kind of better updates are continuously pushed to publication more often. The currently available tools and technology have also made it possible to automate the process, making the innovation by organizations much faster, making it possible for them to maintain competency in the market subtly.

But even though DevOps brought a wide variety of ease to the developers, it still lacked a vital aspect: Security. The pace of the agility of pushing the code to production, showing how the progress in the field of cloud, microservice, and containers had paved the path for the creation of a completely new domain of development which the industry people, for the most part, have termed as DevOps culture, just after its creation it has seen an evident rise in the practice of software development. As it arms the developers to provide and scale the infrastructure, they require it without going through the entire different tiresome process where a separate team had to do it for them. As of now, all the major league of cloud providers has adapted the API business where they configure the tools that enable them to use the infrastructure set up as a template of code deployment, or so they, for the most part, thought. But soon, the problem, for the most part, was taken care of by an upgrade to DevSecOps. It kind of was an endeavor to integrate security testing into the Continuous Delivery (CD) and Continuous Integration (CI) pipelines, it also covered the internal by keeping the outcome of testing and the fixing aspect by focusing on the building of the knowledge and skills required by the development team, or so they thought.

3.5   Achieving True Security/Development Integration

The delay in the Security process is because it takes a reasonable amount of time for the developers to fix the bug related to Security without any external help. It requires the developer to sort of build the technical skillset needed to perform the job efficiently. This is handled comparatively in a better manner by keeping a security expert in the team, who is more proficient as qualified in terms of Security in comparison to the other teammates. Even though the entire team must be better equipped with the training on secure programming practices as a part of it, the expert can always look over potential flaws in the system subtly. Not the general protocol, but the above procedure did not constrain the expert from reaching outside for another expert opinion. For instance, the company's application security testing provider might be offering consulting services to customers. Like this, for the most part, is an anomaly from keeping different kinds of development and security teams and having one or more members of the security team embedded into development teams [19].

3.6   Testing and Tools

The tools are available at the early time when the Silicon valley tech-related companies pilot the way to DevSecOps into the process where it's not simple to use by the developers. The requirement essentially was to automate the command line tools, which would aid them in altering a variety of configurations and whose results could be transported into the bug trackers. This was later on taken up by the conventional security scanners, which were designed with security teams and CISOs as focus, with the aim of governance, security policy compliance, and risk management in a significant way. Soon, the developers generally started making and marketing advanced tools for the developers that could be integrated into the development environment and the next CI/CD workflows. But even though the solved requirements of the developers, they did not satisfy the points of CISO any longer. Some of these tools kind of were open-source. Still, some were turned into accurate start-up business models built around them, further showing how soon the developers started making and marketing advanced tools that could be integrated into the development environment and the following CI/CD workflows. The wide variety of reasonably open source tools being used for the process creates a sense of satisfaction for the team. They can mainly cover what generally was required for all intents and purposes to be covered. The DevSecOps tools that are present in the market and being used by the companies in the DevOps pipeline are Codacy, Accunetix, GitLab, Aqua Security, XebiaLabs, Contrast Security, Logz.io, SonarQube, and WhiteSource [19]. But in real life, from the perspective of an administration, it becomes tough for the security team to map the distinguished software's made with different intent to adhere to the company policies, which is significant generally. But considering the requirements and situation in the past, it has been observed that the customary application security vendors have altered their products to address the problem by providing analytical and CISOs reports and providing the freedom and convenience required as per the developer's choice. Some providers have started adding security testing to their services, such as GitHub and git labs. Which is radially available into the service's marketplace by an add-on from the third party; when it is not present, there is an inherited feature, which is quite significant. According to Brian Fox, CTO of DevOps automation and open-source governance firm Sonatype, there is a pattern in DevSecOps that repeats itself. It is like a pendulum that swings between people who wanted one vendor and an all-compassing tool suite to people who are assembling best-of-breed toolchains [19].

These practices are not flawless as they invite an unforeseen situation that the organizations need to be prepared to deal with. The problem with these practices from suites specifically is that they bring some other functionalities with them that were not even intended but generally were free and can leverage, but not necessarily are the best option available out there. This step in the future can lead to the emerging sub-divisions inside the corporation, which will start testing and utilizing other tools that met their requirement better than the company-approved suite provides, which is significant.

3.7   Adoption of DevSecOps

"Security Debt" would be the reason for no immediate result even though the number of companies integrating the automated fashion of security scans as a sub-part of the CI/CD pipelines is rising. The number of vulnerabilities that get passed through to the production phase. The prime reason for this is the negligence of the developers, and it happens due to not fixing the bugs in a significant way. This can be due to a variety of reasons such as not being able to fix them immediately or sometimes the poor planning of when to fix the bugs or the severity of the bug at that time doesn't seem particularly much in a major way. According to the 2019 State of Software Security report, reveals that the average time taken to particularly solve a bug a decade ago, for the most part, was 59 days when the first report came out, which now, in turn, has changed to 171 days, this was collaborated by performing scans on 85,000 applications per annum in a major way. However, this is skewed by the accrued security debt, and the median time to fix it has essentially remained about the same. The data collected has also revealed that the applications scanned daily had a particularly median time duration of 19 days compared to the 68 days for the monthly reviewed applications, which is significant. That proves that the scanning is done for the most part; the chances of it getting fixed sooner increases. As an increased number of times of scanning can be achieved by the integration of automated scanning in CI/CD workflow, showing how the data collected has also revealed that the applications scanned daily had a median time duration of 19 days when compared to the 68 days for the monthly scanned applications [19].

When security is included from the beginning of the process, i.e., building security into requirements, design, code, and deployment stages of DevOps, it is called DevSecOps. The code for the program can be the starting point for scanning vulnerabilities. The CI/CD process is always the best option for integrating the vulnerabilities scanning step. It will ensure the security of code at every significant stage of the delivery pipeline. It is necessary to ensure that the parties involved in these steps have the training and the tools they need to perform the task.

For detecting vulnerabilities in your proprietary code, SAST is the relevant technology to go with it. For open-source, SCA tools can be used. Integration to CI servers, build tools, repositories, and some also integration to IDEs are readily offered by some vendors who can help developers find issues as early as possible [17].

4   AI Enabled DevSecOps

In this part, an AI paradigm is merged to facilitate and improvise the DevSecOps operation as shown in Fig. 2. The primary aim of the model is to enable the developers and security professionals to practice and implement the detection of insecure functions and potential vulnerabilities in a paradigm that has been developed with C/C++ language. This model has been paved on the grounds of the previous works on security as well as DevOps. The data-set used in the project has been sewed with the insecure functions and potential vulnerabilities of C/C++, which is according to the SEI CERT Coding Standard [1], as it provides rules for secure coding in the C/C++ programming language. The objective of these standards and proposals is to foster protected, dependable, and secure frameworks, for instance by disposing of indistinct practices that can prompt unclear program practices and exploitable vulnerabilities. Conformance to the coding rules characterized in this standard is important to guarantee the reliability, dependability, safety, and security of programming frameworks created in the C/C++ programming language. Thus this unique and outstanding Data-set is solely at the disposal of the authors of this research.

Model Preparation and Tuning: An offline process that starts with creating a dataset consisting of vulnerable and non-vulnerable code of C/C++ language derived from SEI-CERT Coding Standard.

1. **Pre-processing:** An offline process where the code is analyzed. The sample for feature extraction is created by performing various processing such as removing any irrelevant information i.e., comments in code.
2. **Feature Extraction:** It is a phase where the insecure/vulnerable functions and patterns of C/C++ with high and moderate CVSS (Common Vulnerability Scoring System). The generated dataset (.csv format) is ready for the Machine Learning Models.
3. **Training, Testing, and Saving Models:** The generated dataset is then used to train and test the ML models using sklearn.model-selection.train-test-split. The trained models are then saved as a pickle file to interact with the REST API easily.

System Architecture: The core of the project is its architecture which comprises trained models, extracted features, analysis, and pre-processing. The service is offered using the REST API Interface.

1. **REST API Interface:** The user (developer/Tester) can interact with the REST API to send their code to find vulnerable patterns in their code.
2. **Pre-processing:** Pre-processing is an online process where the submitted code is processed (for instance, removing irrelevant information, i.e., description/comments in code) and producing the code in the sample feature format.
3. **Analysis And Logging:** An important module where the code is analyzed produces valuable insights and shows the patterns correlated to the vulnerable, insecure and safe code. Currently, its shows uncertain functions and entropy as a result.
4. **Models:** Models are the first component of this workflow. It consists of all the trained models (described in Model Preparation and Tuning). Its main engine interacts with the workflow's analysis and logging and REST API to produce desired results.
5. **Interface:** The REST API is built using a flask to provide a convenient service to the users to access the platform for testing and securing the code more efficiently and fast than other tools present in the market.

Feature extraction is the phase where the insecure functions and vulnerabilities of C/C++ with high and moderate CVSS (Common Vulnerability Scoring System (CVSS). It is an open framework for communicating the characteristics and severity of software vulnerabilities [10] scores from the data-set are extracted according to the SEI CERT standards. Directly, this data-set will be fed to our Supervised machine learning model for the subsequent processing. Further, the data-set using sklearn.model-selection.train-test-split is bifurcated from the training and testing of the model.

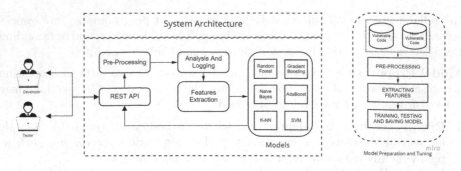

Fig. 2. Architecture diagram.

4.1   Implementation

For the implementation of the project, we have used Scikit-learn 0.22 (version), Python 3.8 (version), Spyder IDE, and the Anaconda framework. The project is built on the system Windows 10 Home (64 bits Operating System) running with Intel (R) Core (TM) i5-7200U processor and 12 Gigabytes RAM. The below-mentioned supervised machine learning classifier models are implemented here.

Random Forest: A random forest is a meta estimator that fits various choice tree classifiers on different sub-examples of the information collection and to improve the predictive accuracy and control over-fitting [18]. With the random state of 42 and train test split with the ratio of 7:3, it produces an accuracy of 88%.

Support Vector Machine: Support vector machines (SVMs) are a set of supervised learning methods used for classification, regression, and outliers detection [25]. The Benefits Support Vector Machine provides Potent high dimensional spaces. However effective in cases where several dimensions are greater than the number of samples, it utilizes a subclass of training points in the decision function (called support vectors) memory efficient with versatility. Specified decision functions can have different Kernal functions. Common kernels are provided, but it is also possible to specify custom kernels. SVM with the kernel = 'rbf', C = 100, gamma = 0.02, degree = 8 and train test ratio with 8:2 produces 98% accuracy.

KNN: K-NeighborsClassifier implements learning based on the k nearest neighbors of each query point, where k is an integer value specified by the user. RadiusNeighborsClassifier implements learning based on the number of neighbors within a fixed radius r of each training point, where r is a floating-point value specified by the user [8]. With n-neighbors = 2, weights = 'distance', algorithm = 'ball-tree', leaf-size = 30, p = 2, metric = 'minkowski', random state = 42 and train test ratio with 6:4 produces 70% accuracy.

Gradient Boosting: Gradient Tree Boosting or Gradient Boosted Decision Trees (GBDT) is a generalization of boosting to arbitrary differentiable loss

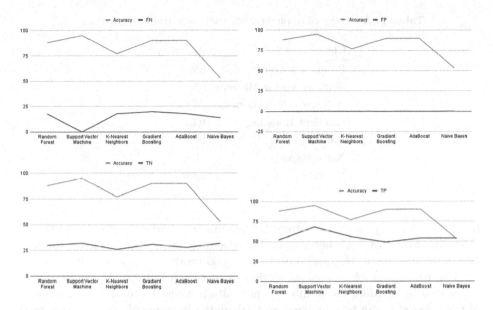

Fig. 3. Accuracy results of different machine learning algorithms implemented with DevSecOps.

functions. GBDT (Gradient Boosted Decision Tree) is an accurate and effective off-the-shelf procedure that can be used for both regression and classification problems in a variety of areas, including Web search ranking and ecology [16]. With n-estimators = 1000, learning-rate = 0.25, max-features = 2, max-depth = 2, random-state = 0 and train test split with the ratio of 7:3 produces the accuracy of 90%.

AdaBoost: The core principle of AdaBoost is to fit a sequence of weak learners (i.e., models that are only slightly better than random guessings, such as small decision trees) on repeatedly modified versions of the data. The predictions from all of them are then combined through a weighted majority vote (or sum) to produce the final prediction [22]. With n-estimators = 400, max-features = "auto", random-state = 0 and train test split with the ratio of 7:3 produces the accuracy of 90%.

Naive Bayes: Naive Bayes methods are a set of supervised learning algorithms based on applying Bayes' theorem with the "naive" assumption of conditional independence between every pair of features given the value of the class variable [20]. The random state of 42 and train test split with the ratio of 7:3 produces an accuracy of 53%.

Bagging: A Bagging classifier is an ensemble meta-estimator that fits base classifiers on random subsets of the original data-set and then aggregates their predictions (either by voting or by averaging) to form a final prediction. Such a meta-estimator can typically be used as a way to reduce the variance of a black-

Table 2. Accuracy of implemented machine learning algorithms.

Classifiers	Accuracy
Random Forest	88%
Support Vector Machine	95%
K-Nearest Neighbors	70%
Gradient Boosting	90%
AdaBoost	90%
Naive Bayes	53%
Bagging	88%

box estimator (e.g., a decision tree) by introducing randomization into its construction procedure and then making an ensemble out of it [2]. With n-splits = 100, random-state = 147, and num-trees = 600 produces an accuracy of 88%.

The percentage of correct prediction of test data is termed accuracy. It is calculated by dividing the number of accurate predictions by the total number of predictions. It can be expressed and calculated in terms of positives and negatives for binary classification. Accuracy denotes the effectiveness of the model to predict the label correctly.

Table 2 and Fig. 3 shows that the Support Vector machine got the highest precision from others, i.e., the kernel trick handled the nonlinear input spaces effectively. Then we have the boosting algorithms giving the high predictions rate, i.e., Gradient boosting and AdaBoost with 90% accuracy. The Random Forest has got 88% accuracy. Random Forest has accuracy lower than boosted trees but higher than decision trees. Like Random Forest, Bagging also predicted the same precision, i.e., 88%. K-nearest Neighbors with the value of K = 2 produce an accuracy of 70%; this signifies that the model does not have an effective result on the test set. Naive Bayes, 53% accuracy, produces the lowest prediction rate.

5   Conclusion and Future Works

When we combine Development, security, and operations, it is termed as DevSecOps. In plain sight, it plans to make everyone responsible for the security objectives administrating security decisions and actions with the same pace of scaling and speed as development and operations decisions and actions. A higher level of security proficiency can be achieved if we can successfully bring professionals of all competencies and abilities across the technology areas to enable the organizations with a stable DevOps framework to shift towards the DevSecOps techniques efficiently.

The DevSecOps framework and the proper guided manner of utilizing DevSecOps tools can ensure that the security has been integrated efficaciously to the very bit of the software application system. It is not just desultorily afterward; it covers from testing for potential security exploits to building business-driven security services. But the DevSecOps tools also generate false positives, and finding the solution after knowing the vulnerability/problems becomes hard. This paper aims to provide high accuracy data-driven machine learning models, which stand significantly in detecting the vulnerabilities in the code developed during the software development. The data-set used by our machine learning models to be trained and tested are a compilation of the insecure functions of the C/C++ programming language, which may cause potential vulnerabilities to the developed software according to the CVSS scoring metrics possing high values. As shown in Table 2, the SVM produces the highest accuracy standing that is 95%, and on the other hand, almost the lowest possible accuracy which the Naive Bayes Algorithm has is 53%.

The presented solution can be integrated with the present tools to reduce false positives and generally provide an effective solution. The research can also mostly be done to provide an effective, fast and accurate solution when the system is encountered with any security problems or vulnerability, which is relatively significant. We have only definitely worked with the insecure and vulnerable functions of the C/C++ programming language. In future work, we work with programming languages to integrate the particular present tools to reduce false positives for all intents and purposes and provide an effective solution subtly.

References

1. Bahaa, A., Abdelaziz, A., Sayed, A., Elfangary, L., Fahmy, H.: Monitoring real time security attacks for IoT systems using DevSecOps: a systematic literature review. Information 12(4), 154 (2021)
2. Breiman, L.: Bagging predictors. Mach. Learn. 24(2), 123–140 (1996)
3. Carter, K.: Francois raynaud on DevSecOps. IEEE Softw. 34(5), 93–96 (2017)
4. Casale, G., et al.: Current and future challenges of software engineering for services and applications. Procedia Comput. Sci. 97, 34–42 (2016)
5. Casola, V., De Benedictis, A., Rak, M., Villano, U.: A novel security-by-design methodology: modeling and assessing security by SLAs with a quantitative approach. J. Syst. Softw. 163, 110537 (2020)
6. Díaz, J., Pérez, J.E., Lopez-Peña, M.A., Mena, G.A., Yagüe, A.: Self-service cybersecurity monitoring as enabler for DevSecOps. IEEE Access 7, 100283–100295 (2019)
7. Edgescan: 2021 Vulnerability Statistics Report. Technical report (2021)
8. Guo, G., Wang, H., Bell, D., Bi, Y., Greer, K.: KNN model-based approach in classification. In: Meersman, R., Tari, Z., Schmidt, D.C. (eds.) OTM 2003. LNCS, vol. 2888, pp. 986–996. Springer, Heidelberg (2003). https://doi.org/10.1007/978-3-540-39964-3_62
9. Hsu, T.H.-C.: Hands-On Security in DevOps: Ensure Continuous Security, Deployment, and Delivery with DevSecOps. Packt Publishing Ltd. (2018)
10. Kumar, R., Goyal, R.: Modeling continuous security: a conceptual model for automated DevSecOps using open-source software over cloud (ADOC). Comput. Secur. 97, 101967 (2020)

11. Laukkanen, E., Itkonen, J., Lassenius, C.: Problems, causes and solutions when adopting continuous delivery-a systematic literature review. Inf. Softw. Technol. **82**, 55–79 (2017)
12. Luz, W.P., Pinto, G., Bonifácio, R.: Adopting DevOps in the real world: a theory, a model, and a case study. J. Syst. Softw. **157**, 110384 (2019)
13. Marsal, J.: What is DevSecOps? And what you need to do it well (2021). https://www.dynatrace.com/platform/. Accessed 19 Aug 2021
14. Mohan, V., Othmane, L.: SecDevOps: is it a marketing buzzword. Department of Computer Science, Technische Universität Darmstadt, Darmstadt (2016)
15. Myrbakken, H., Colomo-Palacios, R.: DevSecOps: a multivocal literature review. In: Mas, A., Mesquida, A., O'Connor, R.V., Rout, T., Dorling, A. (eds.) SPICE 2017. CCIS, vol. 770, pp. 17–29. Springer, Cham (2017). https://doi.org/10.1007/978-3-319-67383-7_2
16. Natekin, A., Knoll, A.: Gradient boosting machines, a tutorial. Front. Neurorobot. **7**, 21 (2013)
17. Ombredanne, P.: Free and open source software license compliance: tools for software composition analysis. Computer **53**(10), 105–109 (2020)
18. Pal, M.: Random forest classifier for remote sensing classification. Int. J. Remote Sens. **26**(1), 217–222 (2005)
19. Rahul, B., Prajwal, K., Manu, M.N.: Implementation of DevSecOps using open-source tools. Int. J. Adv. Res. Ideas Innov. Technol. **5**(3) (2019)
20. Rish, I., et al.: An empirical study of the Naive Bayes classifier. In: IJCAI 2001 Workshop on Empirical Methods in Artificial Intelligence, vol. 3, pp. 41–46 (2001)
21. Sánchez-Gordón, M., Colomo-Palacios, R.: Security as culture: a systematic literature review of DevSecOps. In: Proceedings of the IEEE/ACM 42nd International Conference on Software Engineering Workshops, pp. 266–269 (2020)
22. Schapire, R.E.: Explaining adaboost. In: Schölkopf, B., Luo, Z., Vovk, V. (eds.) Empirical Inference, pp. 37–52. Springer, Heidelberg (2013). https://doi.org/10.1007/978-3-642-41136-6_5
23. Shahin, M., Babar, M.A., Zhu, L.: Continuous integration, delivery and deployment: a systematic review on approaches, tools, challenges and practices. IEEE Access **5**, 3909–3943 (2017)
24. Tomas, N., Li, J., Huang, H.: An empirical study on culture, automation, measurement, and sharing of DevSecOps. In: 2019 International Conference on Cyber Security and Protection of Digital Services (Cyber Security), pp. 1–8. IEEE (2019)
25. Vishwanathan, S.V.M., Murty, M.N.: SSVM: a simple SVM algorithm. In: Proceedings of the 2002 International Joint Conference on Neural Networks. IJCNN'02 (Cat. No. 02CH37290), vol. 3, pp. 2393–2398. IEEE (2002)

A Case Study on Combining Agile and User-Centered Design

Yekaterina Pakhtusova, Swati Megha, and Nursultan Askarbekuly(✉)

Innopolis University, Innopolis, Tatarstan 420500, Russia
{y.pakhtusova,s.megha,n.askarbekuly}@innopolis.university

Abstract. Agile is a dominating software developing technique throughout the world. It promotes high development speed, work in short iterations, and delivering working software as soon as possible.

User-Centered Design is a more traditional approach that puts users and their needs first. It advocates spending more time understanding your users, their needs and wants, while the implementation process can be delayed and last longer. Both approaches try to deliver the best possible software for the users but utilize different means. This paper examines through a case study how Agile and User-Centered Design can be combined and whether this combination brings additional value. A development method is then suggested, combining the two philosophies.

Keywords: Agile · User centered design · Scrum · Product development

1 Introduction

User Centered Design (UCD) is a technique for developing software products, that focuses on users and their needs in each phase of the design process [12]. Agile Software Development (ASD) is a collection of approaches and practices in software development, that aims to maximize the value provided to the customer through early and continuous delivery of working software [15]. These approaches share some similarities [7], like

- They rely on an iterative development process, building on empirical information from previous cycles
- Both techniques place an emphasis on the end-user, encouraging participation throughout the development process
- Both approaches emphasize the importance of team coherence (one of the aspects of UCD is that the whole team should constantly think about the user during the development process)

Both of these methods have a goal of delivering quality software to stakeholders, but there are fundamental differences [7]:

Supported by Innopolis University.

G. Succi et al. (Eds.): ICFSE 2021, CCIS 1523, pp. 47–62, 2021.
https://doi.org/10.1007/978-3-030-93135-3_4

- UCD suggests maintaining specific design products to support interaction with developers, while agile methods look for minimal documentation
- ASD methods are largely against an up-front period of investigation instead of writing code, whereas UCD inspires the team to understand their users as much as possible before the product implementation begins

Several attempts have been made to connect ASD and UCD, but most of them inevitably have trade-offs. This paper focuses on one of such methods called Big Upfront Design (BUD), which supposes that designers must be given sufficient amount of time to find out the basic needs of their users before any code is written.

1.1 Objective

The main goal of the research is to show how to apply Big Upfront Design method of connecting Agile and User Centered Design. Within the study, the research team has implemented an online courses aggregator service called "EduHub" and attempted to apply a combination of Agile and UCD practices in accordance with the BUD method. The study analyses the BUD approach and suggests potential improvements.

1.2 Outline

In Sect. 2 the author describes existing approaches for combining ASD and UCD. In Sect. 3 the methods used for this research are listed. Section 4 is about how UCD and ASD were combined in practice by the author and development team who worked on online course aggregator service. Section 5 lists the results of the research and evaluation of overall work. In Sect. 6 some conclusions about the project are presented, which might be useful for people who conduct similar research work.

2   Related Work

This section describes User Centered Design, Agile Software Development, and existing techniques used for combining them. The author considers 5 most well-known combination techniques and lists its advantages and drawbacks.

2.1   User Centered Design

UCD History. The concept of User Centered Design has been around for a long time [1]. The design of some everyday things sometimes is bad and leaves users frustrated because of the inability to complete a certain task. But when things are designed good and can be used intuitively, we can say that designers used the principles of UCD, that is - constructed things for the users.

But the term UCD originated only in 1986 - from the book "User-Centered System Design: New Perspectives on Human-Computer Interaction" written by

Norman and Draper [19]. Norman continued to develop UCD concepts further in his book "The Psychology Of Everyday Things" published in 1988 [18]. There he suggested 7 principles for facilitating designer's tasks.

Norman's work emphasized the need to thoroughly investigate the necessities and aspirations of the users and the expected uses of the product. The obligation to involve actual users, often in the real-life environment, was a natural evolution in the field of User Centered Design.

UCD. UCD is considered to be one of the most popular frameworks for developing user interfaces. It is based on the active participation of users to improve the understanding of user and task requirements, and the iteration of design and evaluation phases [4,16].

The activities which UCD is composed of [11] (see Fig. 1):

- Define the users' context
- Specify the user requirements
- Design solutions to meet the user requirements
- Evaluate the designs against requirements

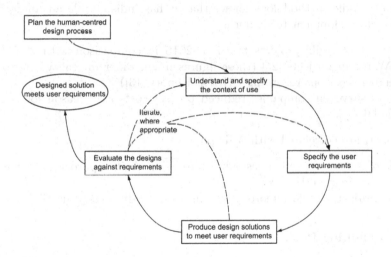

Fig. 1. UCD process as described by the standard ISO 13407

The main principles of UCD are listed below [11]:

- The design is based upon an explicit understanding of users, tasks, and environments
- Users are involved throughout the design and the development
- The design is driven and refined by user-centered evaluation
- The process is iterative

- The design addresses the whole user experience
- The design team includes multidisciplinary skills and perspectives

As a proof of best internationally endorsed practice, UCD processes are also defined in ISO documents, including ISO 13407 and the associated technical report, ISO TR 18529.

To illustrate the effectiveness of UCD, several studies have been conducted. The results show that 72% of the respondents reported UCD methods had made a significant impact on product development in their organizations. The majority said UCD methods had improved the usefulness and usability of products developed in their organizations, 79% and 82% respectively[16].

2.2   Agile Software Development

ASD is a software engineering philosophy that promotes [2]:

- individuals and interactions over processes and tools
- working software over comprehensive documentation
- customer collaboration over contract negotiation
- responding to change over following a plan

Nowadays, Agile methodology shows that it has indisputable advantages over traditional development techniques:

- Only 9% of Agile projects failed in 2015 in comparison with 29% failure for Waterfall projects [25] (these figures might differ in reality due to some arguable occasions regarding CHAOS Report [13])
- 71% of surveyed companies reduced project costs as a reason for adopting Agile [8]

These facts are correlated with ASD popularity:

- 71% of surveyed companies admitted using Agile approaches sometimes, often, or always [21]
- Agile projects are 28% more successful than traditional projects [20].

2.3   Combining Both

For more than a decade, software companies tend to integrate Agile Software Development methods and User Centered Design [22]. Several practitioners integrated UCD in their Agile process with varying degrees of success. This paper will consider the five most successful approaches to integration ASD and UCD.

To organize the work between developers and usability experts, Sy [24] proposes a method called *"Parallel tracks"* that requires developers and user experience designers to work in parallel tracks after the planning iteration also called iteration "0". It gives the opportunity for usability experts to have enough time to gather users' data, analyze that data and to propose design solutions. However, adopting this approach may cause the lack of communication which could lead to misunderstanding and resentment between designers and developers, since there can emerge a situation when designers and developers would work on completely different tasks due to such desynchronization.

Another similar approach was proposed by Armitage [3], but it concerns only the organization of designers' work. *"Design work done on parallel levels"* suggests the design work is done on three parallel levels from unit to global level:

- Provide detailed designs for the requirement developed in the current or next iteration.
- Redesign software developed in previous releases (a release is a set of several iterations).
- Provide overall product vision, to keep a global coherence throughout the project and developed software.

However, it is not clear if the evaluation of the design done in one iteration is conducted by users.

Deuff et al. [10] present another proposition of process for UCD in Agile called *"Sequence of an iterative design phase and an iterative development phase"* that gives a good place to an upfront designing. In classical Agile methodology usability experts have to switch between too many tasks (gather the necessary data, define the design, test) because they do not have time to prepare the data beforehand. To resolve this issue they propose to cut the project in 3 phases: Design, Development and Final test. Due to that reason, we cannot state that the process is iterative, as each phase proceeds after another.

Constantine and Lockwood [9] propose another approach, which is the integration of Usage-Centered Design and Agile. *Usage-Centered Design* is more focused on roles than on users and on usage scenarios also knew as task cases. Roles and tasks are identified by stakeholders. The process is composed of iterations that are all composed of the succeeding steps (see Fig. 2):

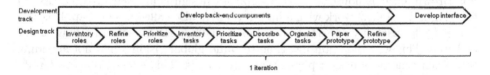

Fig. 2. One iteration of Usage-Centered Design adapted to Agile methods

During this time developers create the back-end components. When the prototype is refined, they develop the interface. The disadvantage is that the evaluation of designs against requirements is not covered in this approach, which goes against the UCD principles.

Big Upfront Design. The fifth approach for combining Agile and User Centered Design is called *"Big Upfront Design (BUD)"*.

Agile methods do not encourage big upfront design [5,17]. In reality, an analysis that is conducted by the product owner before the start of the development process is necessary to compose the product backlog, but no best practice is defined to help the product owner to complete this task. That is why some usability experts propose to conduct a big analysis upfront. Other practitioners are against this practice and prefer to use the iteration "0" to conduct a short analysis and then go deeper throughout the project if the better analysis is needed.

Supporters of BUD
Chamberlain [7] in his work insists on a big upfront design before any development: "UCD practitioners must be given ample time in order to discover the basic needs of their users before any code gets released into the shared coding environment." A lot of work has to be done during one iteration in any Agile methodology so that usability experts do not always have time to ask questions or to take a global view and ensure the homogeneity and consistency of the solution.

For Brown [6], in long projects sometimes it is necessary to devote more time for analysis in order to gather the necessary data.

Opponents of BUD
On the contrary, Armitage [3] insists that it is too risky and time and money-consuming to design deeply in advance and it is totally against Agile practices which encourage "trial and error to reduce the risk of building the wrong thing". A big upfront design might reduce the quality of the software and its design [3].

Another problem is the difficulty to accept changes later when a big upfront design was done, which goes against the Agile values "Responding to change over following a plan" and "Working software over comprehensive documentation" [3,14,17].

Conclusion
For Brown [6], it is nonsense that no upfront design is allowed in Agile-UX. In fact, Agile developers work with a high-level plan also called a roadmap. It is also necessary for usability experts to develop a roadmap in the form of a diagram or a sketch. This way the team has time to build global vision while not spending too much time on a design phase that never ends. This is essential to identify future possible technical difficulties.

BUD covers only three of the four UCD activities: understanding and specifying the context of use, specifying the user and organizational requirements, and producing design solutions. There are no specific recommendations for evaluation of a design against requirements, so there is no guarantee that big upfront design will meet the users' requirements.

BUD does not ensure users' involvement, evaluation, iterativeness, and multidisciplinarity even if they are recommended to be used for a better design. It becomes obvious that the goal of this approach is to implement the first UCD principle: understanding of users, tasks, and context.

2.4   Research Purpose

This research is aimed at applying Big Upfront Design (BUD) on a real project with high user involvement connected with online education. During the research process, the author will try to improve existing BUD practice by ensuring that all the principles of User Centered Design are respected. By applying BUD on the project, it will be possible to see its advantages, disadvantages, and potential improvements to the approach.

3   Methodology

This section provides a detailed overview of the methodologies used by the author for the combination of ASD and UCD.

3.1   Context

To understand how to combine Big Upfront Design and Agile Software Development, the author applied both of these techniques to the development of a real project. The project is an online service for aggregation of Massive Open Online Courses (MOOCs) called EduHub. EduHub provides an opportunity to search for MOOCs from several popular course providers (e.g. Coursera, Udemy, Udacity, etc.) in one place, with the ability to filter and sort them according to some criteria defined by the user. The project was selected due to the high popularity of online education (according to [23] more than 101 million users study online).

3.2   Agile Software Development

The team that is working on EduHub project consists of three people - two software developers and one UI/UX designer (the author). To work effectively, the team selected Agile Software Development as a methodology for creating software. But, for the purpose of genericity and context of the project the team does not stick to some specific framework (e.g. Scrum, Crystal, XP, etc.), but rather selected a set of practices adopted by popular frameworks [8], such as:

- Backlogs - the team maintains an ordered list of product requirements that will be delivered in future sprints. The team has separated product and sprint backlogs.
- User stories - description of a feature of the product written from the perspective of a user.
- Iterative and Incremental Development - development of a system through repeated cycles (iterative) and in smaller portions at a time (incremental), allowing software developers to take advantage of what was learned during development of earlier parts or versions of the system.
- Scrum events: planning, review, and retrospective

- planning - at the beginning of a sprint, the team agrees on the sprint goal, a short description of what they are forecasting to deliver at the end of the sprint
- review - at the end of a sprint, the team hold a review, where the members review the work that was completed and the planned work that was not completed
- retrospective - during this event the team reflects on the previous sprint and discusses what can be improved in the current development process
- Planning poker - the team members make estimations of the difficulty of the tasks and then discuss it
- Velocity tracking - a technique for forecasting the team's performance and planning of the future sprints
- Pair programming - two coders work collectively at one computer. One writes code while the other inspects each line of code as it is typed in. The two programmers shift roles frequently.
- Cross-functional team - a team consisting of people with different functional expertise working toward a common goal.

3.3   User Centered Design

The author uses traditional activities of which UCD consists. These include iterations of the steps:

1. Define the users' context
2. Specify the users' requirements
3. Produce design solutions to meet user requirements
4. Evaluate the designs against requirements

As it was already mentioned in Sect. 2, in Agile there is no best practice for the product owner how to define the product backlog, but this task should be done before the start of the Agile development process. To support the product owner for this task, some usability experts propose to conduct a big analysis upfront. So, the team decided to utilize BUD to analyze what needs to be done.

During Big Upfront Design phase of the design process, the main goal is to capture users' needs, usability goals, the context of use and design criteria. This time is also used to define users or to build personas.

To implement the second step of UCD (specify the users' requirements), several user research methods were utilized:

- Online survey - to understand, who our possible users are, how often they visit resources connected to online education, what difficulties they have while searching for a course, and to get information from as many people as possible, the team conducted an online survey using Google Forms.
- Personas - is a technique of creation of a representative user based on available data and user interviews. Basing on the results of the aforementioned survey, the author created the three most common personas of potential users.

- Heuristic evaluation - is a method for evaluating a website against a list of established guidelines. The team evaluated 5 popular online course providers to analyze how they provide service to users.
- Use Cases - the author created a description of how users use a particular feature EduHub, including the steps users take to accomplish each task.
- Interviews - the author conducted one-on-one discussions with users to get detailed information about a user's attitudes, desires, and experiences.
- Contextual interviews - they enable the observation of users in their natural environment, giving a better understanding of the way users work. For this study, the author observed how people searched for online courses using existing solutions.
- Prototyping - to allows the team to explore ideas before implementing them, the author created mock-ups of the site.

To ensure that the design conforms to the requirements (step 4 of UCD), the team conducted usability testing to identify user frustrations and problems with the site through one-to-one sessions where a user was asked to perform some tasks on the site and their reaction was recorded.

4   Implementation

This section outlines the phases through which the project underwent.

The basic outline of the team's working process can be seen on the following Fig. 3:

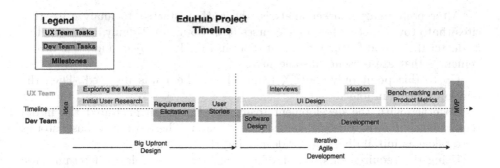

Fig. 3. Project timeline up to the MVP stage

There were two main phases of the development process:

4.1   Big Upfront Design Phase

After the team selected the idea of EduHub project, the author started to conduct market and user research.

During this stage, an online survey was conducted in order to identify who are our potential customers and what are their pains that they encounter during the search for MOOCs. Also, the data about online education and users from the open sources were used to make initial conclusions. The main point of this research is the creation of personas - description of potential customers and their needs:

- Student
  They study at university/school and search for additional materials that can help them to understand their studies. They usually search for free courses as they do not possess a lot of spare money. They expect that an online aggregator will be fast and with a wide choice of courses.
- Professional
  It is a person who usually already has a higher education and work experience. They work in rapidly developing industries where new technologies are emerging every so often, so they have to keep up with changes or they will lose their qualifications. They are ready to pay good money for courses. The most important feature of the site is information content - in order to compare available options and choose the best one.
- Lifelong learner
  Any person who constantly improves their knowledge and expands their horizons can be called a lifelong learner. They like to learn new things just for their curiosity and thirst for knowledge. This makes it harder to highlight some features that are common for lifelong learners as they are varying in age, gender, income and education level, etc. In site, the most important things are a diverse choice of courses and user-friendly interface.

After preliminary market analysis, the author started to analyze existing sites that provide access to online courses (e.g. Coursera, Udemy, Udacity, etc.) to detect their good features to adopt them in EduHub project and avoid inconveniences that are present on some sites.

Up to this point only the UX team (the author) was involved. Then the development team joined.

Together with the development team, the UX team elicitated the initial requirements in order to construct user stories later. These composed user stories were taken as initial direction for developing the system.

Using the requirements, the development team was able to determine the stack of technologies that will be used during the coding stage.

Overall, BUD phase took about one month to complete. During this time, the general roadmap of the project was constructed, the development and UX teams got an understanding of the future work, and initial requirements were gathered, which was enough to start the development.

4.2   Iterative Agile Development Phase

After completing BUD phase, the author started to conduct interviews with real people who resembled some type of personas that were mentioned above.

During the interviews, the author asked questions regarding their pains during the search for MOOCs and what features they would expect from a service that provides access to all the possible online courses at one place. The most common requirements were:

- wide range of available courses
- ease of use
- availability on PC and mobile devices
- ability to sort and filter courses
- ability to read and write feedback about courses

This was a way to validate our requirements and user stories that were constructed previously. Also, it gave ground for further ideation that took place later on.

Simultaneously with the interviews, the UX team started working on UI design production. Firstly, the author produced paper sketches of the future interface for the sake of simplicity and speed. During paper prototyping, the planned design underwent some changes, which was not critical because of the choice of a prototyping tool.

The design was produced with the help of Figma - a free tool for creating digital prototypes. The prototypes that were created include:

- search for online courses
- sorting and filtering results
- viewing course information (details, syllabus, feedback)

The development team worked in parallel, preparing software architecture and design of the system. By the time the software design activities were completed, the UX team already had the first batch of UI sketches ready for use.

The author transferred materials needed for implementation of the design in code to the developers to start coding. The author then continued to work on the design simultaneously with programming work of developers.

As the team worked using Agile practices, every weak at the end of a sprint there was a team meeting, where the team discussed how the sprint went, what was done and not done, aroused questions, and plans for the next sprint. The two teams discussed and assigned priorities to tasks together. The effort estimation for tasks in the product backlog was done by the development team. Based on the priorities and effort estimates tasks were selected tasks for the sprint.

During the development of Minimal Viable Product (MVP) by developers, the author created the design for the rest of the features of EduHub. The design team worked one step ahead of the developers to ensure that the latter would always have UI designs ready to work on. The MVP included the following features:

- possibility to create an account
- profile of the user with personal information and settings
- possibility to leave feedback for a course
- addition of a course to favourite courses list

– email subscription to a newsletter
– display of top-5 courses of the site

In the end of UI Design stage, the author conducted an ideation session in order to generate some ideas for additional features of the EduHub which could be implemented during the future iterations. This ideation session was important because it allowed to create a post-MVP vision for the product development.

At some stage the team realized the need of administrator panel to control the content of EduHub service. The team (as current stakeholders) discussed what features are be needed to be available in the administrator panel. After collecting all the requirements, the author implemented the administrative service using the same principles as for the EduHub service - simplicity and focus on functionality.

When the UI design for the MVP product was finished, the UX team started to develop the product metrics. It was important to create the metrics before the MVP was ready to asses how the product meets user requirements when it would be ready. Having the metrics and results of testing, it is much easier to make improvements.

When the MVP was ready, the author started conducting usability testing to find out if the site is understandable, convenient, and most importantly meets the requirements of the users.

For the sake of usability testing, 20 people who are similar to our target audience were selected. 15 people were students and young specialists who search for online courses for their studying process, other 5 were people who just enjoy self-learning and use online courses to learn something new, not for their job.

The interviewees were given 14 tasks:

1. look through top-5 courses on the main page
2. sign up for a newsletter on the main page
3. search for a course from the home page of a site
4. when results of the search are shown, filter the search to display only free courses
5. select a course that a user likes and go to its details
6. look through the description, syllabus, and feedback
7. go to the site-provider of the course to learn it
8. create an account on the site
9. search for a new course and add it to favourite courses
10. leave feedback for this course
11. go to your profile and look at your favourite courses. Unmark a course from favourites
12. go to settings and add your personal information
13. reset your password
14. log out from your account

While the subjects were performing the tasks, the author observed their behaviour and actions. All the respondents were able to fulfill the tasks correctly and under acceptable time. This can be explained by the fact that all the interviewees were active Internet users and the site utilizes habitual UX design patterns that most of the Internet users have already encountered.

5   Evaluation and Discussion

This section describes the results of the work done and some insights that were received during the project.

5.1   Results

In this section the author enumerates the problems encountered during the project and their possible solutions and the insight that can be useful for the similar projects.

At the initial stage of the project, the UX team worked alone. The reason for it was that user and market research had to be conducted to verify the initial hypothesis before any design and development effort could take place. The hypothesis was that there is a need for an online course aggregator, i.e. online learners are having difficulty with searching for online courses due to a big number of learning platforms and course options. This is the essence of BUD, and the exact circumstance for it to be applied.

During the initial research phase, the UX team faced a problem that there was not enough secondary information (from some other sources) about online education situation in Russia, so the team had to collect it as primary information (from own research). Due to this situation, it took more time for the initial research than it was planned.

The development team was more or less idle during the initial research stage. Since EduHub is an academic project, the development team took advantage of this period to explore the solution space in terms of the state-of-art architectural designs that could be applied during the project. In industrial circumstances, it is a question whether the development team should even be hired/formed/onboarded before the initial user and market research stage produces a conclusive result in regards to hypothesis validation.

Requirements elicitation and documentation has been done through collaboration between the development and UX teams. Starting from this stage the development team could be heavily involved with the project without idle periods.

It is healthy to have both teams collaborating during the production of functional and quality requirements (product backlog) since the development team can assess and estimate the effort needed for developing the functionalities, while the UX team can deal with the prioritization of backlog items.

It should be recognized that BUD in its essence is a sequential approach (and sometimes looks like a Waterfall development model), but this is not a bad idea for kick-starting the project. Once the initial set of requirements is in place, the Agile stage begins, which means that Agile practices can prevail within the development process from this point on.

The gathered and documented requirements were just the initial set, and there was no intention to freeze the requirement and refuse change. They were just a fulcrum that gave a direction for further actions. And the UX team took all the advantages of the agile principle of welcoming changes in the project.

Having the initial set of requirements ready, the development team took their time to make basic architectural choices fitting the project's context and to decide on the appropriate technological stack. The UX team used this time to produce initial UI sketches so that the development team would have the design to implement in the code. This is relevant in the case of software products with graphical user interface. In a similar manner, the UX team was timely supplying the necessary designs to the development team to avoid delays and bottlenecks.

Once the UI designs require less time and effort from the UX team, the designers have to be creative to keep themselves busy until the MVP arrives. The UX team worked on the vision of the future features of EduHub (Ideation session, additional user interviews), as well as developed the metrics for assessment of MVP.

MVP allowed the UX team to conduct further Usability Testing, collect analytics and test the hypotheses that were created during Ideation.

6   Conclusions and Future Work

This section presents the overall conclusions about this research and some plans for the future work.

6.1   Conclusion

In this paper, we have implemented an online course aggregator called EduHub. Two teams were working on that project - UX team and development team. To guide and synchronize a workflow between two teams UCD and ASD methodologies were used. To glue UCD and ASD together, the author proposed to use BUD technique. But the original description of BUD did not fully satisfy UCD process activities and the author had to improve and complement the original BUD method.

To ensure compliance with the fourth step of UCD (evaluation of design against requirements) the author proposes to use usability testing after completing MVP. After that, usability testing can be conducted after any newly added feature.

Overall, we can say that the study is successful. The author with the team achieved the desired results and fulfilled the goal of the project.

We can conclude that application of Big Upfront Design technique for combining UCD and Agile brought beneficial results and allowed to follow the guidelines of both methodologies.

The only disadvantage (though it actually can be an advantage) is that one has to spend some additional time at the beginning of a project for a BUD stage to do preliminary research. This time which UX team spends can be used for searching of developers or deciding on technology stack for the project.

6.2 Future Work

In the future, the author plans to conduct more diversified usability testing, because due to the tight schedule and academic purpose of the research the author had to test students and employees of their university. Since interviewees were from one city and initially predisposed to active Internet usage, the results can be biased.

As a future development of the project, the author and the developers plan to introduce additional features which were extracted from user interviews and created during an Ideation session. One of such features is the introduction of study plans - roadmaps containing a list of courses needed to learn a profession.

References

1. Abras, C., Maloney-Krichmar, D., Preece, J.: User-centered design (2004)
2. Agile Alliance: Agile manifesto (2001). http://www.agilemanifesto.org
3. Armitage, J.: Are agile methods good for design? Interactions **11**(1), 14–23 (2007)
4. Askarbekuly, N., Solovyov, A., Lukyanchikova, E., Pimenov, D., Mazzara, M.: Building an educational product: constructive alignment and requirements engineering. In: Ahram, T.Z., Karwowski, W., Kalra, J. (eds.) AHFE 2021. LNNS, vol. 271, pp. 358–365. Springer, Cham (2021). https://doi.org/10.1007/978-3-030-80624-8_44
5. Blomkvist, S.: Towards a model for bridging agile development and user-centered design. In: Seffah, A., Gulliksen, J., Desmarais, M.C. (eds.) Human-Centered Software Engineering—Integrating Usability in the Software Development Lifecycle. Human-Computer Interaction Series, vol. 8, pp. 219–244. Springer, Dordrecht (2005). https://doi.org/10.1007/1-4020-4113-6_12
6. Brown, D.D.: Five agile UX myths. J. Usability Stud. **8**(3), 55–60 (2013)
7. Chamberlain, S., Sharp, H., Maiden, N.: Towards a framework for integrating agile development and user-centred design. In: Abrahamsson, P., Marchesi, M., Succi, G. (eds.) XP 2006. LNCS, vol. 4044, pp. 143–153. Springer, Heidelberg (2006). https://doi.org/10.1007/11774129_15
8. CollabNet VersionOne: The 13th annual state of agile report (2019). https://www.stateofagile.com
9. Constantine, L., Lockwood, L.: Process agility and software usability: toward lightweight usage-centered design. Inf. Age **8**(8), 1–10 (2002)
10. Deuff, D., Cosquer, M., Foucault, B.: Méthode centrée utilisateurs et développement agile: une perspective & « gagnant-gagnant» au service des projets de R&D. In: Conference Internationale Francophone sur l'Interaction Homme-Machine, pp. 189–196, September 2010
11. ISO DIS: 9241-210:2010 Ergonomics of human system interaction - Part 210: Human-centred design for interactive systems (2009)
12. Endsley, M.R., Jones, D.G.: Design for Situation Awareness. An Approach to User Centered Design. CRC Press, Boca Raton (2004)
13. Eveleens, J., Verhoef, C.: The rise and fall of the chaos report figures. IEEE Softw. **27**, 30–36 (2010)
14. Ferreira, J., Noble, J., Biddle, R.: Up-front interaction design in agile development. In: Concas, G., Damiani, E., Scotto, M., Succi, G. (eds.) XP 2007. LNCS, vol. 4536, pp. 9–16. Springer, Heidelberg (2007). https://doi.org/10.1007/978-3-540-73101-6_2

15. Highsmith, J.: Agile Software Development Ecosystems. Addison-Wesley, Boston (2002)
16. Mao, J.Y., Vredenburg, K., Smith, P.W., Carey, T.: The state of user-centered design practice. Commun. ACM **48**(3), 105–109 (2005)
17. Nodder, C., Nielsen, J.: Agile Usability: Best Practices for User Experience on Agile Development Projects. Nielsen Norman Group, California (2010)
18. Norman, D.A.: The Psychology of Everyday Things. Basic Books, New York (1988)
19. Norman, D.A., Draper, S.W.: User-Centered System Design: New Perspectives on Human-Computer Interaction. Lawrence Earlbaum Associates, Hillsdale (1986)
20. PricewaterhouseCoopers: Agile project delivery confidence (2017)
21. Project Management Institute: Success rates rise. Transforming the high cost of low performance (2017)
22. Schwartz, L.: Agile-user experience design: an agile and user-centered process? In: The Eighth International Conference on Software Engineering Advances, ICSEA 2013 (2013)
23. Shah, D.: By the numbers: MOOCs in 2018 (2018)
24. Sy, D.: Adapting usability investigations for agile user-centered design. J. Usability Stud. **2**(3), 112–132 (2007)
25. The Standish Group International: Chaos report (2015)

An Analysis of the Sensitivity of Software Reliability Growth Models Using Bootstrap and Monte Carlo Simulations

Marina Ivanova[✉]

Innopolis University, Innopolis, Russia
ma.ivanova@innopolis.university

Abstract. A decent characterization of the occurrence of service requests (SRs) for modification is extremely important for software companies because the resolution of SRs is a time and resources consuming process. Software reliability growth models are used in this study to describe SRs arrivals in three open-source mobile operating systems. The systematic literature review was held for purpose of the investigation of two research questions. First, possible methods for constructing confidence intervals for parameters of the software models. Second, measuring the stability of the model to errors in data collection. Confidence intervals were found for model parameters using a bootstrap method. Confidence intervals of estimations support more accurate effort prediction and release time estimation. These predictions have great importance for the software development managing process. Verification of the model resistance to human errors in collecting data was conducted with the application of Monte Carlo simulation with Gaussian noise.

Keywords: Software reliability · Software reliability growth models · Bootstrap · Monte Carlo simulation · Confidence intervals

1 Introduction

The software has become an essential part of business processes and software systems' vulnerabilities and breakdowns might cause unwanted effects on business operations. To reduce the risk of such breakdowns, it is crucial to efficiently predict the behaviour of software systems. Also, to make justified decisions for the resolution of service requests (SRs) caused by the systems' potential breakdowns, project managers need to estimate the number of service requests. The proper estimation of the service requests enables better planning, recognizing the bottlenecks, resource allocation, and precise estimation of the time for the system to become ready to release [7,16,33]. One approach to predict the system's behaviour and supply the necessary estimations is by way of obtaining the confidence intervals for parameters of the software reliability growth models (SRGMs).

Previous research efforts used stochastic differential equations [20,21,34], Bayesian method [35] and adaptive testing [36] for finding the confidence intervals. Though the said methods proved to perform well each on the specific data

© Springer Nature Switzerland AG 2021
G. Succi et al. (Eds.): ICFSE 2021, CCIS 1523, pp. 63–83, 2021.
https://doi.org/10.1007/978-3-030-93135-3_5

distribution, none of them can perform independently from the data distribution. Hence, in this research project, we aim to find ways to determine the confidence intervals of the estimations of SRs and investigate the sensitivity of the models to errors in collecting data. We believe that the outcomes of this research will enable managers to make more accurate calculations of the reliability of software systems [1, 9–12, 18, 19, 22, 26, 28, 31, 37, 38, 41, 42, 46, 47, 51, 52, 57].

To this end, we constructed confidence intervals by using the bootstrap resampling method. Unlike previously used methods [8, 13, 14, 32, 40, 45, 48, 49, 53, 55, 56, 58, 59, 62–65, 67], the suggested method requires no assumptions about the distribution of the input data; this means we can define reliability for the data with any distribution.

2   Background

2.1   Identification of the Relevant Literature

Confidence intervals are used in the different fields such as medicine [2, 39, 43], system dynamics [15], mediation modeling [50, 69], etc. In this study, we will cover only the usage of confidence intervals with implications in the software measures and software models.

The following sections explain the procedure of the Systematic Literature Review (SLR): identification of the research questions, explanation of the search procedure and queries, listing inclusion and exclusion criteria. These sections also provide answers to the research questions of the literature review.

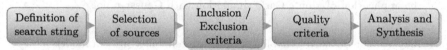

To identify the primary studies that address the topic of our SLR we formulated the research questions (RQ):

RQ1: How is it possible to construct a confidence interval for typical software measures and software models?

RQ2: How is it possible to describe the error in collecting software measures and understand its implication in typical software models?

In the search process, Google Scholar and Springer Link search engines were used. The original search string for RQ1 was:

('construct' OR 'build') 'confidence interval' AND 'software measurement'

The search string for RQ2:

(error OR 'margin of error') AND collect* AND 'software measure*'

Table 1. Identified keywords

Area	Keywords
RQ1	Confidence interval, sample statistic, bootstrap, software measures, software models, confidence interval for typical software measures and software models, confidence interval for software measures
RQ2	Margin of error, error in collecting software measurement, implication of error in software models

For each RQ, the keywords were extracted and the proper search queries were specified using the keywords. The overall web were inspected using Google engine. The resulting keywords are shown in Table 1. After searching and retrieving the set of potentially interesting papers, we have applied the following inclusion and exclusion criteria on the set.

Inclusion Criteria

- *Type of intervention:* Articles that are oriented on software measures and software models
- *Type of outcome:* Described methods and approaches for building confidence interval
- *Topic/scope:* Software reliability growth models
- *Language:* English
- *Type of publication:* Original research, book, review research, papers

Exclusion Criteria

Any paper that fails to meet any of the inclusion requirements
- Papers that do not have the full text will be excluded

These criteria have been applied in three phases leading to a final selection of eighteen papers (Table 2):

Phase 1: All publications were evaluated by title and abstract.
Phase 2: The result was renewed considering introduction and conclusion.
Phase 3: A final selection was performed based on a full-text analysis.

Then, we have analysed the results following the guidelines:

- The tags which characterise each publication in terms of the topic that it covers were added.
- All papers were separated according to their affiliation to RQs.

We used Zotero research assistant, where we store all found publications. Figure 1 shows the distribution of papers by year.

Table 2. Filtering results

RQs	Phase 1	Phase 2	Phase 3
RQ1	33	20	9
RQ2	30	14	9
Total	63	34	18

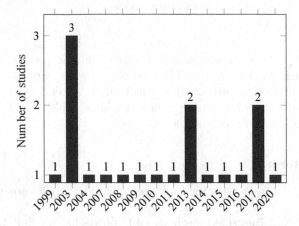

Fig. 1. Distribution of papers by years

The data extracted from the reviewed papers were:

- The research question(s) of the study
- The authors of the research
- The summary of the research
- The gaps in the research and the areas of further studies

We manually searched 63 papers. After the second stage of the filtering, we had 34 papers. After the third stage, we rejected some papers due to lack of relevance to our study and fully analysed 18 papers. The full list for the Final review for each RQ is presented in Tables 3, 4. In Fig. 2 we can see a distribution of papers across conferences. The distribution of studies per journal is depicted in Fig. 3.

2.2   Existing Techniques for Constructing the Confidence Intervals

For purpose of constructing the confidence intervals, we studied previous researches on this topic. We found out that confidence intervals are used in:

- Software Reliability modelling [20,21,25,34–36]
- Software Effort estimation [5,44]
- Optimal Release Time estimation [21,25]

There are several methods for estimation of confident intervals for software metrics. The construction of confidence intervals for *reliability assessment* and *Optimal Release Time estimation* can be done with:

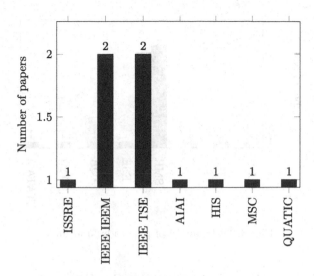

Fig. 2. Distribution of papers by conferences

- Bootstrap methods [25,60]
- Stochastic differential equations [20,21,34]
- Bayesian method [35]
- Adaptive testing [36]

For *effort estimation* the following methods are used:

- Ridge Regression Conformal Predictors [44]
- Robust Confidence Intervals [5]

Skylar et al. in the work [60] evaluate different bootstrap metrics for the calculation of the confidence intervals of the basic software metrics [17]. It was found that confidence intervals for median, mean, and Spearman correlation coefficient were accurately estimated. The confidence intervals for variance and kurtosis were underestimated. In contrast with our work, Skylar et al. do not apply the bootstrap method in the case of software reliability models.

Inoue et al. [25] discuss a bootstrap method for estimating confidence intervals of software reliability and cost-optimal software release time. For this purpose, the authors utilize the discretized exponential software reliability growth model. The mentioned model is the discrete analogue of the continuous-time exponential software reliability growth models, that our research is focused on.

Unlike previous researches that used stochastic differential equations [20,21, 34], Bayesian method [35] and adaptive testing [36], our method do not require assumption about distribution of the data.

In papers [5,44] the machine learning methods are applied for finding the confidence intervals of effort estimation. Though, we concentrate on defining the confidence intervals for parameters of software reliability growth models. These parameters denote the number of SRs and the speed of their detection.

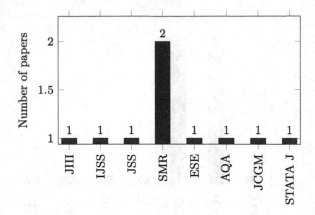

Fig. 3. Distribution of papers by Journals

2.3 Overview of Methods to Describe the Error in Collecting Measurements

We found that measurement error can be calculated by:

- Multiple Imputation (MI) and its extension Multiple Overimputation (MO) [3,4]
- Generalized linear models [24]

Measurement uncertainty can be found according to the:

- "Guide to the Expression of Uncertainty in Measurement" (GUM), Convolution method and Monte Carlo method [6]
- Analysis of variance (ANOVA) [30,54]
- An extension of UML and OCL types [66]

Blackwell et al. proposed the MI and MO methods [3,4] to handle observed data measured with error. The MI and MO methods can be used when the degree of measurement error can be analytically determined. In our case, the goal is to find the degree of measurement error. Thus, we chose a different method to reach our goal.

Hardin et al. introduce additive measurement error in a generalized linear-model context [24]. However, we consider non-linear models in our work.

The GUM, convolution and Monte Carlo methods were evaluated in [6] for estimating the uncertainty for individual measurement processes errors. All three methods can be used and showed comparable results.

Also, uncertainties arising at different stages of a measurement process can be estimated using analysis of variance (ANOVA) on duplicated measurements (Table 5).

3   Method

3.1   The Proposed Methodology

1. Collect data about defects from the issue tracking system.
2. Fit SRGM curve with collected data.
3. Find confidence intervals of parameters of the software model with a bootstrapping method.
4. Check model sustainability to errors in collecting data by conducting Monte Carlo simulation.

3.2   Software Reliability Growth Models

Software reliability growth models [68] account for indicating the number of cumulative failures that may be found after the software was released and thus can specify the time when the software is ready to be released. SRGMs contain concave and S-shaped models. Concave models are described with concave function. S-shaped models are formulated by convex function and after reaching maximal error-detection point by concave function. S-shape models are justified by peculiarities of the software testing process such as firstly the team does not know the software in details, it causes a slow process of the defect removal.

Table 3. Studies included in the final review for RQ1

Ref.	Authors	Year	Title	Venue
[21]	C. Fang, C. Yeh	2011	Confidence Interval Estimation of Software Reliability Growth Models Derived from Stochastic Differential Equations	IEEE IEEM
[30]	J. Lv et al.	2014	Estimating confidence interval of software reliability with adaptive testing strategy	JOS
[35]	L. Yin, S. Trivedi	1999	Confidence Interval Estimation of NHPP-Based Software Reliability Models	ISSRE
[34]	T. Lee, C. Fang	2013	Confidence Interval Estimation of Software Reliability Growth Models based on Ohba's Inflection S-shaped Model	JIII
[60]	S. Lei, M. Smith	2003	Evaluation of Several Nonparametric Bootstrap Methods to Estimate Confidence Intervals for Software Metrics	IEEE TSE
[25]	S. Inoue, S. Yamada	2013	Interval Estimations of Software Reliability and Optimal Release Time Based on Better Bootstrap Confidence Intervals	IEEE IEEM
[20]	C. Fang, C. Yeh	2015	Effective confidence interval estimation of fault-detection process of software reliability growth models	IJSS
[44]	H. Papadopoulos et al.	2009	Reliable Confidence Intervals for Software Effort Estimation	AIAI
[5]	P. Braga, A. Oliveira	2007	Software Effort Estimation using Machine Learning Techniques with Robust Confidence Intervals	HIS

Table 4. Studies included in the final review for RQ2

Ref.	Authors	Year	Title	Venue
[4]	M. Blackwell et al.	2015	A Unified Approach to Measurement Error and Missing Data: Overview and Applications	SMR
[30]	T. Khoshgoftaar	2004	Comparative Assessment of Software Quality Classification Techniques: An Empirical Case Study	ESE
[54]	P. Rostron et al.	2020	Confidence intervals for robust estimates of measurement uncertainty	AQA
[3]	M. Blackwell et al.	2017	A Unified Approach to Measurement Error and Missing Data: Details and Extensions	SMR
[60]	S. Lei, M. Smith	2003	Evaluation of Several Nonparametric Bootstrap Methods to Estimate Confidence Intervals for Software Metrics	IEEE TSE
[66]	A. Valecillo et al.	2016	Expressing Measurement Uncertainty in Software Models	QUATIC
[29]	Joint Committee for Guides in Metrology	2008	Evaluation of measurement data - Guide to the expression of uncertainty in measurement	JCGM
[24]	J. Hardin, R. Carroll	2003	Measurement error, GLMs, and notational conventions	STATA J
[6]	S. Castrup	2010	Comparison of Methods for Establishing Confidence Limits and Expanded Uncertainties	MSC

When the team have acquainted with the software the defects start to be removed faster.

In our work we consider the SRGMs described in Table 6 with the respectively mentioned formulas. The Table 6 was adopted from [61,68]. We fit each of SRGMs curves with data about system failures. By calculating the goodness of fit metric proposed by [61] we assess the quality of the models.

According to the conducted SLR, the bootstrap method demonstrates consistent results across different metrics. The bootstrap method does not require an assumption on the distribution of the input data. We use the bootstrap method for constructing confidence intervals of parameters a, b, c in Software reliability growth models.

Table 5. Summary of findings for RQs

Research question	Summary of findings
RQ1: Construction of confidence intervals	The construction of CI for *reliability assessment* and *optimal release time estimation* can be done with: – Bootstrap methods – Stochastic differential equations – Bayesian method – Adaptive testing For *effort estimation* the following methods are used: – Ridge Regression Conformal Predictors – Robust Confidence Intervals
RQ2: Ways of description of the error in collecting software measurement	Measurement error can be calculated by: – Multiple Imputation and its extension Multiple Overimputation – Generalized linear models Measurement uncertainty can be found according to: – "Guide to the Expression of Uncertainty in Measurement", Convolution method and Monte Carlo method – Analysis of variance – An extension of OCL and UML types

Parameter a usually represents a total number of SRs, parameters b and c describe the speed of receiving SRs. It should be noted that parameters b and c are not comparable between models due to their different impacts on the models.

For evaluation of sensitivity to human mistakes, we use Monte Carlo simulation with added Gaussian noise represented in the number of service requests.

3.3 Collected Data

We use data from issue tracking system about service requests (SRs) for modifications in three open-source mobile operating systems: Tizen[1], CyanogenMod[2] and Sailfish[3]. SRs arise during the development process, code reviews and testing phase. Our data contain SRs on the early usage stage of the software. We have an assumption that all SRs influence the system equally.

The projects are written in multiple programming languages, such as Java, C, C++. The sizes of the projects are 97,041,969 lines of code (LOC) for Sailfish,

---

[1] https://bugs.tizen.org/.
[2] https://jira.cyanogenmod.org/.
[3] https://bugs.nemomobile.org/ and https://bugs.merproject.org/.

Table 6. Software reliability growth models

Model name	Model type	Formula
Goel-Okumoto (GO)	Concave	$a(1 - e^{-bt}), a \geq 0, b > 0$
GO S-Shaped (GoS)	S-Shaped	$a(1 - (1 + bt)e^{-bt}), a \geq 0, b > 0$
Logistics (L)	S-Shaped	$\frac{a}{(1+be^{-ct})}, a \geq 0, b > 0, c > 0$
Hossain-Dahiya (HD)	S-Shaped	$a\frac{(1-e^{-bt})}{(1+ce^{-bc})}, a \geq 0, b > 0, c > 0$
Weibull (W)	S-Shaped	$a(1 - e^{-bt^c}), a \geq 0, b > 0, c > 0$
W more S-Shaped (WS)	S-Shaped	$a(1 - (1 + bt^c)e^{-bt^c}), a \geq 0, b > 0, c > 0$
Yamada Exp. (YE)	Concave	$a(1 - e^{-b(1-e^{ct})}), a \geq 0, b > 0, c > 0$
Yamada Raleigh (YR)	S-Shaped	$a(1 - e^{-b(1-e^{-c\frac{t^2}{2}})}), a \geq 0, b > 0, c > 0$

122,166,906 LOC for Tizen and 50,523,609 LOC for Cyanogen dataset as mentioned in [27]. For the Sailfish operating system, we have data from two projects - Sailfish-Nemo and Sailfish-Mer. The information about SRs was transformed into a cumulative number of SRs per date. Then, data were normalized to reach the convergence faster.

3.4   Implementation of Software Reliability Growth Models

We are fitting SRGM curves by using the nlstools package[4] in R language. We fit SRGM to the dataset with nonlinear least-squares Levenberg-Marquardt (nlsLM). The formula is transformed into a function that returns a vector of residuals whose sum of squares is minimized by nlslm. The optimized parameters are then transferred to nlsModel in order to obtain an object of class 'nlsModel'. The least-squares problems appear in the situation of fitting a parameterized mathematical model to a set of data points by minimizing an objective expressed as the sum of the squares of the errors between the model function and a set of data points.

The Levenberg-Marquardt algorithm [23] couples two numerical minimization methods: the gradient descent algorithm and the Gauss-Newton algorithm. In the gradient descent method, the sum of the squared errors is reduced by updating the parameters in the steepest-descent direction. In the Gauss-Newton method, the sum of the squared errors is reduced by assuming the least-squares function is locally quadratic in the parameters and finding the minimum of this quadratic. The Levenberg-Marquardt method acts more like a gradient-descent method when the parameters are far from their optimal value, and acts more like the Gauss-Newton method when the parameters are close to their optimal value.

---

[4] https://cran.r-project.org/web/packages/nlstools/nlstools.pdf.

3.5 Bootstrapping and Building Confidence Intervals

We apply bootstrap resampling [25] by using nlstools package in R. The mean-centered residuals are bootstrapped 100 times. The bootstrap method creates multiple resamples (with replacement) from a single set of observations, and calculates the effect size of interest on each of these resamples. The bootstrap resamples then can be used to determine the 95% CI. The resampling distribution of the difference in means approaches a normal distribution. This is due to the Central Limit Theorem: a large number of independent random samples will approach a normal distribution even if the underlying population is not normally distributed.

Bootstrap resampling provides two benefits. First, there is no need to assume that our observations, or the underlying populations, are normally distributed. The resampling distribution of the effect size will approach normality because of the Central Limit Theorem. Second, easy to build the 95% CI from the resampling distribution.

4 Evaluation and Discussion

4.1 Curve Fitting

The results of the fitting process are depicted in Fig. 4, 5, 6, 7 for each dataset. Time in days and cumulative number of SRs were normalized for reaching convergence faster.

According to empirical results, we can conclude that for Tizen and Cyanogen datasets models L, YR, HD, W, WS succeed in fitting the data. Models GO, GoS and YE do not show acceptable results. Because of this reason, we do not consider GoS model in our evaluation of confidence intervals for each dataset. Models GO and YE we do not evaluate on Tizen and Cyanogen datasets.

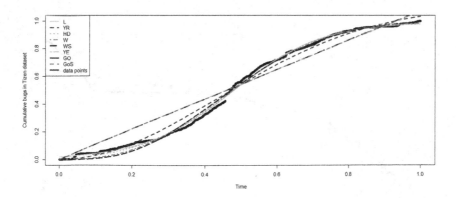

Fig. 4. Fitting cumulative normalized SRs in Tizen dataset with SRGMs

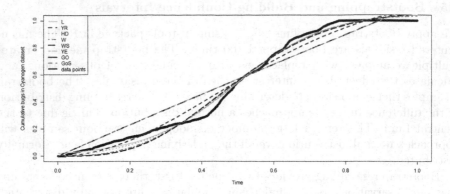

Fig. 5. Fitting cumulative normalized SRs in Cyanogen dataset with SRGMs

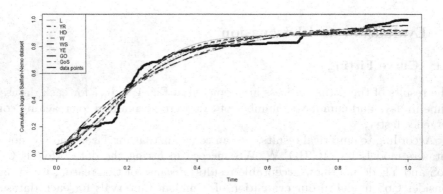

Fig. 6. Fitting cumulative normalized SRs in Sailfish-Nemo dataset with SRGMs

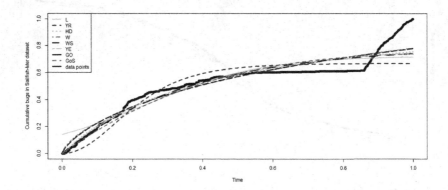

Fig. 7. Fitting cumulative normalized SRs in Sailfish-Mer dataset with SRGMs

We chose the metric *Goodness of fit (GoF)* for the evaluation of fitting results. The goodness of fit shows how well the model fits the data. The unit used for GoF in Table 7 is the number of SRs. This criterion is measured using the root mean square error, the standard deviation of residuals.

For Tizen and Cyanogen datasets Logistics model demonstrates the best values for GoF. For Sailfish-Nemo and Sailfish-Mer the WS model indicates the best results. For Sailfish datasets all models are showing comparably similar results and fitting the data well. For Tizen and Cyanogen datasets models GO, GoS, YE displayed the worst results that make a sign that these models do not fit the data properly. In Table 8 the ranking of the models is presented according to the *Goodness of fit* metric.

Table 7. Goodness of fit for each dataset

Model	Tizen	CyanogenMod	Sailfish-Nemo	Sailfish-Mer
GO	470.0	1031.0	49.9	98.5
GoS	471.5	1033.6	51.3	105.9
L	84.8	314.6	45.0	116.0
YR	202.8	570.4	44.2	124.3
HD	95.3	355.6	43.4	93.2
W	128.7	431.8	43.7	92.9
WS	143.9	486.0	42.4	92.2
YE	474.3	1038.7	49.9	95.5

Table 8. Ranking of SRGMs according to goodness of fit metric

	Tizen	CyanogenMod	Sailfish-Nemo	Sailfish-Mer
1	L	L	WS	WS
2	HD	HD	HD	W
3	W	W	W	HD
4	WS	WS	YR	YE
5	YR	YR	L	GO
6	GO	GO	YE	GoS
7	GoS	GoS	GO	L
8	YE	YE	GoS	YR

4.2 Confidence Intervals Evaluation

In Tables 9, 10, 11, 12 we demonstrate the built 95% confidence intervals for parameters a, b, c (if available) for each dataset. The tightest confidence intervals are encountered with the Logistics method across all datasets for parameter a. The widest confidence interval was noticed in model YR for Tizen, Sailfish-Nemo and CyanogenMod datasets. In Sailfish-Mer the widest CI is produced by HD model. Parameters b and c are not comparable between models because their interpretation varies in different models.

Table 9. Confidence intervals for parameters of SRGMs in Tizen dataset

Model	a(2.5%)	a(97.5%)	b(2.5%)	b(97.5%)	c(2.5%)	c(97.5%)
L	5538	5563	49,46	51,65	8,15	8,25
YR	6174	6278	73,20	263,98	0,02	0,07
HD	5583	5610	7,68	7,80	37,73	39,87
W	5525	5572	4,71	4,94	2,58	2,63
WS	5650	5713	5,65	5,89	1,65	1,69

Table 10. Confidence intervals for parameters of SRGMs in CyanogenMod dataset

Model	a(2.5%)	a(97.5%)	b(2.5%)	b(97.5%)	c(2.5%)	c(97.5%)
L	11256	11352	51,13	55,83	7,90	8,10
YR	12569	12915	62,79	267,42	0,06	0,36
HD	11287	11409	7,58	7,86	41,36	47,07
W	11036	11169	4,87	5,28	2,73	2,82
WS	11302	11487	5,70	6,07	1,73	1,80

Table 11. Confidence intervals for parameters of SRGMs in Sailfish-Nemo dataset

Model	a(2.5%)	a(97.5%)	b(2.5%)	b(97.5%)	c(2.5%)	c(97.5%)
GO	854	868	3,28	3,44		
L	765	772	11,43	13,35	12,26	12,98
YR	781	921	1,84	4,73	8,02	18,55
HD	781	789	8,29	9,00	3,09	3,90
W	792	799	6,35	7,02	1,35	1,42
WS	797	808	7,23	7,86	0,90	0,94
YE	857	878	16,70	165,77	0,02	0,20

4.3   Sensitivity of the Models

The process of data collection can be influenced by human errors. We assessed the resistance to errors in collecting data by one of the methods mentioned in RQ2. We conducted a Monte Carlo simulation with Gaussian noise with a standard deviation varying from 1 up to 800 errors. The simulation is executed

Table 12. Confidence intervals for parameters of SRGMs in Sailfish-Mer dataset

Model	a(2.5%)	a(97.5%)	b(2.5%)	b(97.5%)	c(2.5%)	c(97.5%)
GO	1082	1116	2,65	2,85		
L	993	1022	3,79	4,39	5,62	6,23
YR	920	1246	1,33	7,48	4,83	21,83
W	1633	2380	0,61	1,09	0,62	0,71
WS	1674	2460	1,50	2,18	0,38	0,45
YE	1145	1972	0,91	9,03	0,31	1,80

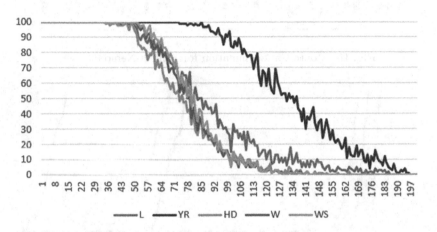

Fig. 8. Monte Carlo simulation for Tizen dataset

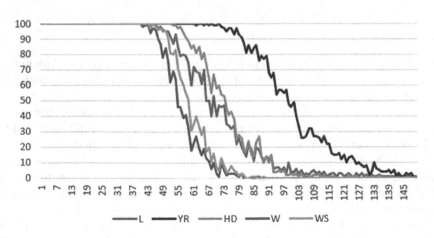

Fig. 9. Monte Carlo simulation for CyanogenMod dataset

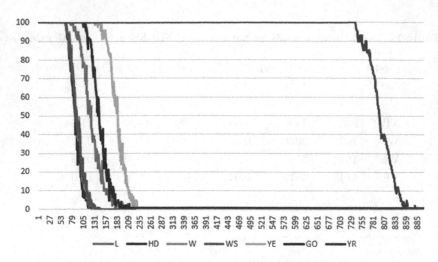

Fig. 10. Monte Carlo simulation for Sailfish-Nemo dataset

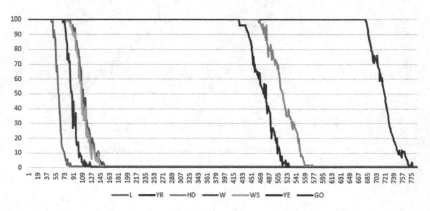

Fig. 11. Monte Carlo simulation for Sailfish-Mer dataset

for each value of standard deviation 100 times. From every simulation, we find the parameters of the model. We check if the parameters fall inside 95% confidence intervals of the original models, we evaluate percentile.

We apply the Monte Carlo simulation technique only to models that showed sensible results in previous steps of the research such as the empirically valid fit of the data points and positive values for parameters of the models.

In Figs. 8, 9, 10, 11 the x-axis is the standard deviation of the added noise, expressed in the number of errors. The y-axis represents the percentage of the total number of simulation runs, for the given standard deviation, with the parameters of the resulting model within the confidence interval.

For the Tizen dataset, all the evaluated models have good resistance to noise up to standard deviation equals to 50 errors, the percentile is bigger than 95. For Cyanogen dataset the standard deviation of 43 errors is an acceptable level of noise to not significantly influence the model. The standard deviation of fewer than 66 errors let all models in the Sailfish-Nemo dataset stay in the 95 percentile. For the dataset Sailfish-Mer, 49 errors in standard deviation value of noise is possible to resist. Basically, the models with wide confidence intervals show the strongest resistance to the noise (YR model). However, such models are not highly useful in giving valuable information about the occurrence of failures.

5 Conclusion

In this work, we used a non-linear least squares technique to model software reliability curve. We applied bootstrap method to construct the confidence intervals of estimations of the software reliability growth models. We tested our method on datasets of SRs that appeared in the three operating systems.

For Tizen and Cyanogen datasets Logistics model demonstrates the best values for the goodness of fit. For Sailfish-Nemo and Sailfish-Mer the WS model indicates the best results. The worst results for the goodness of fit metric are shown by GO, GoS and YE models for Tizen and CyanogenMod datasets.

With the usage of the bootstrap resampling technique, we found confidence intervals for parameters of the SRGM models. The Logistics model showed the tightest confidence intervals across all examined datasets for parameter a that indicate information about the number of failures. The widest confidence intervals are produced by GO, GoS, YE for Tizen and CyanogenMod systems. For the Sailfish project, the YR and HD models displayed the widest confidence intervals.

After testing on all datasets, models L and WS appeared to be the best performing models in terms of GoF, confidence intervals range and resistance to errors in collecting data. The worst performing models are GO, GoS, YE for Tizen and Cyanogen datasets, YR and HD for the Sailfish dataset.

We assessed the sensitivity of the models by conducting a Monte Carlo simulation with added noise. All models showed acceptable results and were able to resist mistakes with a standard deviation of up to 50, 43, 66, 49 errors for Tizen, CyanogenMod, Sailfish-Nemo and Sailfish-Mer datasets, respectively.

The assumption of this study is that the number of releases equals one. This assumption provides an opportunity for further research on multi-stage models with several releases.

References

1. Atonge, D., et al.: The development of data collectors in open-source system for energy efficiency assessment. In: Ivanov, V., Kruglov, A., Masyagin, S., Sillitti, A., Succi, G. (eds.) Open Source Systems. OSS 2020. IFIP Advances in Information and Communication Technology, vol. 582, pp. 14–24. Springer, Cham (2020). https://doi.org/10.1007/978-3-030-47240-5_2
2. Bender, R.: Calculating confidence intervals for the number needed to treat. Control. Clin. Trials **22**(2), 102–110 (2001)

3. Blackwell, M., Honaker, J., King, G.: A unified approach to measurement error and missing data: details and extensions. Sociol. Methods Res. **46**(3), 342–369 (2017)
4. Blackwell, M., Honaker, J., King, G.: A unified approach to measurement error and missing data: overview and applications. Sociol. Methods Res. **46**(3), 303–341 (2017)
5. Braga, P.L.: Software effort estimation using machine learning techniques with robust confidence intervals. In: 7th International Conference on Hybrid Intelligent Systems (HIS 2007), pp. 352–357 (2007)
6. Castrup, S.: Comparison of methods for establishing confidence limits and expanded uncertainties. In: Proceedings of the 2010 Measurement Science Conference, p. 23 (2010)
7. Ciancarini, P., et al.: Analysis of energy consumption of software development process entities. Electronics **9**(10), 1678 (2020)
8. Clark, J., et al.: Selecting components in large cots repositories. J. Syst. Softw. **73**(2), 323–331 (2004)
9. Coman, I.D., Robillard, P.N., Sillitti, A., Succi, G.: Cooperation, collaboration and pair-programming: field studies on backup behavior. J. Syst. Softw. **91**, 124–134 (2014)
10. Corral, L., Georgiev, A.B., Sillitti, A., Succi, G.: A method for characterizing energy consumption in android smartphones. In: Green and Sustainable Software (GREENS 2013), 2nd International Workshop on, pp. 38–45. IEEE (May 2013)
11. Corral, L., Georgiev, A.B., Sillitti, A., Succi, G.: Can execution time describe accurately the energy consumption of mobile apps? An experiment in Android. In: Proceedings of the 3rd International Workshop on Green and Sustainable Software, pp. 31–37. ACM (2014)
12. Corral, L., Sillitti, A., Succi, G.: Software assurance practices for mobile applications. Computing **97**(10), 1001–1022 (2015)
13. Corral, L., Sillitti, A., Succi, G., Garibbo, A., Ramella, P.: Evolution of mobile software development from platform-specific to web-based multiplatform paradigm. In: Proceedings of the 10th SIGPLAN Symposium on New Ideas, New Paradigms, and Reflections on Programming and Software, pp. 181–183. Onward! 2011, ACM, New York, NY, USA (2011)
14. Di Bella, E., Sillitti, A., Succi, G.: A multivariate classification of open source developers. Inf. Sci. **221**, 72–83 (2013)
15. Dogan, G.: Bootstrapping for confidence interval estimation and hypothesis testing for parameters of system dynamics models. Syst. Dyn. Rev. **23**(4), 415–436 (2007)
16. Ergasheva, S., Ivanov, V., Khomyakov, I., Kruglov, A., Strugar, D., Succi, G.: InnoMetrics dashboard: the design, and implementation of the adaptable dashboard for energy-efficient applications using open source tools. In: Ivanov, V., Kruglov, A., Masyagin, S., Sillitti, A., Succi, G. (eds.) OSS 2020. IAICT, vol. 582, pp. 163–176. Springer, Cham (2020). https://doi.org/10.1007/978-3-030-47240-5_16
17. Ergasheva, S., Kruglov, A.: Software development life cycle early phases and quality metrics: a systematic literature review, vol. 1694, p. 012007 (2020). https://doi.org/10.1088/1742-6596/1694/1/012007
18. Ergasheva, S., Kruglov, A., Shulhan, I.: Development and evaluation of gqm method to improve adaptive systems. In: ITTCS (2019)
19. Ergasheva, S., Strugar, D., Kruglov, A., Succi, G.: Energy efficient software development process evaluation for MacOS devices. In: Ivanov, V., Kruglov, A., Masyagin, S., Sillitti, A., Succi, G. (eds.) OSS 2020. IAICT, vol. 582, pp. 196–206. Springer, Cham (2020). https://doi.org/10.1007/978-3-030-47240-5_20

20. Fang, C.C.: Effective confidence interval estimation of fault-detection process of software reliability growth models. Int. J. Syst. Sci. 16 (2016)
21. Fang, C.C., Yeh, C.W.: Confidence interval estimation of software reliability growth models derived from stochastic differential equations. In: 2011 IEEE International Conference on Industrial Engineering and Engineering Management, p. 5 (2011)
22. Fitzgerald, B., Kesan, J.P., Russo, B., Shaikh, M., Succi, G.: Adopting open source software: A practical guide. The MIT Press, Cambridge, MA (2011)
23. Gavin, H.P.: The Levenberg-Marquardt algorithm for nonlinear least squares curve-fitting problems, pp. 1–19. Department of Civil and Environmental Engineering, Duke University (2019)
24. Hardin, J.W., Carroll, R.J.: Measurement error, glms, and notational conventions. Stand Genomic Sci. $3(4)$, 329–341 (2003)
25. Inoue, S., Yamada, S.: Interval estimations of software reliability and optimal release time based on better bootstrap confidence intervals. In: 2013 IEEE International Conference on Industrial Engineering and Engineering Management, p. 5 (2013)
26. Ivanov, V., Kruglov, A., Sadovykh, A., Succi, G.: Scenarios for the evaluation of the energy efficiency of mobile applications. In: 2019 IEEE 10th Annual Information Technology, Electronics and Mobile Communication Conference (IEMCON), pp. 0595–0601 (2019)
27. Ivanov, V., Reznik, A., Succi, G.: Comparing the reliability of software systems: a case study on mobile operating systems. Inf. Sci. 423, 398–411 (2018)
28. Janes, A., Succi, G.: Lean Software Development in Action. Springer, Heidelberg (2014). https://doi.org/10.1007/978-3-642-00503-9, http://dx.doi.org/10.1007/978-3-642-00503-9
29. Joint Committee for Guides in Metrology: JCGM 100: Evaluation of measurement data - guide to the expression of uncertainty in measurement. JCGM, pp. 1–116 (2008)
30. Khoshgoftaar, T.M., Seliya, N.: Comparative assessment of software quality classification techniques: an empirical case study. Empir. Softw. Eng. $9(3)$, 229–257 (2004)
31. Kivi, J., Haydon, D., Hayes, J., Schneider, R., Succi, G.: Extreme programming: a university team design experience. In: 2000 Canadian Conference on Electrical and Computer Engineering. Conference Proceedings. Navigating to a New Era (Cat. No.00TH8492), vol. 2, pp. 816–820 (May 2000)
32. Kovács, G.L., Drozdik, S., Zuliani, P., Succi, G.: Open source software for the public administration. In: Proceedings of the 6th International Workshop on Computer Science and Information Technologies (October 2004)
33. Kruglov, A., Strugar, D., Succi, G.: Tailored performance dashboards—an evaluation of the state of the art. PeerJ 7, e625 (2021)
34. Lee, T.Q., Fang, C.C., Yeh, C.W.: Confidence interval estimation of software reliability growth models based on ohba's inflection s-shaped model. J. Ind. Intell. Inf. $1(4)$, 196–200 (2013). https://doi.org/10.12720/jiii.1.4.196-200, http://www.jiii.org/index.php?m=content&c=index&a=show&catid=36&id=62
35. Liang Yin, Trivedi, K.: Confidence interval estimation of NHPP-based software reliability models. In: Proceedings 10th International Symposium on Software Reliability Engineering (Cat. No.PR00443), pp. 6–11. IEEE Computer Society, Boca Raton, FL, USA (1999). https://doi.org/10.1109/ISSRE.1999.809305, http://ieeexplore.ieee.org/document/809305/
36. Lv, J.: Estimating confidence interval of software reliability with adaptive testing strategy. J. Syst. Softw. 15 (2014)

37. Marino, G., Succi, G.: Data structures for parallel execution of functional languages. In: Odijk, E., Rem, M., Syre, J.-C. (eds.) PARLE 1989. LNCS, vol. 366, pp. 346–356. Springer, Heidelberg (1989). https://doi.org/10.1007/3-540-51285-3_51

38. Maurer, F., Succi, G., Holz, H., Kötting, B., Goldmann, S., Dellen, B.: Software process support over the internet. In: Proceedings of the 21st International Conference on Software Engineering, pp. 642–645. ICSE 1999, ACM (May 1999)

39. Montori, V.M., et al.: Tips for learners of evidence-based medicine: 2. Measures of precision (confidence intervals). Can. Med. Assoc. J. 5 (2004)

40. Moser, R., Pedrycz, W., Succi, G.: A comparative analysis of the efficiency of change metrics and static code attributes for defect prediction. In: Proceedings of the 30th International Conference on Software Engineering, pp. 181–190. ICSE 2008, ACM (2008)

41. Moser, R., Pedrycz, W., Succi, G.: Analysis of the reliability of a subset of change metrics for defect prediction. In: Proceedings of the Second ACM-IEEE International Symposium on Empirical Software Engineering and Measurement, pp. 309–311. ESEM 2008, ACM (2008)

42. Musílek, P., Pedrycz, W., Sun, N., Succi, G.: On the sensitivity of COCOMO II software cost estimation model. In: Proceedings of the 8th International Symposium on Software Metrics, pp. 13–20. METRICS 2002, IEEE Computer Society (June 2002)

43. Noce, L., Gwaza, L., Mangas-Sanjuan, V., Garcia-Arieta, A.: Comparison of free software platforms for the calculation of the 90% confidence interval of f2 similarity factor by bootstrap analysis. Eur. J. Pharm. Sci. **146**, 105259 (2020)

44. Papadopoulos, H., Papatheocharous, E., Andreou, A.S.: Reliable confidence intervals for software effort estimation. In: AIAI workshops, pp. 211–220 (2009)

45. Paulson, J.W., Succi, G., Eberlein, A.: An empirical study of open-source and closed-source software products. IEEE Trans. Softw. Eng. **30**(4), 246–256 (2004)

46. Pedrycz, W., Russo, B., Succi, G.: A model of job satisfaction for collaborative development processes. J. Syst. Softw. **84**(5), 739–752 (2011)

47. Pedrycz, W., Russo, B., Succi, G.: Knowledge transfer in system modeling and its realization through an optimal allocation of information granularity. Appl. Soft Comput. **12**(8), 1985–1995 (2012)

48. Pedrycz, W., Succi, G.: Genetic granular classifiers in modeling software quality. J. Syst. Softw. **76**(3), 277–285 (2005)

49. Petrinja, E., Sillitti, A., Succi, G.: Comparing OpenBRR, QSOS, and OMM assessment models. In: Ågerfalk, P., Boldyreff, C., González-Barahona, J.M., Madey, G.R., Noll, J. (eds.) OSS 2010. IAICT, vol. 319, pp. 224–238. Springer, Heidelberg (2010). https://doi.org/10.1007/978-3-642-13244-5_18

50. Preacher, K.J., Selig, J.P.: Advantages of monte carlo confidence intervals for indirect effects. Commun. Methods Meas. **6**(2), 77–98 (2012)

51. Ronchetti, M., Succi, G., Pedrycz, W., Russo, B.: Early estimation of software size in object-oriented environments a case study in a CMM level 3 software firm. Inf. Sci. **176**(5), 475–489 (2006)

52. Rossi, B., Russo, B., Succi, G.: Modelling failures occurrences of open source software with reliability growth. In: Ågerfalk, P., Boldyreff, C., González-Barahona, J.M., Madey, G.R., Noll, J. (eds.) OSS 2010. IAICT, vol. 319, pp. 268–280. Springer, Heidelberg (2010). https://doi.org/10.1007/978-3-642-13244-5_21

53. Rossi, B., Russo, B., Succi, G.: Adoption of free/libre open source software in public organizations: factors of impact. Inf. Technol. People **25**(2), 156–187 (2012)

54. Rostron, P.D., Fearn, T., Ramsey, M.H.: Confidence intervals for robust estimates of measurement uncertainty. Accredit. Qual. Assur. **25**(2), 107–119 (2020)
55. Scotto, M., Sillitti, A., Succi, G., Vernazza, T.: A relational approach to software metrics. In: Proceedings of the 2004 ACM Symposium on Applied Computing, pp. 1536–1540. SAC 2004, ACM (2004)
56. Scotto, M., Sillitti, A., Succi, G., Vernazza, T.: A non-invasive approach to product metrics collection. J. Syst. Architect. **52**(11), 668–675 (2006)
57. Sillitti, A., Janes, A., Succi, G., Vernazza, T.: Measures for mobile users: an architecture. J. Syst. Architect. **50**(7), 393–405 (2004)
58. Sillitti, A., Succi, G., Vlasenko, J.: Understanding the impact of pair programming on developers attention: a case study on a large industrial experimentation. In: Proceedings of the 34th International Conference on Software Engineering, pp. 1094–1101. ICSE 2012, IEEE Press, Piscataway, NJ, USA (June 2012)
59. Sillitti, A., Vernazza, T., Succi, G.: Service oriented programming: a new paradigm of software reuse. In: Gacek, C. (ed.) ICSR 2002. LNCS, vol. 2319, pp. 269–280. Springer, Heidelberg (2002). https://doi.org/10.1007/3-540-46020-9_19
60. Skylar Lei, Smith, M.: Evaluation of several nonparametric bootstrap methods to estimate confidence intervals for software metrics. IEEE Trans. Softw. Eng. **29**(11), 996–1004 (2003). https://doi.org/10.1109/TSE.2003.1245301, http://ieeexplore.ieee.org/document/1245301/
61. Succi, G.: An investigation on the occurrence of service requests in commercial software applications. Empir. Softw. Eng. **8**(2), 197–215 (2003)
62. Succi, G., Benedicenti, L., Vernazza, T.: Analysis of the effects of software reuse on customer satisfaction in an RPG environment. IEEE Trans. Softw. Eng. **27**(5), 473–479 (2001)
63. Succi, G., Paulson, J., Eberlein, A.: Preliminary results from an empirical study on the growth of open source and commercial software products. In: EDSER-3 Workshop, pp. 14–15 (2001)
64. Succi, G., Pedrycz, W., Marchesi, M., Williams, L.: Preliminary analysis of the effects of pair programming on job satisfaction. In: Proceedings of the 3rd International Conference on Extreme Programming (XP), pp. 212–215 (May 2002)
65. Valerio, A., Succi, G., Fenaroli, M.: Domain analysis and framework-based software development. SIGAPP Appl. Comput. Rev. **5**(2), 4–15 (1997)
66. Vallecillo, A., Morcillo, C., Orue, P.: Expressing measurement uncertainty in software models. In: 2016 10th International Conference on the Quality of Information and Communications Technology (QUATIC), pp. 15–24. IEEE, Lisbon, Portugal (September 2016). https://doi.org/10.1109/QUATIC.2016.013, http://ieeexplore.ieee.org/document/7814510/
67. Vernazza, T., Granatella, G., Succi, G., Benedicenti, L., Mintchev, M.: Defining metrics for software components. In: Proceedings of the World Multiconference on Systemics, Cybernetics and Informatics, vol. XI, pp. 16–23 (July 2000)
68. Wood, A.: Software reliability growth models. Tandem Tech. Rep. **96**(130056), 900 (1996)
69. Zhang, Z.: Monte Carlo based statistical power analysis for mediation models: methods and software. Behav. Res. Methods **46**(4), 1184–1198 (2014)

A Study: Design Patterns Detection Approaches and Impact on Software Quality

Danil Shilintsev and Gcinizwe Dlamini[✉]

Innopolis University, Innopolis, Russia
g.dlamini@innopolis.university

Abstract. The influence of design decisions on quality characteristics has been studied extensively in research with various viewpoints, aims, measurements, and quality attributes, resulting in contradictory and difficult-to-compare conclusions. Until now, the results on the effect of design patterns on software quality are controversial. There are two objectives of conducting this study. The first one is to analyze the impact of design patterns on software quality. The second is investigating the approaches used for detecting design patterns. All the analysis is done with the use of a technique called systematic literature review (SLR). The SLR findings demonstrate that pattern documentation, pattern class size, and pattern dispersion degree have a significant effect on the quality of software. Similarity scoring, graph-based, and machine learning-based approaches are the existing proposed methods for detecting design patterns. The results have shown that there is a need for benchmarking design patterns detection proposed approaches.

Keywords: Software design · Design patterns · Quality assurance · Software development

1 Introduction

Object-oriented design decisions were presented in the1990 s as a systematic list of typical solutions to ordinary design problems, and are examined as a level of "good" projects [12]. Alexander[3] first presented the concept of patterns in the architecture area. Later Gamma et al. [12] also known as the gang of four (GoF), modified design patterns idea to match with product design in the field of software development. The researchers [12] listed 23 design decisions, categorized by two factors namely: purpose and area. Purpose, describes the motivation of the design pattern. Area, determines the level on which a design pattern is implemented (class or object level). Using the two aforementioned factors the gang of four proposed three main categories of design patterns: behavioral, structural, and creational patterns.

The use of design patterns over the years has proved to be an important aspect of software development. In [12], the researchers offer that using determining product design decisions provides simpler reusability and easier possibilities

© Springer Nature Switzerland AG 2021
G. Succi et al. (Eds.): ICFSE 2021, CCIS 1523, pp. 84–96, 2021.
https://doi.org/10.1007/978-3-030-93135-3_6

to support, clearer implementation, and more flexible scopes. Here it is important to illuminate that Gang of Four patterns are not the only design decisions in existing literature related to software development.

There also exist a number of design decisions from different scopes, such as game design patterns, computational patterns, computational patterns, and others. Many researchers have been taken attempts to analyse the influence of GoF decisions on product quality in recent years. Exploring the existing papers on the impact of design solutions application on program quality produces contentious outcomes. Up to this day, researchers tried to explore the results of design patterns application concerning software conditions through experimental techniques, such as surveys or case studies, but due to results leading to various directions, reliable conclusions cannot be made. As introduced in [8] and [1], design solutions suggest developing patterns for common tasks that can be performed with easier solutions.

The aim of paper is to analyse the influence of different design decisions on the quality of software and existing approaches for design patterns detection. To reach our goal we conduct a systematic literature review that aims to answer the following research questions:

1. RQ1: When design patterns are applied, what confounding circumstances, practices, or programming structures impact quality attributes?
2. RQ2: What are the quality attributes that are examined and measured, and what are the metrics that are employed?
3. RQ3: What is the link connecting design patterns and software quality?
4. RQ4: What are the existing design patterns detection approaches?

The rest of this paper is organised as follows. Section 2 presents background information on software Design Patterns and their relationship to software quality. Section 3 describes methodology that was taken for conducting this research. The literature review approach is discussed in detail, listed different steps. Section 4 gives answers to research questions and discusses the quality impact of Design Patterns. The paper is concluded Sect. 5 where future works are also outlined.

2 Background and Related Works

2.1 Design Patterns

A design pattern in software engineering is a typical repeatable solution to a frequently arising issue in product design. A design decision is not a complete solution that can be modified straight inside the code. Pattern is a template for resolving a difficulty that can be applied in a multiplicity of cases. Developers can observe the details of the pattern and create a solution that comes to the realities of the task.

Area of design decisions has been extensively explored in the realm of software and has been shown to increase knowledge conversion [32]. Design patterns can assist software developers in creating better software. Design patterns also capture the experience, offer a consistent glossary for computer scientists throughout range boundaries, and improve software documentation [33]. According to a study conducted by Mcnatt [22], software design decisions are considered as one of the most significant pieces of knowledge for software professionals. Study [20] of researcher Lanza contains the most well-known collection of software design templates.

2.2   Software Quality

Software quality refers to whether or not a piece of software meets its specifications. It is customary to call two types of software requirements - (1) functional and (2) non-functional.

Functional Requirements define what it should be able to perform. Examples of how can such requirements look like are: computations, data processing, data manipulation technical details. All of them are about the process of achieving some desired objective.

Non-Functional Requirements express the way which system was performing how a system should perform. Non-functional criteria, often called as "quality characteristics", include disaster recovery, privacy, portability, security, usability, and supportability.

Software quality is influenced by a number of variables[27]. We will go through the most essential components of software quality, as well as some practical techniques to measure them, so one can make sure the whole code put into production meets its goals. The ISO software quality model is an excellent place to start when learning about software quality. To achieve a comprehensive picture of software quality, integrate the quality characteristics mentioned in this model with additional relevant criteria.

ISO 25010 Quality Model. The ISO 25010 software quality model [10] includes the following eight quality characteristics:

1. **Functional Suitability:** indicates the rate to which a system performs functions that fulfill established and inferred demands.
2. **Performance efficiency:** measures how well a system performs in relation to the number of resources it consumes under certain circumstances.
3. **Compatibility:** The rate to which a system can interact with other components or execute its tasks during dividing the one environment among them.
4. **Usability:** The Degree to which a system can be used by specified users to achieve given goals with efficiency and effectiveness in a specified place of use.
5. **Reliability:** The extent to which a system executes defined functions for a set amount of time under specified conditions.
6. **Security:** The rate to which a product secures data so other components have the proper level of data access for their degrees of permission.

7. **Maintainability:** This feature denotes an ease with which a product or system may be updated to enhance or rectify changes in environment or needs. This quality attribute is the most analyzed by researchers in their papers. They state the connection between the positive impact of design patterns and this quality attribute.
8. **Portability:** The rate at which a product may be moved efficiently from one place to another.

CISQ Quality Model. Another popular quality model is CISQ. Researchers actively investigate the importance of its attributes for the quality of software. To supplement the level of measurement in ISO 25010, CISQ has defined source code level measures of four quality characteristics:

1. **Maintainability:** The simplicity with which one may alter the system, fit it for new uses, and move it from one developer to others is known as maintainability [31]. Software is maintainable when it follows software architecture guidelines and uses consistent code across the program.
2. **Performance efficiency:** The utilization of resources by an application and how it influences user happiness, scalability, and time for response is referred to as performance efficiency. Performance efficiency is aided by design and architecture.
3. **Reliability:** The danger of system halting and the strength of a code when subjected to unforeseen situations are referred to as reliability. There is little downtime, strong data continuity, and no mistakes that impact customers in reliable software.
4. **Security:** of an application is determined by how successfully it protects data from software breaches. A software system's security level is determined by the number and severity of vulnerabilities discovered. Software vulnerabilities are frequently caused by poor coding and architectural flaws.

3   Methodology

'A Systematic Literature Review is a way of discovering, analyzing, and understanding accessible research related to a certain research topic or phenomena of concern,' according to Kitchenham [19]. In this paper, we conduct SLR using Kitchenham's principles [19]. The following are the goals of this SLR:

- Identifying conflicting elements that influence design pattern application.
- Identifying if a design pattern's structure and application have an impact on quality metrics.
- Identifying the metrics from research estimating the influence of design decisions on quality to evaluate quality characteristics.
- Explain the influence of the design patterns on quality of software and how to achieve coherence in this approach.
- Explain methods to identifying and measuring the effect of design patterns on software quality.

- Identifying and recording challenges to reliability that have been observed in research evaluating the impact of design decisions on software quality.

The details of the methodology are presented in the following sections.

3.1 Research Questions

The research questions of this Systematic Literature Review are extracted from the research goals:

- RQ1: When design patterns are applied, what confounding circumstances, practices, or programming structures impact quality attributes?
- RQ2: What are the quality attributes that are examined and measured, and what are the metrics that are employed?
- RQ3: What is the link connecting design patterns and software quality?
- RQ4: What are the existing design patterns detection approaches?

Quality in software is frequently stated as a context-dependent term [26]. There are a number of factors to consider in order to produce high-quality software. Many factors can affect on the quality of software produced. These issues cannot and should not be removed when using design patterns. Furthermore, how developers apply design patterns and their degree of experience might have an impact on how well they use them. By answering this question, we may learn about the aspects that researchers considered when analyzing design patterns from primary studies. We also determine if other criteria should be taken into account.

The second topic concerns the significance of quality parameters, which academics believe are linked to the application of design decisions. The area of software quality contains numerous aspects, some of which may be mutually exclusive. As a result, we should determine which characteristics may be impacted by the application of design patterns, and which have been underestimated. Another key consideration is the measures applied for assessing quality criteria. Such analysis aids to understand why various research provide varied outcomes.

The response to the RQ3 is expected to help organising future work in terms of avoiding faults when conducting empirical assessments on the topic of mapping the impact of design decisions on quality attributes.

Finally, the answer to the fourth research question describes existing design patterns detection approaches and shows challenges the appeared while investigating this topic in the existing literature.

3.2 Search Process

The investigation was conducted in 2 stages. The initial increment was to explore appropriate papers with similar topics in digital libraries. Identifying data sources and selecting search criteria are all parts of this process. The study selection approach is used in the second stage. The inclusion/exclusion criteria, as well as the quality evaluation approach, must be specified in the second phase. The next sections go into the specifics of these procedures.

Keywords and Resources for Search: Using research questions, we came up with the keywords and search phrases. In order to conduct the searching process, we have defined other quarries based on the keywords presented in Table 1.

Table 1. Search keywords

Research questions	Keywords
RQ1	Design patterns, quality attributes, practices, programming structures
RQ2	Quality metrics, quality criteria, quality attributes
RQ3	Design patterns, software quality, impact of GoF patterns
RQ4	Design patterns detection, detection approaches

In order to separate the results of a search process by research questions, I used different keywords for all of my RQs. The keywords which were used for conducting a search are presented in the 1.

The following well-known online resources were searched for relevant articles:

- IEEE Digital Library (ieeexplore.ieee.org)
- Wiley Online Library (onlinelibrary.wiley.com)
- ACM Digital Library (dl.acm.org)
- Google Scholar (scholar.google.com)
- Science Direct (www.sciencedirect.com)

The amount of studies received from all the above-mentioned online libraries is shown in Sect. 4. We searched using above mentioned strings through main parts of metadata such as title, keywords, and abstract. The interval of years was restricted from 2000 to 2021, which corresponds to the time range covered by this work. Because many publications are indexed in many databases (for example, an ACM/IEEE conference paper), there is a significant percentage of duplicated articles. It means that similar articles are present on different search engines. In my research, around 60% of the retrieved articles were redundant.

This is similar to what Chowdhury et al. [6] discovered (~51% of redundant articles). According to Aichberger et al. [1], databases Wiley and Google Scholar, produced similar results of the search to IEEE and ACM. At this point, there are 717 articles that have been retrieved (after removing duplicates).

3.3   Selection of Primary Research

The following criteria for inclusion and exclusion was used:

- Only peer-reviewed publications release in Scopus are included.
- Include studies that investigate the influence of adopting design decisions on object-oriented software programming languages, such as Java.

- Exclude articles about non-GoF [14] design patterns.
- Include only studies written in English language.
- As a primary study, we examine only the journal versions when one article is published in more than one place[9].

Studies that do not match requirements for inclusion are not accepted. Reading the title of paper, abstract, and keywords determines whether or not an article is relevant.

From all the retrieved studies based on the search quires, we used the inclusion and exclusion criteria and we were left with 57 papers as a result for deeper analysis. The remaining papers were then subjected to the quality evaluation strategy.

The following factors were used to evaluate the 57 potential main studies:

1. The paper contains specific goals that are relevant to our research.
2. The study technique is fully described in the publication.
3. The study defines the factors that are used to assess criteria of quality and explains their measurement.
4. Threats to validity of research constraints are discussed in this article.

To perform the quality evaluation, one must read the whole text of each candidate's primary research. We organized the candidate's primary papers by publication date in ascending order to conduct a quality assessment. Starting with the oldest articles on the list, we compiled a list of potential main studies. A number of factors influence the number of articles in each category.

4   Results and Discussion

This section presents the results achieved by applying methodologies for examining the impact of design patterns on the quality of software development. Applying techniques of conducting a systematic literature review, the process began with searching for existing articles in online libraries. On the 2 results of search in each of them are shown.

Removing duplicates, that appeared in different search engines, the resulting amount of retrieved papers was 717. These 717 were taken for further analysis. After applying the study quality assessment the number of studies reduced to 57. Visualisation of these results are shown on Fig. 1.

4.1   RQ1: When Design Patterns Are Applied, What Confounding Circumstances, Practices, or Programming Structures Impact Quality Attributes?

The software's quality is influenced by a number of variables. Other elements that impact the usage of patterns must be found when researching the influence of design decisions on quality. The factors, programming structures, or practices that impact product quality in the presence of design decisions are discussed in the following sections.

Table 2. Summary of search process

Research questions	Search engines							
	ACM-DL		IEEE xplore		Science direct		Google scholar	
	Hits	Relevant	Hits	Relevant	Hits	Relevant	Hits	Relevant
RQ1	423	7	118	6	273	5	460	11
RQ2	352	8	681	14	523	3	160	12
RQ3	265	6	58	19	478	18	398	9
RQ4	197	8	95	3	285	8	542	7

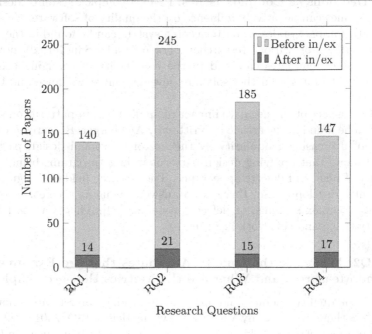

Fig. 1. Comparing the number of papers before in/ex criteria and after

Documentation: It is hard to overestimate the importance of the documentation for the product development, efficiency and maintenance. Many articles described the impact of discussing design decisions construction inside the documentation. Below presented some of them.

Aichberger [1] describes the results of a survey conducted on fifty software developers on the importance of describing the design solutions used in the project code. According to the survey, 80% of developers voted for their colleagues to describe in detail the reasons for using certain design patterns. Aichberger sums it up by talking about the positive effects of documentation and the strengths of documented code.

Weyuker [34] outlines the benefit of documentation in terms of maintainability. Programs with good quality of documentation tends to decrease the expense on maintainability. This article clearly conveys the idea that the likelihood of a developer understanding the code significantly increases, regardless of what type of documentation was provided to him. The results of the analyzed articles are similar. All articles have concluded that documentation of design decisions plays a positive role in the process of improving product quality. Unfortunately, the studied articles did not analyze the weakness or absence of documentation of design patterns, which may be a subject for future work.

Design Decisions as Complex Issues: Being a complex systems, design patterns sometimes can negatively influence on the quality of software. Evidence of such negative impact of design patterns on a system can be found in the existing literature written by various researchers. For example, Sandhu [29] notes that the use of code templates can lead to the complexity of changing the implementation in the future. Further software development slows down and becomes more costly.

Another aspect of the negative impact of applied design patterns on software quality can be found in the article [1] written by Aichberger. Researcher discovers the idea of decreasing modularity by the use of creational design patterns in code. He shows that applying design patterns in huge programs brings to high possibility of bugs and defects appearance. The research field of design patterns is constantly developing, so, there is no answer - what is the reason of defect proneness, complex systems, or defects proneness [24]. This is a good field for possibility to expand this work in future.

4.2   RQ2: What are the Quality Attributes that are Examined and Measured, and What are the Metrics that are Employed?

The topic of quality models and metrics are widely investigated nowadays. In Sect. 2.2 there were briefly discussed two models - ISO 25010 and CISQ. Researches are constantly taking attempts on exploring the connection between quality attributes of these models and metrics. In order to visualize findings of different researches, we summarised all studies where various quality attributes were examined by appropriate metrics in Table 3.

Alebrahim et al. [2] assessed the three quality criteria recommended by ISO 25010. Maintainability, performance and correctness are the factors that were assessed. Quality was evaluated in both libraries and independent apps, according to the researchers. The researchers concluded, that the results are controversial. Some design decisions have a larger impact on quality, while others have the opposite effect.

4.3   RQ3: What is the Link Connecting Design Patterns and Software Quality?

The link between the study of design patterns and the topic of software quality can be seen in many articles published between 2000 and 2021. Researchers

Table 3. Quality attributes summary

Quality attribute	Study	Metrics
Maintainability	[2,5,7,16,21,31]	LoC, amount of changes, time for maintenance, comprehension
Performance	[4,11,17,25,36]	Number of violation of rules, amount of changes, time for response
Effectiveness	[2,30,31]	Faults per class, time for response
Correctness	[2,12,31]	LoC, coupling, amount of defects

are studying the impact of applying design decisions on the quality of the code written by the developer. The quality of the code, in turn, is assessed by various metrics.

Qamar and Nosheen [28], in their article on the impact of design patterns on complexity and size, noted that metrics as cyclomatic complexity quite successfully evaluates the state of the code after the insertion of various design patterns into it. The researchers summarize by talking about the difference in results among different types of design patterns such as creational, behavioral, and structural.

4.4   RQ4: What are the Existing Design Patterns Detection Approaches?

The field of recognizing design patterns in code has become the subject of study by many researchers lately. There are many methodologies based on machine learning, graph analysis, deep learning and others. Scientists note that the great difficulty in creating an ideal method for recognizing design patterns is the lack of a benchmark dataset that would allow training the model.

According to [18] the graph-based approach has a limitation in testing on huge datasets. It was tested only on small cases, there is no certainty that it will work for large ones with the same accuracy. Gueheneuc and Antoniol [13] investigated the quality of the learning-based approach in their article. They outlined the excellence of results of the application of this method on different size datasets. Though this approach has one important disadvantage - it took a lot of time to train the machine learning model before it produced an accurate result.

Moha et al. [23] outlined the importance of the similarity scoring approach in the field of design patterns detection. The limitation of this method is concentrated in the types of design patterns detection, i.e. it is possible to detect only behavioral and creational patterns. This is explained by the definition of the Structural design patterns - they are about objects' interactions [14].

A variety of prediction patterns in the code is widely studied. Each of them requires different compiling times, datasets of various sizes. Fehmi [15] showed a distinction between the results of the use of methods in accordance with the size of datasets. Many approaches have similar challenges [35] in conducting an ideal detection process. A benchmark dataset is required for analysis of the accuracy of the proposed detection methods in order to achieve high precision and recall. For now - there is no such a dataset. Another important limitation, which refers to Deep learning approaches - the need for big-size data. In order to train the machine learning model of design patterns detection, these approaches require a huge dataset. Creating such a big dataset costs much time and resources.

5   Conclusion

Understanding the effects of using design patterns in the coding process could be helpful for developers who want to achieve a good quality of the software. With the aim to investigate and present the effect of using design decisions in development process, this thesis combines design patterns detection, quality models analysis, and evaluating the impact of creational design patterns on software quality. The thesis work concentrates on studying the influence of design patterns on the quality of software by applying the methodology of systematic literature review of the available literature.

Using the aforementioned methods, we came to the results of the work in the form of answers to research questions. Among them: describing confounding circumstances, practices, and programming structures influencing quality attributes, which are examined and measured by different metrics. In order to explore these topics as well as the relationship between design patterns and software quality, we conducted a systematic analysis of the available literature, which led to a result of 717 articles, and after applying the inclusion and exclusion criteria, we received 57 articles that were carefully analyzed. Also, in our analysis of existing approaches used to detect design patterns in source code, we found a that there is a lack of benchmark datasets. As future work we plan to compile a benchmark dataset from open source projects and evaluate the existing design patterns detection approaches. In addition to compiling a benchmark dataset, we plan to analyse if there is any energy impact that comes with implementation of different design patterns.

Acknowledgement. This research project is carried out under the support of the Russian Science Foundation Grant № 19-19-00623.

References

1. Aichberger, J.: Mining software repositories for the effects of design patterns on software quality (2020)
2. Alebrahim, A., Fassbender, S., Filipczyk, M., Goedicke, M., Heisel, M.: Towards systematic selection of architectural patterns with respect to quality requirements. In: Proceedings of the 20th European Conference on Pattern Languages of Programs, EuroPLoP 2015. Association for Computing Machinery, New York (2015). https://doi.org/10.1145/2855321.2855362
3. Alexander, C.: A Pattern Language: Towns, Buildings, Construction. Oxford University Press, Oxford (1977)

4. Brown, W.H., Malveau, R.C., McCormick, H.W.S., Mowbray, T.J.: AntiPatterns: Refactoring Software, Architectures, and Projects in Crisis, 1st edn. Wiley, USA (1998)
5. Cardoso, B., Figueiredo, E.: Co-occurrence of design patterns and bad smells in software systems: an exploratory study. In: Anais do XI Simpósio Brasileiro de Sistemas de Informação, pp. 347–354. SBC, Porto Alegre (2015). https://doi.org/ 10.5753/sbsi.2015.5836
6. Chowdhury, M.I., Katchabaw, M.: Improving software quality through design patterns: a case study of adaptive games and auto dynamic difficulty. Game–ON 2012 (2012)
7. Christopoulou, A., Giakoumakis, E., Zafeiris, V.E., Soukara, V.: Automated refactoring to the strategy design pattern. Inf. Softw. Technol. 54(11), 1202–1214 (2012). https://doi.org/10.1016/j.infsof.2012.05.004
8. Dong, J., Yang, S., Zhang, K.: Visualizing design patterns in their applications and compositions. IEEE Trans. Software Eng. 33(7), 433–453 (2007). https://doi.org/ 10.1109/TSE.2007.1012
9. Elbaz, K., Chaoui, A.: An empirical study to improve software quality through design patterns. Int. J. Ind. Syst. Eng. 29(1), 74–94 (2018)
10. Estdale, J., Georgiadou, E.: Applying the ISO/IEC 25010 quality models to software product. In: Larrucea, X., Santamaria, I., O'Connor, R.V., Messnarz, R. (eds.) EuroSPI 2018. CCIS, vol. 896, pp. 492–503. Springer, Cham (2018). https://doi. org/10.1007/978-3-319-97925-0_42
11. Fontana, F., Zanoni, M., Marino, A., Mäntylä, M.: Code smell detection: towards a machine learning-based approach. In: 2013 IEEE International Conference on Software Maintenance, pp. 396–399 (2013)
12. Gamma, E., Helm, R., Johnson, R., Vlissides, J.: Design Patterns: Elements of Reusable Object-Oriented Software. Addison-Wesley Longman Publishing Co. Inc., Boston (1995)
13. Guéhéneuc, Y.G., Antoniol, G.: Demima: a multilayered approach for design pattern identification. IEEE Trans. Software Eng. 34(5), 667–684 (2008). https://doi. org/10.1109/TSE.2008.48
14. Izurieta, C., Bieman, J.M.: A multiple case study of design pattern decay, grime, and rot in evolving software systems. Software Qual. J. 21(2), 289–323 (2013). https://doi.org/10.1007/s11219-012-9175-x
15. Jaafar, F., Guéhéneuc, Y.G., Hamel, S., Khomh, F., Zulkernine, M.: Evaluating the impact of design pattern and anti-pattern dependencies on changes and faults. Empirical Softw. Engg. 21(3), 896–931 (2016). https://doi.org/10.1007/s10664- 015-9361-0
16. Jaafar, F., Guéhéneuc, Y.G., Hamel, S., et al.: Analysing anti-patterns static relationships with design patterns. Electronic Communications of the EASST 59 (2014)
17. Khaer, M.A., Hashem, M., Masud, M.R.: On use of design patterns in empirical assessment of software design quality. In: 2008 International Conference on Computer and Communication Engineering, pp. 133–137. IEEE (2008)
18. Khomh, F., Guéhéneuc, Y.G.: Do design patterns impact software quality positively? In: 2008 12th European Conference on Software Maintenance and Reengineering, pp. 274–278. IEEE (2008)
19. Kitchenham, B.A., Charters, S.: Guidelines for performing systematic literature reviews in software engineering. Technical Report EBSE-2007-001. Keele University and Durham University Joint Report (2007)

20. Lanza, M., Marinescu, R.: Object-Oriented Metrics in Practice: Using Software Metrics to Characterize, Evaluate, and Improve the Design of Object-Oriented Systems, 1st edn. Springer, Heidelberg (2010). https://doi.org/10.1007/3-540-39538-5
21. Martin Fowler, K.B.: Refactoring: Improving the Design of Existing Code. Addison-Wesley Longman Publishing Co. Inc, USA (1999)
22. McNatt, W.B., Bieman, J.M.: Coupling of design patterns: Common practices and their benefits. In: 25th Annual International Computer Software and Applications Conference, COMPSAC 2001, pp. 574–579. IEEE (2001)
23. Moha, N., Gueheneuc, Y.G., Duchien, L., Le Meur, A.F.: Decor: a method for the specification and detection of code and design smells. IEEE Trans. Softw. Eng. **36**(1), 20–36 (2010). https://doi.org/10.1109/TSE.2009.50
24. Muraki, T., Saeki, M.: Metrics for applying GOF design patterns in refactoring processes. In: Proceedings of the 4th International Workshop on Principles of Software Evolution, pp. 27–36. IWPSE 2001. Association for Computing Machinery, New York (2001). https://doi.org/10.1145/602461.602466
25. Nahar, N., Sakib, K.: Automatic recommendation of software design patterns using anti-patterns in the design phase: a case study on abstract factory. In: QuA-SoQ/WAWSE/CMCE@ APSEC, pp. 9–16 (2015)
26. Nikolaeva, D., Bozhikova, V.: One approach to improve the software quality by applying software design patterns. In: 2019 16th Conference on Electrical Machines, Drives and Power Systems (ELMA), pp. 1–6. IEEE (2019)
27. Ozkaya, I., Bass, L., Sangwan, R., Nord, R.: Making practical use of quality attribute information. IEEE Softw. **25**(2), 25–33 (2008). https://doi.org/10.1109/MS.2008.39
28. Qamar, N., Malik, A.: Impact of design patterns on software complexity and size. Mehran Univ. Res. J. Eng. Technol. **39**, 342–352 (2020). https://doi.org/10.22581/muet1982.2002.10 https://doi.org/10.22581/muet1982.2002.10
29. Sandhu, P.S., Singh, P.P., Verma, A.K.: Evaluating quality of software systems by design patterns detection. In: 2008 International Conference on Advanced Computer Theory and Engineering, pp. 3–7. IEEE (2008)
30. Vokac, M.: Defect frequency and design patterns: an empirical study of industrial code. IEEE Trans. Softw. Eng. **30**(12), 904–917 (2004). https://doi.org/10.1109/TSE.2004.99
31. Wagey, B.C., Hendradjaya, B., Mardiyanto, M.S.: A proposal of software maintainability model using code smell measurement. In: 2015 International Conference on Data and Software Engineering (ICoDSE), pp. 25–30. IEEE (2015)
32. Weiss, M.: Patterns and their impact on system concerns. In: EuroPLoP (2008)
33. Wendorff, P.: Assessment of design patterns during software reengineering: lessons learned from a large commercial project. In: Proceedings of the Fifth European Conference on Software Maintenance and Reengineering, p. 77. CSMR 2001. IEEE Computer Society (2001)
34. Weyuker, E.: Evaluating software complexity measures. IEEE Trans. Softw. Eng. **14**, 1357–1365 (1988). https://doi.org/10.1109/32.6178
35. Yang, S., Tzerpos, V.: A model for analysis and presentation of design pattern detection results. In: Proceedings of the 33rd Annual ACM Symposium on Applied Computing, pp. 1500–1509. SAC 2018. Association for Computing Machinery, New York (2018). https://doi.org/10.1145/3167132.3167292
36. Yasir, R.M., Asad, M., Galib, A.H., Ganguly, K.K., Siddik, M.S.: GodExpo: an automated god structure detection tool for Golang. In: Proceedings of the 3rd International Workshop on Refactoring, pp. 47–50. IWOR 2019. IEEE Press (2019). https://doi.org/10.1109/IWoR.2019.00016

Skills Development Through Agile Capstone Projects

Evangeli Boti[1], Vyron Damasiotis[1] (ID), and Panos Fitsilis[1,2(✉)] (ID)

[1] University of Thessaly, Gaiopolis Campus, 41500 Larissa, Greece
{eboti,damasiotis,fitsilis}@uth.gr
[2] School of Science and Technology, Hellenic Open University, Parodos
Aristotelous 18, 26335 Patras, Greece

Abstract. Agile development, which has been accepted by many organizations in the area of management and software engineering in the last two decades, nowadays, tends to become an emerging teaching and learning methodology in higher education. A great number of educational institutions are offering courses in programming and software engineering using agile methods, setting aside the traditional teaching. This paper attempts to point out the impact of agile methodology in skills' development on university students. Its aim is to explain Scum's application in university students of a computer science program in a capstone project. It tries to identify the role of agile methods in improving students' transversal skills such as communication, collaboration, team cohesion, team self-organization and autonomy, problem-solving, creativity, and generally project planning skills as well as the need for training in agile methods. The research is based on a survey concerning a capstone project implemented by students of Hellenic Open University (HOU). Results indicate that implementation of agile methods can benefit project team members and help them develop both their transversal skills and team working characteristics.

Keywords: Agile methodology · Higher education · Transversal skills

1 Introduction

During the last years, a new teaching and learning methodology based on Agile methodology tends to enjoy acceptance by plenty of educational organizations in higher education. Agile methods are widely accepted in software engineering industry as traditional processes in software engineering and information systems development cannot cope with the increased complexity, constant changes and challenges that occur in modern software development. Project stakeholders are required to work as a team in order to deliver higher quality projects in less time [3]. With the great impact and the growing implementation of agile methodologies such as eXtreme Programming and their processes such as Scrum and Kanban, graduates can gain the knowledge and skills needed to be productive and successful in their future professional activity [40]. According to Lang [20], Agile Learning is "the application of the processes and principles of agile software development to the context of learning". The use of agile methodologies can help them to communicate and collaborate better in order to

© Springer Nature Switzerland AG 2021
G. Succi et al. (Eds.): ICFSE 2021, CCIS 1523, pp. 97–112, 2021.
https://doi.org/10.1007/978-3-030-93135-3_7

overcome the challenges they face in their student project teams [15, 43]. Relevant researches has shown a great impact of Project-based learning to computer science, software engineering and information systems students [9, 24, 38] and teaching agile methods continues to gain prominence for information systems projects [39]. Also, in software engineering, agile methodologies, as they include continuous communication and iterative development, can promote knowledge management [21]. Educating students in a communicative environment through agile development is a key goal for the instructors in computer science programs in higher education [19]. It also constitutes a more dynamic and effective approach to teamwork/project management compared to traditional management [25]. For these reasons this research implemented a new didactic approach based on Agile Methodology by engaging students of the computer science program from HOU in a capstone project, using the Scrum method, as part of their software engineering/programming curriculum.

In the next section the relative literature of agile concepts in education in general and of Scrum methodology in particular, as well as their impact in team members skills are presented. In continuous the research questions set and the research methodology followed are described in detail. Next, the survey and its results are analyzed both quantitatively and qualitatively. Finally, conclusions are drawn in the final section.

2   Theoretical Background

2.1   Agile Mindset

Although agile software development has been around over the last decade, implementation of agile methodologies in a learning and teaching context is in its infancy, but it has drawn a lot of attention in educational and research conferences. Researchers emphasize that software engineers need to develop not only technical skills but also a set of soft skills that are required to make their work more efficient. They also emphasize the same for the field of education arguing that students have to apply agile methods to their projects because theoretical lectures are not enough for their personal development [5]. Traditional teaching and learning produce graduates with skills and knowledge but don't provide a context for applying those skills. In contrary, agile methods provide active learning by having students to work in a way that makes them to face real problems like they will do on their future jobs [19].

Agile mindset includes a set of methods and procedures that try to engage students with real world experiences in an iterative team-based approach which focuses on team communication and interaction. It diffuses the values and principles from Agile Manifesto [4]. According to it, agile means iterative, quick response to changes, interactive, incremental development and quick feedback. Quick and continuous feedback is among the most important principles in Agile, as the enablers learn from the previous iterations and improve every next iteration, detecting their mistakes early and fixing them as soon as they can. Creative problem solving is also encouraged by continuous feedback through sprint retrospective in the Scrum Framework [19]. Feedback from all stakeholders leads to continuous improvement for any organization [17]. In Agile there is no concept of best practices. More and better practices will emerge through continuous iterations [17]. There is no need to follow a specific plan but always shape the plan according to the changes that occur.

The Agile principles and values in the context of learning, as Peha's [33] version says are:

- "individuals and interactions over processes and tools
- meaningful learning over the measurement of learning
- stakeholder collaboration over constant negotiation
- responding to change over following a plan" (Peha [33]:23; [30]).

Agile methodologies include quite a few software development and project management processes, such as Scrum, eXtreme Programming (XP), Kanban, Dynamic Systems Development Method (DSDM) and others. The most popular agile approach to software development is Scrum.

2.2 Scrum Framework

Scrum is a framework for developing, delivering, and sustaining complex products. Applying as an alternative educational methodology for team work increases students' perception of learning by allowing self-managing of their time and resources for meaningful active learning [27]. It consists of short project cycles, called "sprints". The team members have to deliver a designed, built, tested, reviewed and useful product iteratively and incrementally through continuous feedback. If students understand Scrum rules they will be able to overcome any occurred obstacles, and to tackle management and teamwork as real professionals. All these imply an increased need for soft skills, as success depends on effective and efficient communication and fast execution [10].

2.3 Skills Development Through Agile Methodologies

According to a variety of researches, soft skills are as important as hard skills [32]. All required soft skills are described in the conference "Supporting Key Competence Development: Learning approaches and environments in school education" about Education and Training from European Commission which took place in November 2019 at Brussels, Belgium, in which it is highlighted that key competences are best developed in systems, which promote and use a variety of learning approaches and environments, support their teachers and assess and validate key competences [29]. The implementation of an agile approach in the context of learning contributes to personal and team development. Further, according to the Association of American Colleges & Universities, the majority of hiring managers believes that graduates cannot succeed in entry-level positions because of their poor soft skills, locating the problem within higher education (Association of American Colleges & Universities 2019 [2]), emphasizing that graduates are not able to apply learning in real-world settings. That's why employers try to hire graduates with soft skills in order to contribute to today's economy [7]. Because of the social dimension of agile practices, skills such as collaboration, communication, teamworking, self-managing, trust and transparency are being developed.

An empirical study about an implementation of eXtreme Programming (XP) in a laboratory course, focused on disseminating knowledge through collaborative practices such as pair programming, has shown that there is a huge potential to enhance the development of collaborative skills. Because the fact that it relies upon sharing knowledge and information, leads to the development of organizations [18], it could help teachers and students share technical knowledge through their teamworking. In pair programming students as partners discuss and work on the given problem while sharing their experience and knowledge [47]. Thus, agile learning becomes a self-regulated learning process because the students learn through iterative cycles and continuous knowledge exchange among them according to their needs. Traditional teaching cannot arouse students' interests, which results in less active engagement in learning. Therefore, teaching students by embracing changes with agile practices, is appropriate both for students' needs and also for improving teaching quality [45].

In an adaptation of a Scrum process has been found that interpersonal communication has been developed. The regular and early meetings helped students improve their communication. It, also, helped them to develop problem solving skills, and creative solution skills through complex adaptive systems methods, leading them to continuous improvement addressing the issue and improving the confidence among the team members [25]. The adoption of Scrum can be very helpful for the student learning processes, empowering their teamworking [14]. It increased students' commitment allowing them to self-reflect on their performance in the Sprint Retrospective meetings [35]. Continuous communication through iterations contributes to mutual learning and increasing progress among team members [45].

Universities are required to develop students' skills needed to have a successful hands-on experience in a software engineering environment close to the real world [31]. Thus, in another case study on a capstone project in a Scrum-based training it has been found that students maximize their performance and develop their problem-solving skills [36].

During a research project where agile-method learning tools were used, project participants, by employing their personal abilities, developed their skills in cooperation and creativity. This happened as the project kept them engaged itself, because of the common understanding about the goals which have been set [26].

According to Hof et al. [16], collaboration and communication are key to successful agile software development through agile values as respect, openness, transparency and trust in a multiweek Scrum simulation project, the evaluation showed that students enjoyed more fun, and the collaboration in the team.

Agile working promotes a psychologically safe working environment. Agile meetings lead students to improve communication, and increase a shared sense of responsibility and respect among them [25]. Because of the fact that the agile approach has no strict rules but is based on useful principles, it seems to suit perfect skill development [5].

3   Research Methodology

The aim of this research is to identify if teaching agile can improve transversal skills such as communication skills, collaborative skills, and team cohesion, team self-organization and autonomy, problem-solving, creativity, and generally project planning skills.

More specifically, in this research we would like to examine the following research questions:

RQ1: Which are the skills that are developed during the implementation of a project using agile methods?

RQ2: Is necessary team members training in agile methods before participating in an agile project?

RQ3: Are the agile team organization and team roles easily comprehended and what are the challenges faced by students?

RQ4: In which way is the agile software development process affected by factors such as a) the team's geographical distribution, b) task switching between project work and other activities, c) lack of team members' commitment?

To achieve the objectives set a survey was conducted with students of Hellenic Open University (HOU). In particular, students of the computer science program of studies were asked to take part in a survey with regard to the skills they developed after the implementation of the capstone project using Scrum methodology. During their third year of study, these students were taught agile methods by engaging themselves in a capstone project as part of their software engineering/programming curriculum. HOU students are mainly distance learning students. Students of two separate years of studies were asked to participate in order to be able to see differences that arise with modality. Specifically, the survey included all students that attended the module during academic years 2019–2020 and 2020–2021. Students were organized into groups. Each group had between 20 to 30 students leading to 8 to 9 student groups per academic year. Finally, students asked to form their own capstone project team using the "self-selection method" that consisted of 3 to 4 persons. The "self-selection" method is a method that gives full responsibility to the students in contrast to random selection or alphabetical methods. Further, it allows the formation of excellent and/or poor performing teams, in contrast with a random selection that produces usually "average" performing teams [1].

In this capstone project, students were given a product backlog for developing a java application and they were asked to implement this application using agile practices. The product backlog contained approximately ten user stories. The user stories described a software system that contained a simple graphical user interface, the use of a restful API, storage and retrieval of data to a relational database, the creation of an XLM file, and the creation of threads.

The teaching team was directing the students to use the SCRUM method. The duration of the capstone project lasted roughly two months, giving them sufficient time to run up to three sprints. However, the duration of each sprint was at the discretion of the team. Teams usually consisted of three to four members, and they were self-organized, meaning selection of members of the team and as well the assignments of the roles to members of the team. A member of the teaching team was assigned to the position of product owner, while another member of the team was assigned to the role of scrum master. Each team was required to submit reports on a variety of software engineering topics, such as system design, requirements prioritization, sprint backlog, and risk management.

More specifically students were asked as a deliverable of their capstone project to provide the following:

1. Calculation of the required effort per requirement documentation in detail how to calculate the effort. It was suggested to use the planning poker method [23].
2. Calculation of the priorities of the receivables documenting in detail the way of calculating the priority. More specifically, for prioritization, the teaching team recommended the priority poker method, which is a variant of planning poker, where participants, instead of choosing effort estimates for each user story, choose priorities. The method can be ap-plied using "T-Shirt Sizes" cards with the assumption that XXS (eXtra-eXtra-Small) corresponds to the lowest priority and XXL (eXtra-eXtra-Large) to the highest [37].
3. The sprint backlog as it was formed after each iteration.
4. For each of the user stories of the product backlog, the acceptance criteria.
5. The assignments of responsibilities to the team members in each repetition (sprint).
6. The implementation time per user story/per sprint compared to what was planned, as well as the burnt down chart
7. A retrospective review report.

As an output of the retrospective report students were asked to evaluate several factors that relate to the difficulties they faced either concerning the project techni-calities or about teamwork. As well, they were asked to report on how they would improve their work taking into account the acquired experience. These reports were used as a qualitative input for this research. More specifically, students were asked to report on:

1. the problems the team encountered during the implementation of the capstone project,
2. the deviations of the actual implementation from the sprint planning,
3. the usefulness of the online collaboration tool that was used to assist the team in their daily work
4. the risks that occurred during the project, and their response to them,
5. to propose changes in the work practices for a next subsequent project, and on
6. the knowledge, competences, and skills acquired.

This research had two parts. The quantitative part was conducted with the devel-opment and administration of a questionnaire and the qualitative part which was based on the views as they were expressed by students at the retrospective review report.

3.1 Quantitative Research

The research took place by uploading the questionnaire online using Google Forms and sending it out to the selected students. Before sending out the questionnaire, it was tested internally with a pilot group to ensure its validity as in its structure, language and questions asked. During the pilot research, it was confirmed that the questions were easily comprehensible, engaging, and offered answers relative to the scope of the research. The questionnaire was sent out to 239 current (the academic year 2020–2021) and 238 from previous academic year students (2019–2020) at the Hellenic Open University (https://www.eap.gr/en/). All of the students had or are currently attending a computer science course at the university that included agile software engineering. The students had 30 days to answer and of the total 477 students, 115 replied to the questionnaire, a percentage of 24.1%.

The questionnaire that was distributed had three sections:

- The first section included questions regarding the level of familiarity of the former students with the agile concepts both in university courses as well as in their work environment and some personal information about them.
- The second section consisted of questions regarding the perceived improvement of students' communication skills after the implementation of the project. This section included questions such as, if the students' ability to communicate with other project stakeholders and to understand customer needs or requirements has improved. It was asked if the use of scrum practices and roles helped organize their work and overall improved the communication.
- The third section of the questionnaire focused on the efficiency of agile methods and their use to improve collaboration and overall team cohesion. Students were asked to evaluate the active participation of each member of the team in the planning of the project goals in each sprint, if sprint retrospectives helped to identify the weaknesses of the team and each member individually, or to improve team members' commitment, etc.
- The next section was focused on how agile methods affect team self-organization and group autonomy. Students were asked to evaluate if Scrum affected their ability to create their own sustainable work pace, how the ownership of the decision making affected project execution etc.
- The fifth section was related to problem-solving and creativity skills. The questions in this section were evaluating if agile methods can affect the ability of the team members to solve problems and to be more creative.
- Finally, the sixth section of this questionnaire was related to planning skills and if agile methods affect the ability of team members to manage time, to evaluate the effort estimations required per sprint or user story, etc.

3.2 Qualitative Research

The questions asked in the retrospective review report were the basis of the qualitative analysis. The retrospective review reports were similar to interview questions. Usually, in a semi structured interview, a set of 5–7 topics is formed and the respondents are prompted to talk about, while the interviewer is taking notes [46].

Further, these reports were considered as student feedback. Student feedback is used systematically by all universities to assess the quality or to assess if the learning outcomes were met.

Considering that this was a group assignment where teams had between 3 to 4 team members and the fact that some students have not submitted their assignment at all, and some assignments were incomplete in this section, a total number of 109 assignment reports were evaluated.

In the literature, it is suggested that one effective way to analyze qualitative input is the use of Computer Aided Qualitative Data Analysis Software programs (CAQDAS) such as NVivo and SPSS, etc. Such tools implement learning analytics algorithms that enable researchers to discover insights by qualitatively analyzing student feedback [13]. However, the student input language that was Greek did not allow us to use such tools.

For the above reason, an inductive research approach was used. When the inductive approach is used, research findings emerge from the raw data. Usually, the topics that emerge are the most frequent, dominant, or significant themes [22, 44]. Consequently, interpretation of themes is done by comparison. The inductive approach is flexible since it is not strongly guided such as grounded theory, narrative research, or case study.

When the inductive approach is used [44] five are the main steps:

1. studying the raw data which in our case were the retrospective reports,
2. identification text that is related to the specific research questions
3. labelling text to relate the text with the initial research categories and addition of new emerging categories,
4. reducing overlapping categories, and
5. creating a model consisting of the major most influential categories.

The data collected were statistically analyzed with descriptive statistics for summarizing the findings.

4   Research Analysis

4.1   Quantitative Survey Analysis

In total 115 responses received during the survey. Initially participants were asked to declare if they had any prior experience in software development projects and assess this experience according to a 5-scale Likert scale ranging from "No experience" to "Excellent experience". According to responses 47.8% had none or insignificant experience, 23.9% had moderate experience and 28.3 had very good or excellent experience in software projects (see Fig. 1).

Next, they were asked to evaluate the experience gained from their participation in the project using the same Likert scale. According to their responses, 7.9% declared that they still had none or insignificant experience, 34.2% declared that they now have moderate experience and 57.9% declared that they have very good or excellent experience in software projects (see Fig. 2).

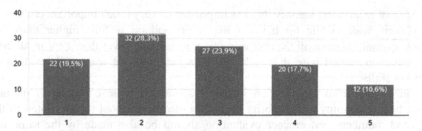

Fig. 1. Level of experience in software projects before participating in project

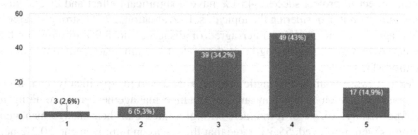

Fig. 2. Level of experience in software projects after participating in project

The project was conducted using Agile methods and specifically the SCRUM methodology. It is worth notice that only 14.9% of the participants had previous experience in agile methods while 85.1% of them had no previous experience in using Agile methods. The survey tried to identify if agile methods helped them to improve their transversal skills such as communication, collaboration, team working and the effectiveness of Scrum method in teamworking improvement.

Respondents could answer using a 5 point Likert scale in all questions. In all cases, more than 65% of the responders declared that their transversal skills were improved or very much improved, about 25% declared that had a moderate improvement and less than 10% declared that had no or insignificant improvement.

Specifically, 74.6% declared that they had improved or very much improved their personal communication skills, 21.9% had a moderate improvement and only the 8.8% said that had no or insignificant improvement. Regarding the effectiveness of Scrum in team level communication either through role assignment to team members or sprints more than 65% of participants declared that Scrum methodology significantly contributed to team communication improvement while less than 12% said that there was insignificant improvement. The rest declared that there was indeed an improvement although in moderate level. As that, it can be undoubtedly concluded that team members' communications skills can be improved by their participation in an agile (Scrum) project.

Participants were asked to evaluate the importance of team members participation in setting sprint backlog, the role of sprints and retrospections in revealing personal and team weaknesses, the contribution of sprints in team members commitment and willingness to concentrate both to personal and team success. Regarding the first two, more than 85% of responders identify them as important or very much important (values 4 or 5 in Likert scale) while for the rest the same opinion is little higher than 70%. Responses that consider all the above as insignificant are lower than 12% in all cases. This sets a grounded base that agile methods can improve team collaboration and cohesion skills.

Considering team organization issues, respondents believe that team members should have autonomy and authority in making decisions about topics related to their work and members performance evaluation should be also made by the same team members and this approach can improve project progress. Specifically, 25.7% of responders believe that teams' self-autonomy and authority to make decisions have a moderate effect in project success, 45.1% have a significant effect and 26.5% have an extreme effect on it. Considering the topic of self-evaluation, 27.7% strongly agree with it, 33% agree with it, 30.4% neither agree or disagree and 8.9% disagree or totally disagree. According to these, agile methods foster team team-autonomy and self-evaluation skills.

Next, it was examined if agile methods and scrum specifically can improve transversal skills such as problem analysis, change management and providing feedback. Specifically, 16.7% of responders strongly agree that their change management capabilities were improved, 55.3% agree that there was an improvement, 20.2% neither agree or disagree and the rest do not believe that there was any improvement. Regarding improving problem analysis skills, about 70% of the participants believe that their capabilities to analyze problems, evaluate alternatives and merging different approaches and proposals were clearly improved (values 4 or 5 in Likert scale) due to requirements for repetitions and retrospectives set by Scrum methodology. As for their capabilities improvement in providing feedback, 51.8% of responders believe that there was indeed an improvement, 18.8% consider there was an extreme improvement, 17.9% believe that was a small improvement and 11.6% believe that essentially there was no improvement. These also consist of a solid base that the aforementioned skills can also benefit from agile methods application.

Finally, participants were asked to evaluate the effect of Scrum methodology and generally of agile methods in planning and management skills of team members. They were asked to evaluate to what degree Scrum structure and processes e.g. sprints, user stories, burndown charts, actions for task prioritization improve their time management skills. In all relative questions, at least 70% of the responders declared that their time management capabilities were significantly or very much improved, about 25% declared that they had a moderate improvement while only 5% responded that there was no or insignificant improvement. Considering the improvement in planning and effort estimation capabilities, about 55% of responders declared that they had more than a significant improvement, about 25% declared that had a moderate improvement and less than 10% declared that had no or insignificant improvement. As such, it can be concluded that planning and management skills can also be improved.

From data analysis and considering RQ1 can be concluded that the implementation of agile methods in a project can benefit project team members and help them develop and grow both their transversal skills and team working characteristics such as cohesion, collaboration, effective communication, clear role assignments and mutual understanding.

4.2   Qualitative Analysis of Students' Feedback

As it was mentioned in the research methodology section, students were asked to provide a critical assessment of their work and on the challenges that they faced during their work. More specifically, they were asked to report on the challenges they faced, the risks that occurred, and their response to them, and, also, on the possible changes in their work practices that they could recommend. Finally, they were asked to report on the knowledge, competences, and skills acquired during this project.

According to the feedback received by students the most frequent problems/challenges the teams encountered were the following:

Student initial education and information: Initially, students were not familiar with the agile principles and the culture behind these principles. Even though agile practices were easily comprehensible, the adoption of them was challenging for most of the teams. Some students mentioned that the agile methods were introduced quickly and thus the provided material and guidance was inadequate in the beginning. We can provide numerous examples of the challenges faced by students in their projects. For example, this lack of agile culture or agile experience was expressed with many different symptoms:

- Inability to deliver user stories according to the planning and keep up a constant delivery pace
- Inability to deliver working and tested software at the end of each day (daily build) or the end of the sprint
- Daily communication with the product owner
- Use of visual tools for reporting the progress of the team (the team were instructed to use a collaborative online tool (e.g. Trello)
- Etc.

Similar findings have been reported in other studies such as in Gandomani et al. [11] and Nuottila et al. [28]. The aforementioned provides a clear answer in RQ2 about the necessity of agile education prior project execution.

Team organization and roles. It was a mandatory project requirement for all student teams to use agile roles. However, there were problems in team organization and assignment of roles, since students could not comprehend in practice the responsibility of each role. A typical paradigm, and maybe the most common, for a software development team, is that team members are assuming a vertical role e.g. acting as analysts, as designers, as programmers, etc. This is not the case in agile software development that requires cross-lifecycle developers, developers that execute all steps of a software development process. This fact caused confusion and communication difficulties, especially during the first weeks of the project. Further, in many cases, the roles of scrum master and product owner were not clear to the students, since scrum masters were reluctant to contact product owners (a role assumed by members of the teaching team) asking for clarifications or decisions. Finally, there were cases where the scrum master was acting as a project manager since he/she was dictating to other team members assignments and deadlines. The project manager is a role that is not supposed to exist in an agile project. The existence of a project manager in agile projects that has been revealed in this research indicates a gap between theory and practice that is in line with the findings of other studies [41].

Nevertheless, these problems were expectable to a certain extent since capstone projects are short, in duration, projects, which implies that the team has not sufficient time to be well organized. The above analysis provides a clear answer to RQ3 that the agile team organization and team roles are difficulty to comprehend, especially in the beginning of the implementation, adversely affecting project execution.

Student commitment: HOU students are part-time students attempting to combine in most of the cases work, personal life, and studies, which is directly linked with time constraints. As was expected, most teams reported that the available time was not sufficient. From this fact, we can conclude that agile methods are better applicable when team members are working full-time on a project. This is in line with agile lean principles where context switching is considered as a source of waste [34].

Student distributed location. According to Calefato and Ebert [6], "Today, software engineering is characterized by two strong trends: agile and distributed. Both together are increasingly demanding and challenging teams and projects due to lack of discipline, insufficient transparency, agile "ping-pong," and thus overheads and rework." This was the case for all these capstone projects since they were administered during the spring semester of the academic years 2019–2020 and 202–2021, academic years where the HOU used exclusively distance learning, due to the COVID-19 pandemic. According to literature [42] distributed agile teams suffer from some problems, such as inadequate communication, insufficient knowledge sharing, project and process management discrepancies, technical issues, etc. All the above symptoms were present and they were reported by the students and especially insufficient knowledge sharing, project and process management discrepancies.

User stories effort estimation. Planning poker is an agile software estimation technique that has two main prerequisites: a) software developers have experience from previous projects, so they can estimate the size of the user story and b) they are familiar with group decision-making techniques that require consensus. Both the above were important constraints that were faced by the students since in most cases they didn't have relevant experience. Reaching consensus on the size of user stories is the core principle of Planning Poker [23]. To overcome the challenge of reaching consensus, students used averaging which is not considered an accurate method [12]. Overall, the application of effort estimation didn't produce accurate results since most of the teams reported deviations of the actual implementation from the sprint planning.

For many of the students, it was the first time they worked as part of a team during their studies and especially in a project that had technical, tooling, methodological and organizational challenges. As it was reported:

- The successful implementation of the project improved their collaborative skills, teamwork skills along with their technical skills, and this was considered as one of the most positive outcomes of the project. In relation to the above outcome, we are quoting from one of their reports that "Finally, with the delivery of the project, we have the feeling of satisfaction for the successful completion of such a demanding project."

- Knowledge sharing was considered as an important benefit from this capstone project and according to some of them, knowledge sharing and distribution of work accelerated the overall work outcome. This is in line with personal efficiency improvement objectives "to do more work in less time".
- The fact that the teams were self-organized allowed the students to assume full responsibility for their work including the planning. This empowered them and improved their organizational and planning skills.
- The fact that students had to work in a distributed fashion enabled them to use modern collaborative tools and to improve their ability to work within a team remotely, which was considered quite important.

The aforementioned provides a clear answer to RQ4 that project execution can be negatively affected by factors such as geographical distribution, task switching between project work and other activities and lack of team members' commitment.

5 Conclusion

This paper presents an implementation of a Scrum training model in an agile learning environment for university students. The methodology was implemented in a capstone project, using the Scrum method, as part of their software engineering/programming curriculum. To evaluate the impact of the agile methodology implementation a survey and a retrospective review were completed by with the students and analyzed by data analysis.

The results of the analysis indicated a great level of student satisfaction with the agile method implementation. It also have been indicated a positive impact on their performance as well as they improved both their software development skills and their transversal skills such as communication, collaboration, team cohesion, team self-organization and autonomy, problem-solving, creativity, and generally project planning skills. They became very responsible for their work by using collaborative tools, improving their ability to work within a team.

Knowledge sharing was considered as an important benefit from this capstone project as agile methodologies including continuous communication and iterative development, can promote knowledge management as stated also by Levy et al. [21].

Although there were problems in team organization and assignment of roles causing confusion and communication difficulties, especially in the beginning of the project continuous communication through iterations contributed to mutual learning and increasing progress among team members as also stated by Yang et al. [45].

In conclusion, according to the above findings, it can be assumed that Agile methodology could be of interest to anyone planning to implement agile procedures to projects in a context of software engineering curriculum, as well as in other disciplines in higher education [8], in order students to develop not only technical skills but also a set of transversal skills that are required in today's economy.

References

1. Aller, B.M., Lyth, D.M., Mallak, L.A.: Capstone project team formation: mingling increases performance and motivation. Decis. Sci. J. Innov. Educ. **6**(2), 503–507 (2008)
2. Association of American Colleges and Universities: Fulfilling the American dream: liberal education and the future of work (2018). https://aacu.org/research/2018-future-of-work. Accessed 07 Sept 2021
3. Bica, D.A.B., da Silva, C.A.G.: Learning process of agile scrum methodology with Lego blocks in interactive academic games: viewpoint of students. IEEE Revista Iberoamericana de Tecnologias del Aprendizaje **15**(2), 95–104 (2020)
4. Beck, K., et al.: The Manifesto for Agile Software Development (2001). http://agilemanifesto.org/. Accessed 25 Aug 2021
5. Bruegge, B., Reiss, M., Schiller, J.: Agile principles in academic education: a case study. In: 2009 Sixth International Conference on Information Technology: New Generations, pp. 1684–1686. IEEE, April 2009
6. Calefato, F., Ebert, C.: Agile collaboration for distributed teams [software technology]. IEEE Softw. **36**(1), 72–78 (2019)
7. Coates, K.: The value of soft skills: preparing the next generation of workforce for future work (2020)
8. Cubric, M.: An agile method for teaching agile in business schools. Int. J. Manag. Educ. **11**(3), 119–131 (2013)
9. Ding, D., Yousef, M., Yue, X.: A case study for teaching students agile and scrum in capstone course. J. Comput. Sci. Coll. **32**(5), 95–101 (2017)
10. Fitsilis, P., Lekatos, A.: Teaching software project management using agile paradigm. In: Proceedings of the 21st Pan-Hellenic Conference on Informatics, pp. 1–6, September 2017
11. Gandomani, T.J., Zulzalil, H., Ghani, A.A., Sultan, A.B.M., Sharif, K.Y.: How human aspects impress Agile software development transition and adoption. Int. J. Softw. Eng. Appl. **8**(1), 129–148 (2014)
12. Gandomani, T.J., Faraji, H., Radnejad, M.: Planning Poker in cost estimation in Agile methods: averaging vs. consensus. In: 2019 5th Conference on Knowledge Based Engineering and Innovation (KBEI), pp. 066–071. IEEE, February 2019
13. Gottipati, S., Shankararaman, V., Gan, S.: A conceptual framework for analyzing students' feedback. In: 2017 IEEE Frontiers in Education Conference (FIE), pp. 1–8. IEEE, October 2017
14. Grimheden, M.E.: Can agile methods enhance mechatronics design education? Mechatronics **23**(8), 967–973 (2013)
15. Harding, L.M.: Students of a feather "flocked" together: a group assignment method for reducing freeriding and improving group and individual learning outcomes. J. Mark. Educ. **40**(2), 117–127 (2017)
16. Hof, S., Kropp, M., Landolt, M.: Use of gamification to teach agile values and collaboration: a multi-week scrum simulation project in an undergraduate software engineering course. In: Proceedings of the 2017 ACM Conference on Innovation and Technology in Computer Science Education, pp. 323–328, June 2017
17. Kamat, V., Sardessai, S.: Agile practices in higher education: a case study. In: 2012 Agile India, pp. 48–55. IEEE, February 2012
18. Kavitha, R.K., Ahmed, M.S.I.: Knowledge sharing through pair programming in learning environments: an empirical study. Educ. Inf. Technol. **20**(2), 319–333 (2013). https://doi.org/10.1007/s10639-013-9285-5

19. Kumar, S., Ureel, L.C., Wallace, C.: Agile communicators: cognitive apprenticeship to prepare students for communication-intensive software development. In: 2015 Agile Conference, pp. 71–75. IEEE, August 2015
20. Lang, G.: Agile learning: sprinting through the semester. Inf. Syst. Educ. J. 15(3), 14 (2017)
21. Levy, M., Hadar, I., Aviv, I.: Agile-based education for teaching an agile requirements engineering methodology for knowledge management. Sustainability 13(5), 2853 (2021)
22. Liu, L.: Using generic inductive approach in qualitative educational research: a case study analysis. J. Educ. Learn. 5(2), 129–135 (2016)
23. Mahnič, V., Hovelja, T.: On using planning poker for estimating user stories. J. Syst. Softw. 85(9), 2086–2095 (2012)
24. Mahnic, V.: A capstone course on agile software development using scrum. IEEE Trans. Educ. 55(1), 99–106 (2012)
25. Marder, B., et al.: 'Going agile': exploring the use of project management tools in fostering psychological safety in group work within management discipline courses. Int. J. Manag. Educ. 19(3), 100519 (2021)
26. Mihalik, J.: Agile approach in higher education-a collaborative research project report. Opus et Educatio 6(4), 470–476 (2019)
27. Milićević, J.M., Filipović, F., Jezdović, I., Naumović, T., Radenković, M.: Scrum agile framework in e-business project management: an approach to teaching scrum. Eur. Proj. Manag. J. 9(1), 52–60 (2019)
28. Nuottila, J., Aaltonen, K., Kujala, J.: Challenges of adopting agile methods in a public organization. Int. J. Inf. Syst. Proj. Manag. 4(3), 65–85 (2016)
29. O'Shea, M., Frohlich Hougaard, K.: Supporting key competence development: learning approaches and environments in school education. Input Paper (2019)
30. Parsons, D., MacCallum, K.: Agile education, lean learning. In: Parsons, D., MacCallum, K. (eds.) Agile and Lean Concepts for Teaching and Learning, pp. 3–23. Springer, Singapore (2019). https://doi.org/10.1007/978-981-13-2751-3_1
31. Paasivaara, M., Lassenius, C., Damian, D., Raty, P., Schroter, A.: Teaching students global software engineering skills using distributed scrum. In: Proceedings of 35th International Conference on Software Engineering, May 2013, pp. 1128–1137 (2013)
32. Patacsil, F., Tablatin, C.: Exploring the importance of soft and hard skills as perceived by IT internship students and industry: a gap analysis. J. Technol. Sci. Educ. 7, 347 (2017)
33. Peha, S.: Agile Schools: How Technology Saves Education (Just Not the Way We Thought It Would) (2011). https://www.infoq.com/articles/agile-schools-education/. Accessed 10 Sept 2021
34. Poppendieck, M., Poppendieck, T.D.: Implementing lean software development: from concept to cash. Softw. Qual. Prof. 9(3), 45 (2007)
35. Rodriguez, G., Soria, Á., Campo, M.: Virtual scrum: a teaching aid to introduce undergraduate software engineering students to scrum. Comput. Appl. Eng. Educ. 23(1), 147–156 (2015)
36. Rodríguez, G., Soria, Á., Campo, M.: Measuring the impact of agile coaching on students' performance. IEEE Trans. Educ. 59(3), 202–209 (2016)
37. Sachdeva, V.: Requirements prioritization in agile: use of planning poker for maximizing return on investment. In: Latifi, S. (ed.) Information Technology – New Generations. AISC, vol. 558, pp. 403–409. Springer, Cham (2018). https://doi.org/10.1007/978-3-319-54978-1_53
38. Saltz, J., Heckman, R.: Exploring which agile principles students internalize when using a Kanban process methodology. J. Inf. Syst. Educ. 31(1), 51 (2020)
39. Schmitz, K.: A three cohort study of role-play instruction for agile project management. J. Inf. Syst. Educ. 29(2), 93–103 (2018)

40. Sharp, J.H., Mitchell, A., Lang, G.: Agile teaching and learning in information systems education: an analysis and categorization of literature. J. Inf. Syst. Educ. **31**(4), 269–281 (2020)
41. Shastri, Y., Hoda, R., Amor, R.: The role of the project manager in agile software development projects. J. Syst. Softw. **173**, 110871 (2021)
42. Shrivastava, S.V.: Distributed agile software development: a review. arXiv preprint arXiv: 1006.1955 (2010)
43. Takai, S., Esterman, M.: Towards a better design team formation: a review of team effectiveness models and possible measurements of design-team inputs, processes, and outputs. In: ASME 2017 International Design Engineering Technical Conferences and Computers and Information in Engineering Conference (2017)
44. Thomas, D.R.: A general inductive approach for analyzing qualitative evaluation data. Am. J. Eval. **27**(2), 237–246 (2006)
45. Yang, J., Zhang, X.L., Su, P.: Deep-learning-based agile teaching framework of software development courses in computer science education. Procedia Comput. Sci. **154**, 137–145 (2019)
46. Wilkinson, S., Joffe, H., Yardley, L.: Qualitative data collection: interviews and focus groups. In: Marks, D., Yardley, L. (eds.) Research Methods for Clinical and Health Psychology, pp. 39–55. SAGE Publications, London (2004)
47. Williams, L.A., Kessler, R.R.: All I ever needed to know about pair programming I learned in kindergarten. In: Communications of the ACM. Association for Computing Machinery (ACM), New York (2000)

Impact of the Communication Issues:
A Case Study of IT Start-Up

Artem Kruglov[✉] [ID]

Laboratory of Industrial Software Production, Innopolis University,
Universitetskaya st., 1, Innopolis, Russia
a.kruglov@innopolis.ru

Abstract. This case represents a brief story of a start-up company producing innovative IT solutions for the forest industry. The start-up was launched in 2015 as experts had suggested the necessity of the digital transformation for the industry. The development process was accompanied by a number of management faults which ultimately led to the lack of commercial success of the developed product. The most critical mistakes were made in the sphere of project communication management with almost all the stakeholders in the project. Thus, the analysis from the viewpoint of communication management is given here followed by some recommendations.

Keywords: Case studies · Business-case analysis · Project management · Collaboration exchanges · Patterns

1 Introduction

To the date of the 1st of November, 2018 the total income of Xemeria company was 87 000 rubles. Thus, I had to fire all the personnel and begin the bankruptcy procedure. Looking back, I am trying to remember all milestones and twists on our path to the current catastrophic situation.

It started 3 years earlier, at the beginning of 2015, when the grant for innovative project development was won and, as a result, Xemeria company was founded. The R&D project was aimed to develop a complex solution for forest enterprises that will allow them to monitor and control the turnover of raw material, such as roundwood, in automated mode. The idea of this project has come from one of the industry experts, ex-owner of a logging plant. He helped with the grant application and act as an investor in the project. With the investor's money and grant, I was able to initiate this ambitious project.

The project for automatic monitoring and control of forest enterprise activity consists of two parts:

1. Manufacturing execution system (MES) for dispersed data processing for the purpose of forest enterprise operations management, i.e. automatic processing of such operations as:

© Springer Nature Switzerland AG 2021
G. Succi et al. (Eds.): ICFSE 2021, CCIS 1523, pp. 113–132, 2021.
https://doi.org/10.1007/978-3-030-93135-3_8

- Accounting of incoming timber products from the declared cutting areas as a result of the logging team output and wood skidding,
- Accounting of the timber processing operations at the roundwood yard connected with transportation and crosscutting,
- Accounting of the timber shipment in terms of vendor contract and destination,
- Low landing stockpile analysis,
- Generating of the shipping document,
- Generating reports on productivity of logging chews, handling chews and truckers.

2. Software for automatic calculating of volume of the log batches via image processing.

According to the plan, the primary product to be developed is software for automatic volume calculation which can be used as a separate product. Xemeria had hired two programmers, so at the beginning, it consisted of four persons: a director, two programmers, and an accountant. Due to the limited size of the team and the lack of management experience, the development process was ad hoc, with periodical (usually, weekly) reporting of programmers to me about current progress. The approximate plan was established in grant application, so the team was aware of current progress of the project.

In 9 months the first version of the software for the PC was produced, so it was a time for industrial testing of the program. Hopefully, two months before this date I met the director of the medium-sized logging enterprise Nova-LesProm, who became interested in our project and agreed to test our programs at his plant. In October, 2015 we provide the employees of Nova-LesProm with software and cameras for tests. The communication with the responsible person of the plant was established via email. The feedback that we obtained shown us that the solution has a low level of usability - it is uncomfortable to make a photo on the camera, upload an image to the computer, and process it in our software. Thus, I decided that the software should be adapted to mobile devices. Unfortunately, it involved a complete redesign of the GUI and some modules of the algorithm. It was the end of 2015, thus I decided to start a new development iteration the next year.

In 2016 we started with the development of a new version of automatic volume calculating software - for mobile devices. The grant was prolonged for one more year with additional funding. This time Nova-LesProm had become the investor of the project. Because of the re-development of the software, I found the project behind the schedule. Furthermore, it became clear that the project is much more complex than I thought at the beginning. These facts led to the decision to outsource the development of the MES system. On the recommendations, I contact the local IT company Polus, who has experience in the development of such systems. They agreed to modify their own solution to our area (the forest industry) and add interfaces for interaction with our software for the purpose of a completely automated monitoring and control process. We start from the several interviews with the director and personnel of the Nova-LesProm to elaborate the activity diagrams and use cases for the developing system. We provide three meetings - one in February and two in March - to gather all necessary information and after that Polus was working on the system alone with monthly reports to me.

In parallel with it, our key partner introduced me to the rector of the Forest Engineering University (FEU). I assumed it as an opportunity for the rapid growth of Xemeria, since this university has many contacts with enterprises all over the country. The rector found our project extremely important for the industry and expressed a willingness to support it. We agreed on presenting of our software at some industrial exhibitions and directly to particular companies. At this time, in the middle of 2016, one of the programmers left the project. It was a massive blow to the company, and I devoted 2 months to find new personnel for this project. Thus, it was September when we presented our new software to the Nova-LesProm. Polus delivered their system in November.

The industrial tests of the software and system were conducted till the end of April, 2017. The director of Nova-LesProm explained such a huge delay with the high workload of the staff and inability to introduce new technologies in the manufacturing process in this period - i.e. high season. Finally, I received feedback on our complex solution with several shortcomings described, mostly on system performance. This feedback was addressed to Polus and Xemeria, in turn, started modifying several parts of the software. As far as Xemeria still has no sales, I transferred employees to piecework.

During the modification stage I conducted several meetings with directors of forest plants which contacts were given to me by the rector of FEU. The result of this meeting was that the idea is interesting and perspective, but each enterprise needs some specific features and not ready to buy our solution right now.

Therefore, I decided to concentrate all effort to Nova-LesProm, but the process of our solution implementation still was extremely slow. Employees of the Nova LesProm were accustomed to Excel and discovered the new system hard to use. Tallymen were afraid of using innovative technology for log batches measurement and it was hard to convince them. In fact, the introduction of a novel approach was faced with rejection from employees, and the director, in spite of his interest in the project, was not ready to force it against the will of employees.

I spent the rest of 2017 and the beginning of 2018 in negotiation with Nova-LesProm. Finally, all complaints were resolved and in June 2018 Xemeria was ready to deliver the whole system to its primary client. At this moment I found out that the director of Nova-LesProm decided to sell his company to the large forestry concern against the background of an unstable economic situation. Up to this moment, Xemeria has only several sales of the software for automatic volume calculating of the log batches. The funds, received in 2015–16 years come to an end and there is still no customer for our system. There were a lot of mistakes done in the management process for Xemeria project. However, in my opinion, the most important one is that I gave too little effort to the development and management of the communication along with the project. Investors, partners, development team, new clients - for the overall success of the project, it was necessary to pay more attention to all the stakeholders, even it looks impossible for me at the moment.

In the next chapters, I will try to provide an analysis of possible techniques and approaches to project communication management, which can help you to avoid the described mistakes and lead to a successful project.

2 Literature Review

Principles of communication management are discussed in a broad number of sources. Foremost, Project Management Institute (PMI) provides a thorough description of tools and techniques involved in project communication management [17]. In [15] a number of articles present current trends in digital communications as well as analysis of their impact on various types of organizations. More details on communication tools and techniques and communication obstacles analysis are given in [20]. Paper [23] describes some communication management practices, which apply not only for the given domain but in any sphere as well. Focus on communication between project team members is given in [12] where specific practices which help to significantly improve cross-communication among team members also provided. A survey on the implementation of communication management techniques in companies with different organizational structures is provided in [19]. Impact of communication on organizational processes during its change investigated in [21] in respect to postmodernism, chaos and complexity theories of management. Problems of communication management faced by project managers are thoroughly observed in [13].

Some research papers are devoted to the problem of communication management in the software development process. These are the most relevant to the described problem. In [5] several approaches for effective communication are proposed: active listening, consistent understanding of the development effort, and communication infrastructure. VCSD tool for visualizing various types of communication flows between developers is presented in [22]. The problem of weaknesses in definitions of project-critical terms as a critical aspects of the communication process is observed in [24] with a novel method for a higher-quality glossary construction. Some fundamental aspects of communication in agile projects are investigated in [11, 16], indicating the hidden threats of external communications in SCRUM and XP practices. The investigation of communication management in the agile projects continues in [3, 8, 14], where authors analyze the impact of communication channels and practices in Agile Software Development.

3 Case Study Analysis

This chapter provides a thorough explanation of the drawbacks of communications management. Communication channels are investigated. As far as communication management is about the exchange of information, this aspect of the project (the lack of infrastructure) is also taken into account. At the end of the chapter, the decision on the critical level and possibility for surveillance of the case project is provided.

Let's return back to the given case study and perform its thorough analysis in the context of communications. Foremost, the stakeholders of the project should be structured in some way for further analysis. One well-known approach is stakeholder register [17, p. 514] which includes the classification of stakeholders based on their relation to project or impact, identification, and assessment information, like the name, role, expectation, etc. The initial stakeholder register can be created as given in Table 1.

Table 1. Project's primary stakeholders

Company	Name	Position	Role	Time period
Xemeria	Kirill	Senior developer	Development of core functionality of the software	Untill June, 2016
	Ilya	Developer	Software functionality and GUI development	All along
	Stepan	Developer	Development of interfaces for MES and software integration	Since August, 2016
	Svetlana	Accountant	Bookkeeping	All along
Nova-Les Prom	Oleg	Director, investor	Contract execution. Successful example for future sales	Jul., 2015–Jun., 2018
	Pavel	Tallyman	System (MES + software) acceptance	Oct., 2015–Jun., 2018
Polus	Irina	Senior developer	Contact partner from organization who responsible for MES development	Feb., 2016–Apr., 2017
FFU	Evgeniy	Rector	Provide support for product testing, sales. Direct contacts with logging companies. Collaboration in sales	Since Feb., 2016
–	Daniil	Expert, investor	Mentoring, participating in company development. New investors engagement	All along (periodically)
Fund	Ksenia	Inspector	Contact person from government investment fund	Mar., 2015–Sep., 2017

This table serves as the basis of the stakeholder register for our communications problem analysis. It can be expanding in terms of stakeholders' numbers (we can also include additional investment funds and logging enterprises) and their descriptions. However, it is excessive effort as far as the main goal here is to keep all stakeholders in mind during communications analysis. To characterize project communications, we need to define their possible grouping categories, or dimensions [17, p. 361]:

- Internal/external - stakeholders within organization or external stakeholders.
- Formal/informal - reports and formal meetings or general daily communications.
- Upward/downward/horizontal hierarchy - the comparative position of the stakeholder in social hierarchy.
- Official/unofficial - reports to regulators and government bodies and contracts or establishing and maintaining of the project and building strong relationships.
- Written/oral.

Also for communications description it is important to take into account such factors as [17, p. 364]:

- physical location of stakeholder - whether they are in the same geographical zone or globally separated; distance and time zones are taken into account,
- communication technology - tools and techniques for direct and indirect communication,
- language and culture differences - usage of one or more languages, specific vocabulary.

Fortunately, the given project is a local one, so physically stakeholders were located in one region (except the investment fund, which located in Moscow) with a maximum distance of 150 km (to Nova-LesProm). The language barrier is absent, however, there are sufficient cultural differences as far as some stakeholders related to IT industry and others - to forest one. Regarding the communication technologies, the commonly used are telephone calls and face-to-face communication for oral communications and emails for a written one. Based on this classification the determination of Xemeria director communication channels with each stakeholder can be performed. (Table 2).

Table 2. Communications' classification

Name	Internal (I)/external (E)	Formal (F)/informal (I)	Hierarchy	Official (O)/unofficial (U)	Written (W)/oral (O)	IT/Forest (F) Domain	Location
Kirill	I	I	D	U	O	IT	Ekaterinburg
Ilya	I	I	D	U	O	IT	Ekaterinburg
Stepan	I	I	D	U	W	IT	Pervouralsk
Svetlana	I	F	D	U	W	–	Ekaterinburg
Oleg	E	I	U	U	O	F	Rezh
Pavel	E	F	D	U	W	F	Rezh
Irina	E	F	D	U	W	IT	Ekaterinburg
Evgeniy	E	I	U	U	O	F	Ekaterinburg
Daniil	E	I	U	U	O	F	Ekaterinburg
Ksenia	E	F	H	O	W	–	Moscow

Another instrument for communication analysis is the communication matrix (who-to-who matrix) [10]. It shows how many contact channels on the project exist and to which extend each stakeholder is involved in project communication. The rows in the table show the initiation of the communication by this person. For better understanding, the analysis is given for the 3 time periods: 2015,

Table 3. Communication matrix 1 (2015)

	Artem	Kirill	Ilya	Stepan	Svetlana	Oleg	Pavel	Irina	Evgeniy	Daniil	Ksenia
Artem		+	+	-	?	+	-	-	-	+	?
Kirill	+		+	-	-	-	-	-	-	-	-
Ilya	+	+		-	-	-	-	-	-	-	-
Stepan	-	-	-		-	-	-	-	-	-	-
Svetlana	?	-	-			-	-	-	-	-	-
Oleg	?	-	-		-		?	-	-	-	-
Pavel	-	-	-	-	-	?		-	-	-	-
Irina	-	-	-	-	-	-	-		-	-	-
Evgeniy	-	-	-	-	-	-	-	-		-	-
Daniil	?	-	-	-	-	-	-	-	-		-
Ksenia	?	-	-	-	-	-	-	-	-	-	

+ - the person often initiates communication (on daily or weekly basis)
? - the person rarely initiate communication (on monthly basis or less often)
− - - the person never initiate communication
▓ - the person was not involved in project at the moment

Table 4. Communication matrix 2 (2016–2017)

	Artem	Kirill	Ilya	Stepan	Svetlana	Oleg	Pavel	Irina	Evgeniy	Daniil	Ksenia
Artem		?	+	+	?	?	?	+	+	?	?
Kirill	-		-	-	-	-	-	-	-	-	-
Ilya	+	-		-	-	-	-	-	-	-	-
Stepan	+	-	-		-	-	-	?	-	-	-
Svetlana	+	-	-	-		-	-	-	-	-	-
Oleg	-	-	-	-	-		?	-	-	-	-
Pavel	?	-	-	-	-	?		-	-	-	-
Irina	+	-	?	?	-	?	?		-	-	-
Evgeniy	?	-	-	-	-	-	-	-		+	-
Daniil	-	-	-	-	-	-	-	-	-		-
Ksenia	?	-	-	-	-	-	-	-	-	-	

Table 5. Communication matrix 2 (2016–2017)

	Artem	Kirill	Ilya	Stepan	Svetlana	Oleg	Pavel	Irina	Evgeniy	Daniil	Ksenia
Artem		-	?	+	?	?	?	-	?	-	-
Kirill	-		-	-	-	-	-	-	-	-	-
Ilya	?	-		-	-	-	-	-	-	-	-
Stepan	?	-	-		-	-	-	-	-	-	-
Svetlana	?	-	-	-		-	-	-	-	-	-
Oleg	-	-	-	-	-		-	-	-	-	-
Pavel	-	-	-	-	-	-		-	-	-	-
Irina	-	-	-	-	-	-	-		-	-	-
Evgeniy	-	-	-	-	-	-	-	-		-	-
Daniil	-	-	-	-	-	-	-	-	-		-
Ksenia	-	-	-	-	-	-	-	-	-	-	

2016–17, and 2018 years. Some of the relations are given approximately, as far as communication rate was not constant and stable, but has peaks and gaps. Thus, these tables show an approximate evaluation of the communication rate.

From the data given above and some additional explanations on case study the following statements could be given:

1. Communication of the project manager with team members was based on the informal agile approach, which seems to be a good solution for a small start-up company. However, some necessary ideas of agile were not fulfilled, for example, Product Owner was never presented in the team, and it is not a good practice when the project manager takes this role. The project had a government contract in form of grant in 2015–16, which means the detailed plan of R&D works with clearly defined milestones and set of activities. In this case more formal, waterfall-based approaches seem more suitable [17] for project management. That also leads to more formal communications between the team and the project manager.

2. In fact, it was a reason why Kirill had left the company. Initially, he started work with relative freedom of what and how to do in the project. Over the course of the project, his tasks had become more strict and prescriptive, which also result in a formal way of communications between him and the director. He was not ready to accept a new model, so the conflict had arisen and he quitted.

3. Another aspect related to the proper usage of formal and informal communication styles is communication with Oleg, director of Nova-LesProm. As can be seen from Table 2 the most often used style was an informal one. It is natural and only welcome in the case of first client, when relations are usually based on enthusiasm and emotional aspect. However, during the project, this communication channel should become more formal at certain point, which means the contract negotiations. The mistake of Xemeria director was that he postponed this activity until it became too late. That is the result of the missing project communication plan and schedule [17, p. 378].

4. By analysis of the communication matrix, it can be concluded that about 90% of all project communications were held with the participation of one person - the director. It is a common situation for project communications, as far as the primary role of a project manager is communications. In case of a start-up company, the role of communication is even bigger because the manager also involved in technical aspects of the project. This scenario is described in [4] and demonstrated in Fig. 1.

5. It can be seen that all communication threads go from one group to another through the project manager, the technical team is limited to a few people and there is no Project Management team. The case study closely matches this template. However, the communication rate is low for most stakeholders: only with the technical team, it keeps on a sufficient level.

6. Regarding the communication within the team, we can also see that contacts between members were weak. In fact, all conversations were performed through the director - even the development and testing issues for the phase

Fig. 1. Project manager's communications

of MES and software integration pass from one developer to another through the director. That is a big problem of project communications, as far as an extra node in the communication chain significantly reduces the effectiveness of communication due to noise and additional factors [17, p. 373].

7. Analysis of the communication matrix also demonstrates the decline of involvement of the stakeholders in the project. It is reasonable for such persons as Kirill (leave the project), Irina and Ksenia (complete their work). However, for others, it may mean a loss of interest in a project. It is critically important to control this parameter on regular basis and perform correction actions.

8. For example, Oleg, director of Nova-LesProm, has started with a moderate interest in the project, as far as it was not critically important for his own business. The primary task of Xeneria director was to maximize the involvement of Oleg by providing him with weekly reports on current status, performing interviews and regular industrial tests. However, as we can see from Tables 3, 4, the communication rate become low in a few months which finally led to an overall decrease of Nova-LesProm involvement in the project. The same results obtained for other influential stakeholders - expert and rector. The problem is again in proper managing of communications: it is highly important to maintain a high communication level with all key stakeholders of the project. This problem is thoroughly observed in [7], where the stakeholders analyzed through an influence/interest matrix (see Fig. 2) to choose the appropriate way of interaction.

The last communication matrix (Table 5) demonstrates the overall decline of the project as far as most communication channels do not work and key stakeholders show no interest to the project. It means that project is at the hazard of being terminated. However, some positive aspects also exist:

- Product successfully developed and ready for industrial testing and installation
- Communication channels with key stakeholders are not completely lost yet

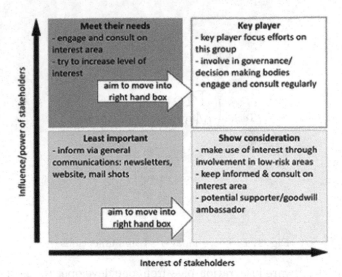

Fig. 2. Stakeholders' interaction strategy based on their influence/interest

Thus, by taking into consideration the current situation and trends in project communications, the project closure hazard is highly possible. Nevertheless, it seems still possible to get project back on track by performing some corrective actions related to project communications management.

4   Recommendations on Communications Management

Tools and techniques for project communications management provided in this chapter. It starts from the observation of up-to-dated tools. They will be analyzed in the view of the given case study and the most appropriate ones will be suggested for implementation.

In [18] it is said that "communication is the basis for project performance in any organization". The author analyzed project communications management based on the "Triple C model", where project success based on communication, cooperation and coordination [6]. The result of this analysis are 5 main areas of project communication that should be simultaneously taken into consideration (see Fig. 3).

There are two main approaches for performing project communication management were discovered:

– International standards and methodologies [1, 2, 17], and
– Project Communication Management patterns [12].

4.1   Communication Management Patterns

Each described pattern consists of the following fields: context, problem, solution, q-effect (what communication quality aspects are affected by the pattern

Table 6. Pattern "Clear rules at the start"

Context	While planning various aspects of the project, the area of communication and documentation management is neglected. There is no regular contact with the client to inform them about the progress of the project and for keeping in touch for quick reaction to possible changes and new requirements
Problem	There are no designated persons and tasks related to planning and managing communication and documentation processes. Team members feel no need to communicate the status of their tasks, nor do they feel responsible for informing the client about the status of the project
Solution	Development of a clear, practical and high-quality communication plan with assigned persons responsible for communication management, description of communication and documentation tasks
Q-effect	Positive on the following communication quality aspects: meeting needs of communicating participants. Possibly negative on the following communication quality aspects: in case of excessive formalism and bureaucracy participants may be discouraged to communicate effectively and all communication quality aspects can be threatened
Applicability	The pattern should be used for any kind of project and team, although it is especially useful for teams with different working cultures and fixed price projects. The pattern applies to all stakeholders. All persons assigned to any communication and documentation tasks should be clearly informed of their responsibilities
Consequences	Ensures that all team members and project stakeholders know their communication and documentation responsibilities. Client is instantly informed about the status of the project tasks. It is important to let the communication plan evolve and alter throughout the project to make it better tailored to the given project and team
Implementation	Preparing a high-quality communication plan requires time and effort, so that it is then easy to realize and not burdensome for the project team; too much formalism may discourage the team; the communication plan should be communicated already during the project kick-off meeting, or at least during the initiation phase of the project

and if it is a positive or a negative influence), applicability, consequences, and implementation. There are some patterns [12, pp. 10–14] presented in Tables 6, 7 and 8 that fit the case study project.

Based on given patterns the strategy of project communications management could be established and appropriate practices and tools chosen.

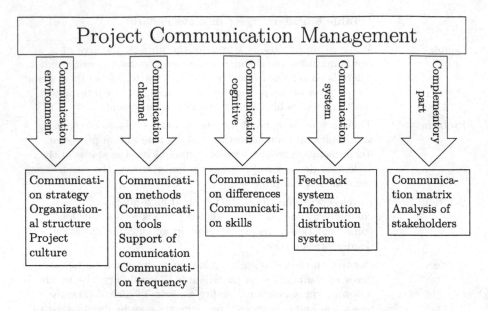

Fig. 3. Main areas of project communication management

Table 7. Pattern "Visits and team rotations"

Context	Project is characterized by having a distributed team and a long realization time. The direct contact of the contractor's team with the client's team is limited to the kick-off meeting and a few other project meetings
Problem	Lack of trust and willingness to communicate within the project team, because of the lack of direct contact and familiarity of team members
Solution	Regular visits of individual team members at the client's site, as well as delegating team members to the client's site for a longer period of time. Rotation can also be used, so that different team members can get to know each other and break the communication barrier
Q-effect	Positive on the following communication quality aspects: meeting needs of communicating participants, communication workflow supporting openness, feedback
Applicability	The pattern is designed for big projects with distributed teams. Only willing team members should be chosen for delegation to other locations, to avoid discontent and frustration. Shorter visits should be realized by all key team members
Consequences	Building non-professional relations among team members fosters effective and direct communication. Delegated team members facilitate communication between the client's team and the contractor's team
Implementation	Realization of the pattern should be preceded by an analysis of predispositions and willingness of individual team members to delegations, so that appropriate plan of visits and team rotation can be developed and included in the budget

4.2   Standards and Methodologies

There are several methodologies consider project communications management. In [18] three of them are analysed: ICB, PMBoK and PRINCE2 (see Table 9).

Table 8. Pattern "Basic communication principles"

Context	The team consists of inexperienced members. Basic principles of communication are not respected
Problem	Misunderstandings, hostility or animosity among team members
Solution	Reminding team members about the basic principles of transparent, effective and positive communication, and desired behavior, that is, among others: justifying requests, asking rather than telling, keeping promises and showing up for appointments, writing positive e-mails (even criticisms and dissatisfaction in a positive way)
Q-effect	Positive on the following communication quality aspects: clearness and cohesion, meeting needs of communicating participants
Applicability	The pattern can be used for any kind of project and team, although it is especially useful for immature and inexperienced teams, or where there are many introverts, team members are age or culture diversified
Consequences	Good atmosphere in the team, clear and positive relations among team members and their responsible behavior - all promoting successful project completion
Implementation	Usually the basic principles of transparent, effective and positive communication are something that every person knows and feels, and it should not be required to state it explicitly, but in the cases mentioned above it may be desired to bring them to the attention of some team members. It is also a good practice to set the maximum time for response to an email, to ensure the dynamics of asynchronous communication. If possible communication rules should be agreed upon together by the whole team, preferably during the kick-off meeting

The most engaged one in project communication is PMBoK, its project communications management consists of 3 processes: plan, manage and monitor [17, p 360]. However, by taken into consideration the type of the project and additional factors, it is possible to exclude some parts of communication management. In [18] the analysis of project communications management is given (see Table 10), so the options for small project can be assumed as compulsory for the observed case study.

Thus, standard-based approach with tailoring to small-scale project prescribe the following actions in project communications management, which are also advised for case study project:

Table 9. Comparison of project communication in international methodologies and standards of project management

Monitored elements	Project management methodologies or standards		
	ICB	PMBOK	PRINCE2
Communication environment			
Communication strategy	–	–	✓
Organizational structure	?	?	?
Project culture	–	–	–
Communication channel			
Commnunication methods	?	✓	?
Communication tools	?	✓	?
Support of communication	–	–	–
Communication frequency	?	?	?
Communication cognitive			
Communication differences	–	?	–
Communication skills	–	–	–
Communication system			
Feedback system	?	?	?
System of sharing and distribution of information	–	✓	–
Complementary part			
Communcation matrix	?	?	?
Analysis of stakeholders	?	✓	✓

– - methodology or standard does not include a specific element
? - methodology or standard describes the element only briefly
✓ - methodology or standard describes in detail, what the specific element addresses

- Communication strategy
- Analysis of stakeholders
- List of stakeholders
- Stakeholder's expectations
- Identification of methods, tools and support of communication
- Verbal communication through personal meetings

Table 10. Project communication tailoring to different project scales

Project size	Small project	Medium-sized project	Large project
Main characteristics of the project			
Number of team members	<5	5–9	>9
Number of teams in the project	1–2	2–3	>3
Project duration	min 2 months	min 3 months	min 12 months
Initialization of project communication			
Commnunication strategy	✓	✓	✓
Organizational structure of project communication	?	✅	✓
Planning of project communication			
Analysis of stakeholders	✅	✓	✓
List of stakeholders	✅	✓	✓
Stekeholder's expectations	✅	✅	✓
Responsibility matrix of project communication	?	✅	✓
Identification of methods, tools and support of communication	✅	✅	✅
Groupware matrix	?	✅	✓
Communication schedule	?	✅	✓
Communication matrix	✓	✓	✓
Implementation of project communication			
Rules of personal meetings	✅	✅	✅
Phone call policy	?	✅	✓
Rules of email communication	?	✅	✓
Non-verbal communication	?	✅	✅
Project website	?	✅	✅
Control of project communication			
Report about management of project communication	?	✅	✓
Administrative closure of project communication			
Control of documents	✓	✓	✓

✅ - compulsory

✓ - recommended

? - optional

4.3   Best Tools and Practices

In [23, p 5] author identifies the communication practices as 4 main categories, which are shown in Table 11.

Table 11. Communication management practices

Category of communication management practice	Communication management practice
Strategic (involves communication planning and project environment)	– Clear lines and responsibilities established up front – High-quality communication planning – Good public relations – Adopt common working language among members – Well-defined client authority – High process visibility for clients
Informational (generating, collecting, storing and retrieving project information)	– Shared virtual space, websites, project tracking software – Instant messenger, e-mails – Traditional phone calls – Using various communication channels
Emotional (regarding relationships and trust building)	– Face-to-face communication, audio and video conferencing, more than written communication – Support members to communicate informally with social media – Kick-off, review and stand-up meetings – Feedback from members
Practical (clear, positive communication and behavior rules)	– Employ basic rules for communication – Eligible attitudes and behaviors – Short, asynchronous communication loops

Among the given practices it is necessary to provide additional clarification for some of them.

Shared Virtual Space, Websites, Project Tracking Software. The one of the interesting approach to the shared virtual channels is provided by FOLIO [9]. In this project communication channels divided on primary and secondary ones. The structure of its shared space is given in Fig. 4.

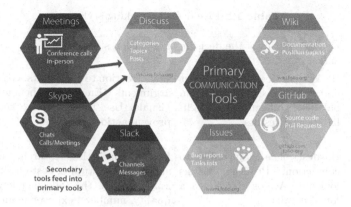

Fig. 4. FOLIO communication spaces

This idea and tools could be successfully implemented in case study project for improving internal communications.

Adopt Common Working Language Among Members. This problem is thoroughly investigated in [24]. The idea is in creating the vocabulary with definitions of specific turns, as far as project involve stakeholders from IT and forest disciplines. The method consists of following steps:

– Determine which meaning elements are required to identify the concept and distinguish it from others
– Draft a candidate definition that includes the selected meaning elements.
– Assess the draft for the common weaknesses and renegotiate the content and form accordingly until none of the weaknesses are present.

It is highly important to have the shared domain knowledge among all key stakeholders and to be able to speak with them on the same level of understanding.

Eligible Attitudes and Behaviors. Communication with key external stakeholders, especially at contract negotiation phase is an art of persuasion. For the project manager it is essential to be able to implement specific tools and techniques in this area. It is a large topic which cannot be observed within this paper, however, the 5 general strategies of negotiation with different type of personalities [25, p 5-6] are given in Table 12 for understanding the basic principles.

Table 12. Five decision-making styles

Style	Characteristics of the decision maker	Persuasion strategies
Charismatics	He is easily carried away but makes final decisions based on balanced information. Highlights final results	Pay attention to the results. Give direct arguments. Emphasize benefits with visuals. Use the following keywords: proven, action, easy, clear
Thinkers	Hardest of all amenable to conviction. Prudent, thinks logically. Avoids risk. Need a lot of details	Present marketing research, customer surveys, case studies, cost-effectiveness analysis. Use the following keywords: quality, numbers, experts, evidence
Skeptics	Disputes every data item. Decides intuitively	Establish trust, citing the opinion of the person whom he trusts. Use the following keywords: to capture the essence, power, suspect, trust
Followers	Making a choice in the present based on their own or others' previous decisions. Late accepts new ideas	Use low-risk evidence. Present innovative, yet proven solutions. Use the following keywords: experience, similar, innovative, previous
Controllers	Non-emotional, analytical. Hates uncertainty. Implements only own ideas	Provide highly structured arguments. Make him recognize your idea. Avoid aggressively defending your own opinions. Use the following keywords: facts, reason, strength, just take and make

5   Conclusions

This paper presents the case study of the Xemeria company project related to IT systems for forest industry. During the project a number of mistakes in project management were done, thus the analysis of project communication management is performed. Analysis shows that project is in the critical stage and some corrective actions should be done to improve current situation. For the corrective actions the analysis of two approaches to project communication management is given: by using templates or project management standards. For second variant the list of actions that should be performed is obtained, by taken into account the size of the project and number of current (and potential in short-term period) external stakeholders. The analysis of stakeholder is provided in second section of the paper, with recommendation on future interactions with stakeholders. The only aspect that could be recommended for implementation is weekly analysis of communication matrix as indicator of project status. The description of specific tools and practices is given in third section of the paper. There are a number of tools for online and offline communication. The most appropriate ones for the given project (as IT start-up) are given. Finally, two important aspect of communication process are briefly observed: using of specific language vocabulary as part of shared domain knowledge strategy and negotiation techniques as important skill for interaction with key external stakeholders (clients or investors). This set of practices and tools, being applied to the given case study project may help to get it back on track. This case study is a good example of necessity to plan and control project communications right from the project initiation stage. The result of neglecting communications can be catastrophic. "Communication is a critical part between people, ideas, and information. Therefore, it is necessary to be constantly engaged with communication" [18].

References

1. IPMA standards (2021). https://www.ipma.world/individuals/standard/. Accessed 15 Mar 2021
2. PRINCE2 methodology (2021). https://www.prince2.com/eur/prince2-methodology. Accessed 15 Mar 2021
3. Ahmad, M.O., Lenarduzzi, V., Oivo, M., Taibi, D.: Lessons learned on communication channels and practices in agile software development. In: Proceedings of the 2018 Federated Conference on Computer Science and Information Systems. IEEE (2018). https://doi.org/10.15439/2018f72
4. Ajam, M.A.: How can we define project manager effort in term of project's communications? (2021). http://blog.sukad.com/define-project-manager-communications/. Accessed 15 Mar 2021
5. Atwood, M.E., et al.: Facilitating communication in software development. In: Proceedings of the Conference on Designing Interactive Systems Processes, Practices, Methods, & Techniques - DIS '95. ACM Press (1995). https://doi.org/10.1145/225434.225442
6. Badiru, A.B.: Triple C Model of Project Management. CRC Press (2008). https://doi.org/10.1201/9781420051148
7. Colonna, J.: Forgotten stakeholders (2016). http://www.johncolonna.com/forgotten-stakeholders/. Accessed 29 Nov 2020
8. Coman, I.D., Robillard, P.N., Sillitti, A., Succi, G.: Cooperation, collaboration and pair-programming: field studies on backup behavior. J. Syst. Softw. **91**, 124–134 (2014)
9. A. Inc.: FOLIO communication spaces (2021). https://wiki.folio.org/display/COMMUNITY/FOLIO+Communication+Spaces. Accessed 15 Mar 2021
10. ITWORX: ITWOcx user guide. https://confluence.itwocx.com/pages/viewpage.action?pageId=3080224. Accessed 15 Mar 2021
11. Janes, A., Succi, G.: Lean Software Development in Action. Springer, Heidelberg (2014). https://doi.org/10.1007/978-3-642-00503-9
12. Muszynska, K.: Communication Management in Project Teams: Practices and Patterns, pp. 1359–1366. ToKnowPress (2015). https://EconPapers.repec.org/RePEc:tkp:mklp15:1369-1366
13. Odine, M.: Communication Problems in Management, vol. 4 (2015)
14. Pedrycz, W., Russo, B., Succi, G.: A model of job satisfaction for collaborative development processes. J. Syst. Softw. **84**(5), 739–752 (2011)
15. Peña-Acuña, B. (ed.): Digital Communication Management. InTech (2018). https://doi.org/10.5772/intechopen.70959

16. Pikkarainen, M., Haikara, J., Salo, O., Abrahamsson, P., Still, J.: The impact of agile practices on communication in software development. Empir. Softw. Eng. **13**(3), 303–337 (2008). https://doi.org/10.1007/s10664-008-9065-9
17. PMI (ed.): A Guide to the Project Management Body of Knowledge (PMBOK Guide). Project Management Institute, Newtown Square, PA, 5 edn. (2013)
18. Samáková, J., Babčanová, D., Chovanová, H.H., Mesárošová, J., Šujanová, J.: Project communication management in industrial enterprises (step by step). In: Digital Communication Management. InTech (2018). https://doi.org/10.5772/intechopen.75160
19. Samáková, J., Koltnerová, K., Rybanský, R.: Project communication in functions, process and project-oriented industrial companies. Research Papers Faculty of Materials Science and Technology Slovak University of Technology, vol. 20 (Special-Number), pp. 120–125 (2012). https://doi.org/10.2478/v10186-012-0020-7
20. Sońta-Draczkowska, E.: Project management as communications management. Kommunikationsmanagement in polnisch-deutschen R&D-Projektteams (2015)
21. Ströh, U., Jaatinen, M.: New approaches to communication management for transformation and change in organisations. J. Commun. Manag. **6**(2), 148–165 (2002). https://doi.org/10.1108/13632540210807008
22. Suliman, M., Bani-Salameh, H., Saif, A.: Visualizing communications between software developers during development. Int. J. Softw. Eng. Appl. **10**(3), 131–140 (2016). https://doi.org/10.14257/ijseia.2016.10.3.12
23. Taleb, H., Ismail, S., Wahab, M.H., Rani, W.N.M.W.M.: Communication management between architects and clients. vol. 1891. AIP Conference Proceedings (2017). https://doi.org/10.1063/1.5005469
24. Wasson, K.S., Knight, J.: Development: Identification and Repair of Weak Definitions (2001)
25. Williams, G.A., Miller, R.B.: Change the way you persuade. Harvard Bus. Rev. **80**(5), 64–73, 133 (2002). http://europepmc.org/abstract/MED/12024759

Evolution of Information System Design Methodologies: The IFIP Conference Management Problem Revisited

Anthony I. Wasserman(✉)

Carnegie Mellon University – Silicon Valley, Moffett Field, CA 94035, USA
tonyw@acm.org

Abstract. Hardware and software technologies have evolved greatly throughout the history of computing. This paper illustrates some of those differences by
comparing a modern approach to information systems design to the papers
presented in a 1982 conference that showed 13 different software design
methodologies applied to the problem of creating an information system to
manage a technical conference, including submission and review of technical
papers and overall organization of the conference. Those solutions predated the
World Wide Web, the advent of personal computers, graphical user interfaces,
agile development methodologies, and various modern tools. The goal of this
paper is to create the same application, taking advantage of four decades of
advances in methodologies and tools.

Keywords: Methodologies · Process · Waterfall · Agile · CRIS

1 Background

1.1 Advances in Computing Technology

The world of computing has changed drastically over the decades. Going back four
decades, the IBM PC was new in 1982, and the Macintosh came out two years later,
bringing mass adoption of graphical user interfaces, which came to Microsoft Windows
3.1 in the early 1990s. The Internet evolved from the ARPANET, which adopted
TCP/IP in 1983, leading to the beginning of the World Wide Web in 1991. Smartphones and other mobile devices gained Internet connectivity much later, starting with
the NTT DoCoMo phones and i-mode service in 1999. This ubiquitous connectivity
has also led to dynamically scalable hosted platforms and applications running in the
cloud instead of on fixed hardware.

Software has also evolved rapidly. The first relational databases suitable for
commercial use became available around 1980, and were often accessed across a client-
server network that connected terminals and personal computers to servers. The Unix
operating system was released in 1974, but only received wider use after the release of
Version 4 of the Berkeley Software Distribution (BSD Unix) five years later. New
programming languages and tools emerged, gradually replacing legacy languages such
as FORTRAN and COBOL. Many information system developers used Oracle's

G. Succi et al. (Eds.): ICFSE 2021, CCIS 1523, pp. 133–147, 2021.
https://doi.org/10.1007/978-3-030-93135-3_9

PL/SQL to manage their Oracle databases, which gained a leading share of the database market. Today, a vast quantity of unstructured data is managed by tools such as Hadoop and MongoDB which do not use SQL and relational models.

As the hardware and software foundation changed, so did the processes by which information systems were designed and developed. Schema design focused on relational models of data, and object-oriented design approaches emerged. More importantly, the flaws of the traditional waterfall model of development became apparent, and have been increasingly replaced by iterative and agile development. Beyond that, many organizations have built continuous integration and deployment into their agile processes, combining their development and IT operations (DevOps).

More detail about all of these changes is beyond the scope of this paper. The main point is that systems are designed, developed, and deployed much differently today than they were in the early 1980s.

1.2   The 1982 CRIS Conference

It's very unusual to find old system design artifacts, even when the resulting systems remain in use. The existence of a published set of designs for a single application is particularly rare, and provides an excellent basis for comparison.

In 1980, IFIP Working Group 8.1 (Design and Evaluation of Information Systems) organized a project known as CRIS (Comparative Review of Information Systems Design Methodologies) whereby people could submit a paper showing how their methodology could be applied to the design and development of an information system that could be used to manage all aspects of a technical conference. Thirteen papers were accepted (including one by this author), and seven (including this author's) were presented at a 1982 conference [1].

In general, the accepted papers (excluding this author's) focused primarily on the analysis and design phases of solving the problem, with the methodologists creating elaborate conceptual data models and extensive functional specifications, often including formalisms such as pre- and post-conditions. Most of the methodologies used a method-specific graphical representation to show such things as objects, relationships, and control flow. Many of the solutions were careful to include "edge cases", exceptional situations that could occur in managing the conference.

Some of these methodologies were being used in commercial settings to design systems, but the majority were still in a research stage, with the conference management application allowing the methodologists to test and refine their approaches. Taken as a group, they represented the state of the art in information systems design circa 1982.

Even then, however, it was clear that the waterfall model of system development had significant weaknesses, including the often-lengthy interval between requirements gathering and system availability. Both the requirements and the available technology often changed during the development period. The high rate of system development failures (late delivery, over budget, poor usability) led to extensive efforts in the information systems and software engineering communities to improve the success rate.

The concept of agile development was the most significant approach to emerge from this work. While most readers will be familiar with agile approaches to development, we include here some of the most significant aspects of agile methods as a prelude to showing its use in addressing the CRIS problem.

2 Agile Development

2.1 Basic Concepts

The Agile Manifesto [2] appeared in 2001, and challenged all of the traditional development processes with its preference for individuals and interactions over processes and tools, and working software over comprehensive documentation. The 17 co-authors of the Agile Manifesto enumerated 12 principles of agile software development. Among the more significant principles are:

1. Our highest priority is to satisfy the customer through early and continuous delivery of valuable software.
2. Deliver working software frequently, from a couple of weeks to a couple of months, with a preference to the shorter timetable
3. Business people and developers must work together daily throughout the project.

Agile development downgraded the value of the detailed design documents found in the CRIS papers, and other similar methods of that era. The expectation was that the "business people" had the domain expertise and that developers needed to work closely with them to make certain that the code reflected the customer's requirements. While not every application was well-suited for agile development, the conference management example was a good fit for this approach, while designing the avionics for commercial aircraft was not. The leaders of the agile movement also gave a lot of attention to developers and teams, recognizing the importance of technical excellence. They encouraged empowered, self-organizing teams to produce the best architectures, requirements, and designs. Teams would regularly reflect on how to become more effective, then tune and adjust its behavior accordingly.

The Scrum [3] method was developed by Ken Schwaber and Jeff Sutherland in the 1990s, and has emerged as the most widely used agile method. In a Scrum project, a team, led by a Product Owner and a Scrum Master, would break the project down into sprints, each covering a period of 2–4 weeks. Each sprint begins with a planning meeting to identify the product features (and/or non-functional enhancements) that the team intends to complete during the upcoming sprint. The end of a sprint is marked by deliverable code: a working piece of software. Agile processes rely on a "release early, release often" approach, so interested users can participate in early evaluation and testing of the emerging product, giving feedback to the team. Teams use "burndown" charts to show progress through the sprint, and often use a lightweight management tool, such as Trello or monday.com, and a collaboration tool, such as Slack or Mattermost, for communication and coordination.

Along with the change in process from waterfall to agile, the process for gathering requirements changed, with a much greater focus on "pain points" identified through multiple interviews with potential users and customers. Blank introduced the concept of Customer Discovery as the first of his "four steps to the epiphany [4]." Informally, the idea is for a product designer to "get out of the building", i.e., away from the IT department and into the user's world, ideally in the context of where users are experiencing their pain points. That increases the likelihood that a proposed solution, i.e., a system, will address a significant user issue, and that the user will be more likely to adopt the resulting solution. This concept is also central to the Rapid Contextual Design process [5].

2.2 User Stories

The Customer Discovery process normally proceeds through interviews with people who are seeking solutions to specific problems. For example, the task of buying a new vehicle has multiple pain points, including: 1) the difficulty of creating a short list of candidate vehicles from the large number of options in the market; 2) the effort needed to do research and to visit dealerships to make a choice; 3) the negotiation over the purchase or lease price, and 4) disposing of the owner's old vehicle. (There are other pain points associated with buying a used vehicle.)

The above list provides a foundation for selecting one or more problems to be addressed in a solution, i.e., a system. The planned features for the system can be addressed in short, structured phrases, known as user stories, that describe them from the perspective of the user or customer of the system. For example, some user stories might include: 1) as a user, I want to be able to specify a type of vehicle and see a list of makes and models of that type; 2) as a user, I want to be able to further refine that list to those in a specified price range, and; 3) as a user, I want to create tables and charts that help me compare the refined list.

The product developer presents these user stories to potential users, including those who were initially interviewed, along with others having domain expertise and the ability to validate the ideas or suggest modifications, and other stakeholders. Obtaining these different viewpoints may lead to adjustments in the user stories and thus makes it more likely that a resulting system will satisfactorily address the problems identified in the interview process.

This activity of gathering of user stories is particularly effective for the development of customer-facing applications, where human users with interact with the application.

2.3 User/Developer Communication

Communication between the development team and the various stakeholders is a central issue in gathering system requirements and designing an application. In the early days of information system development, this communication usually took the form of a single lengthy document created at the end of "systems analysis". Many of the information system design methods described in the CRIS Conference papers used complex graphical notations to illustrate the intended system behavior. These notations tended to emphasize the data model associated with the system over the user-centered functionality to be performed by the system. That approach addressed the needs of the system developer and the data modeler, but made it difficult for a potential user to comprehend the planned behavior of the system and thus to suggest changes prior to system development. Agile development, by contrast, emphasizes user-centered communication mechanisms, and makes data modeling an iterative process [6], where each sprint includes evolution of the data model.

One such communication technique is storyboarding, similar to that used by screenwriters and other story tellers, which shows user scenarios in a format resembling comic strips. One popular approach uses two such storyboards for each user story, creating two scenarios, one representing how a process works currently, and the other showing how the process would work in a proposed system. In that way, a potential user can see the surrounding context for each user story in the system. There are numerous tools available for this task, including StoryboardThat [7].

Another approach to user/developer communication is through use case diagrams, originally developed by Ivar Jacobson for his object-oriented software engineering method ObjectOry [8], also included in the Unified Modeling Language (UML) [9]. A use case diagram presents a high level view of a system, bounding its scope and showing the actors and the activities to be performed by the system. The diagram itself doesn't show any control flow or the detailed steps of each activity, which are elaborated later.

Figure 1 shows a use case diagram for an online library system, as created by the developers of the Visual Paradigm modeling and management tools [10]. Without going into detail, one can see Borrower and Librarian actors, a Maintenance subsystem, and a total of 10 different activities. The diagram is well-suited for discussion between a development team and those looking for a solution, i.e., librarians and borrowers.

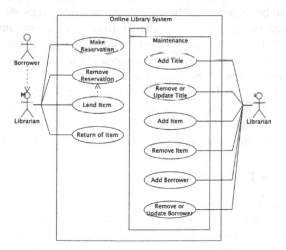

Fig. 1. High level use case diagram for online library system

Use case diagrams and user stories serve a similar purpose. For example, the information in the use case diagram could be addressed by ten user stories, such as: 1) as a Borrower, I want to make a reservation for an Item, and; 2) as a Librarian, I want to add a Title to the system. In both cases, these descriptions serve as mechanisms for communication between the development team and its stakeholders. The team would receive feedback about any problems with the concept, and make any needed adjustments. (There are several problems in the model of Fig. 1.)

The high level descriptions are just a starting point. Each user story or activity must be elaborated, i.e., described in more detail, to show its associated steps. For example, the steps for Lend Item might include: 1) validate Borrower; 2) assign Item to Borrower's record, and; 3) determine the due date for the Item. Those steps enumerate the "normal" operation for that story. Beyond that, it's also necessary to enumerate the exceptional conditions, i.e., the conditions that would prevent the normal operation, and the business rules governing that use case.

Note that the identification and elaboration of the user stories is iterative and does not require a complete description of their steps or the exceptional cases before proceeding. It's not unusual for agile developers to implement the normal case first and return to complete the implementation later. Also, it's common to select a subset of the user stories to be implemented during a specific sprint. In this case, the first sprint might focus on the Maintenance subsystem, since it contains many of the basic activities needed to provide services to Borrowers.

2.4 Business Rules

In following an agile approach, the requirements are typically developed iteratively by working with likely users, customers and experts on the application domain. They have the knowledge about constraints on data values, relationships among data types, industry or government regulations, conditions that trigger associated events, the business process to be implemented by the system, and other relevant information. For example, the rules associated with "validate Borrower" above might include: 1) checking to see that the Borrower's library card has not expired, 2) preventing a Borrower from having more than 10 items checked out at a time, and; 3) preventing a Borrower with unpaid fines to check out any items.

Software developers rarely have such a detailed level of domain knowledge, but proper operation of the resulting system makes it essential to capture such information in the code or in a business rules "engine" that separates the rules from the program logic. Many of these rules emerge from the elaboration of user stories or use cases.

2.5 User Interface Prototyping

An alternative approach to communication between developers and stakeholders is to develop mockups (or live) versions of the intended user interface for the system. Some people gain a better understanding of the features of a planned system by seeing how they will use it. The mockup is designed to show the layout and content of screens, whether for a standalone application, a web application, or a mobile app, and letting potential users view it and possibly work directly with it to see how it would be used in practice. With the appropriate tools, it is possible to design and modify these user interfaces very quickly so that the designer can be highly responsive to user requests and easily demonstrate the planned user experience.

Building these mockups requires the designer not only to have an appropriate tool, but also an understanding of the features to be provided to the users, with the expected inputs and outputs. To do that, the user must usually work through the use cases or user stories and then manually transform that understanding into the user interface design. One effective technique maps a user story into a user command, which may be implemented by text input, menu selection, gesture, or voice input.

In effect, the user interface mockup becomes an alternative approach to require-ments gathering and validation. Some users get a better sense of the system features by working with such mockups rather than with a set of user stories or use case diagrams; there are many tools available for building such prototypes, including Balsamiq Wireframes [11]. That approach is central to the author's User Software Engineering methodology, as presented at the CRIS conference [1, 12].

There are some risks in proceeding with the user interface mockups and bypassing the step of validating user stories with stakeholders. Users of the mockups may have an incorrect impression of progress, thinking that the application is largely built when only the proposed façade has been designed. They may also be less able to find errors or omissions in the overall system. Balsamiq's product helps to overcome this problem, since their wireframes are lower fidelity rather than highly precise.

3   An Agile Approach to the CRIS Conference Problem

The CRIS Conference Problem, as originally stated, is reproduced in the Appendix. Because of space limitations, we will give primary attention to the stories associated with the Program Committee. This approach is in keeping with an agile process, where the stories of the Organizing Committee are addressed in later sprints.

3.1   User Stories

Working from the problem statement leads to the enumeration of the following user stories:

1) As a Program Committee Chair, I will prepare a list of people to whom the call for papers is to be sent;
2) As a Program Committee Chair, I will record the letters of intent from people intending to submit a paper;
3) As a Program Committee Chair, I will register the papers when they are received;
4) As a Program Committee Chair, I will distribute the papers among the referees;
5) As a Program Committee Chair, I will collect the referees' reports and select the papers accepted for the conference program, and;
6) As a Program Committee Chair, I will group the selected papers into sessions for presentation, selecting a chair for each session.

A knowledgeable user would quickly find some important gaps in the problem statement. These include failure to create a Call for Papers, failure to invite people to serve as referees, failure to establish a deadline for referees to return their reviews, failure to identify a decision process when too few reviews are received, absence of a process for notifying authors about the acceptance or rejection of their papers, failure to establish a deadline for submission of the camera-ready copies of the accepted papers, and more. The problem statement refers to referees, with the implicit (and possibly erroneous) assumption that they constitute the Program Committee. Each of these gaps leads to the creation of new actors, user stories, and possibly to modifications of the existing user stories. This, we might add more user stories:

7) As a Program Committee Chair, I will invite people to serve on the Program Committee and be referees for the submitted papers.
8) As a Program Committee Chair, I will prepare a Call for Papers and ask Program Committee Members to review it prior to sending it out.
9) As a Program Committee Member, I will prepare reviews of papers sent to me by the Program Committee Chair and return those reviews before the review deadline.
10) As a Program Committee Chair, I will notify authors about the acceptance or rejection of their submitted paper(s), and provide them with copies of the reviews.
11) As a Program Committee Chair, I will provide authors of accepted papers with information about the procedure for submitting the camera-ready version of their paper.

It's also possible to view some business rules from this list. For example, the system needs a rule to avoid conflicts of interest, making sure that referees are not assigned a paper that they or a close colleague submitted. It's also likely that rules are needed about the maximum length for an accepted paper, the number of papers in a session, and many other constraints and rules.

In this way, it is possible for user stories to serve as the basis for creating a clear, complete, and consistent set of requirements, as well as to identify serious errors in the original problem statement. Even the most rudimentary effort to validate the original problem statement with domain experts and prospective users would easily highlight these gaps, business rules, and missing user stories, long before anyone built complex system models or wrote any code. Because of ongoing interaction with users, the agile approach works better for user-centered development than any of the methods, including this author's, described by the 13 methods in the original CRIS Conference, which collectively failed to find any of the problems so quickly identified here.

3.2   Use Case Diagrams and Their Elaboration

While user stories are a highly effective mechanism for user-centered design, they are not intended to capture system behavior, data produced and consumed by the system, or all of the interactions among the actors and system. A use case diagram can address these issues, as well as illustrating the scope of the system.

Figure 2 shows an incomplete use case model for the IFIP Working Conference, reflecting the user stories shown above and some system actions needed for basic operation of the system, such as providing login/logout capabilities for users, who may be members of the Organising and Program Committees, authors, and members of the sponsoring Working Group(s) and Technical Committee(s). This diagram may be changed frequently, as the application requirements are better understood. Note that these operations, as with the user stories, are shown at a high level of abstraction.

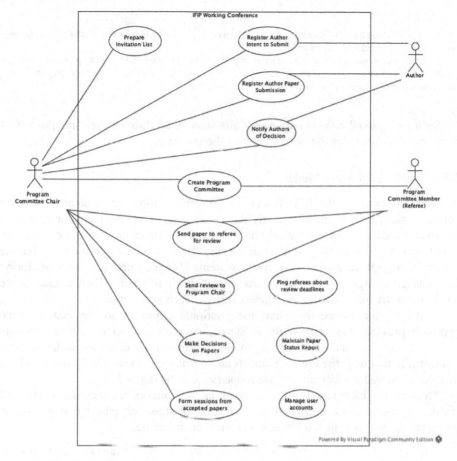

Fig. 2. Preliminary use case model for IFIP working conference problem

Each of these use cases needs further elaboration so that it can be validated and subsequently implemented. For example, the use case "Send review to Program Chair" might be elaborated as:

```
    1. Fill in standard review form with referee name and scores for
quality, originality, and reviewer knowledge of subject area.
    2. Write comments about the paper to be transmitted to the author by
the Program Chair
    3. Write optional comments about the paper to be seen only by the
Program Chair.
    4. Recommend whether the paper should be accepted or rejected.
    5. Transmit the completed review to the Program Chair.
```

While the first implementation of this use case for a Minimal Viable Product [13] may address only the "normal" case, it must eventually address the alternative or exceptional cases, such as:

1. The referee is unable to complete the review before the deadline and does not submit a review.
2. The referee asks a colleague to do the review in their place.
3. The referee is unfamiliar with the subject matter of the paper and is unable to prepare a review.

Such exceptional conditions are typically uncovered through the same process of interviews that provides the normal flow of use case.

3.3   Evolving the Data Model

In earlier solutions to the IFIP Working Conference problem [1], database schema definition played a key role in the early stage of development. With an agile approach, however, the data model is iteratively derived from the use cases and their elaboration, as noted in [6]. Most of the earlier models were relational or entity-relationship, but the advent of NoSQL database management systems [14] provides new ways of storing and managing large volumes of unstructured data. It is much easier to modify the model of unstructured data as developers address each new sprint.

Switching the perspective from the relational approach to the non-relational approach provides the opportunity to store data according to its logical meaning without having to transform the various objects into a set of tables with interrelationships. In that way, the use case models and/or the user stories yield a set of objects that can be stored directly and whose properties can be defined.

Thus, the use case models refer to objects such as authors, invitees, users, letters of intent, papers, reviews, and sessions. For each of those objects, the requirements gathering process provides information about their properties:

```
    Paper (title, abstract, keywords, authors, corresponding_author,
email, paper_body, reviews, decision)
    Session (title, location, date_and_time, length, chair, papers)
```

Once again, these definitions will be refined over time as more is learned about the application and its exceptional situations. For example, it's possible that the Working Conference will have invited papers as well as submitted ones, where the invited papers are automatically accepted without review and scheduled, often in a specially designated session.

3.4   User Interface Mockups

As noted in Sect. 2.5 above, preliminary designs of the user interface are an effective complementary technique for identifying requirements, as well as assuring the usability of the completed application. For example, as shown in Fig. 3 using 123formbuilder.com [15], it's easy to build a "live" high-fidelity mockup of the referee review form that can be tried and reviewed by a user. Many user suggestions can be quickly implemented so that the user can iterate on the design, including doing a/b experimentation of alternatives [16].

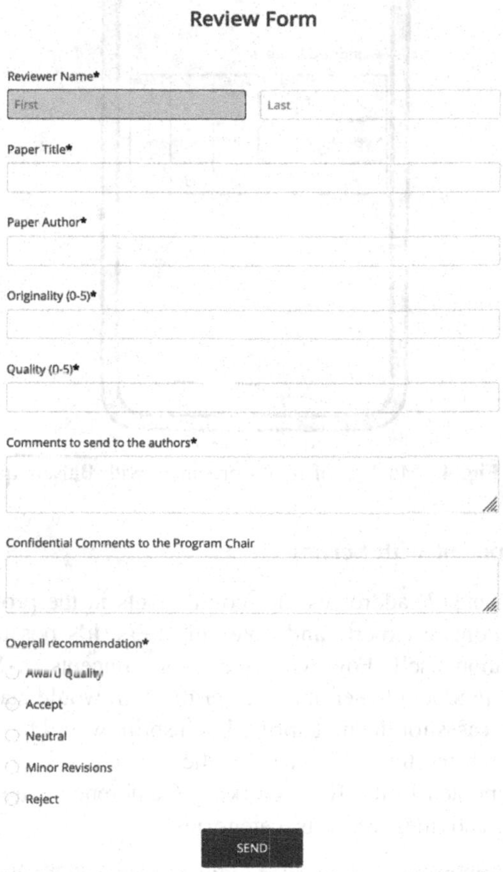

Review Form

Reviewer Name*

| First | Last |

Paper Title*

Paper Author*

Originality (0-5)*

Quality (0-5)*

Comments to send to the authors*

Confidential Comments to the Program Chair

Overall recommendation*

○ Award Quality
○ Accept
○ Neutral
○ Minor Revisions
○ Reject

SEND

Fig. 3. Mockup of a referee review form

There are also numerous tools for building mockups for mobile devices, as needed for mobile app design. Figure 4 shows a preliminary version of a mockup using Balsamiq.

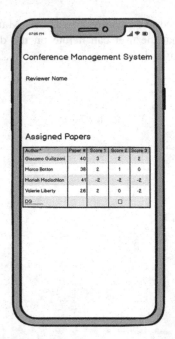

Fig. 4. Mockup of reviewer screen with Balsamiq

3.5   Agile Development with Scrum

As the Product Owner [17] addresses the requirements in the problem statement and reviews them with domain experts and potential users, it's possible to begin implementing the application itself. Following the basic concepts of Scrum described in Sect. 2.1 above, the Product Owner and the Scrum team would start by selecting a set of user stories or use cases for the first sprint. Each sprint would have a backlog of tasks to be completed within the time allocated for the sprint.

One possible approach in the IFIP Working Conference example is to group the Program Committee activities into four categories:

1) Set up basic system infrastructure: user management, establish program committee, manage author submissions (letters of intent and papers);
2) Processing of submitted papers: logging submissions, assigning papers to referees, collecting completed reviews, deciding which papers to accept;
3) Author notifications: send letters of acceptance and rejection, send publication instructions to corresponding authors of accepted papers, and;
4) Session formation: define session titles, appoint session chairs, assign time and location, assign papers to session.

Each of these stories would be refined as needed, with the Product Owner working with domain experts to find and resolve issues. The user stories associated with the activities of the Conference Organizing Committee could be developed in subsequent sprints.

It's long been known that early detection of requirements errors can provide major cost savings over detection of problems later in the process or after application deployment. Even with today's tools for continuous integration and continuous delivery (CI/CD) [18], early error detection can reduce the number of bug fixes and allow the developers to devote more time to enhancements and new features.

With this decomposition of the conference system implementation, the system can be delivered in small pieces. By the end of the second sprint (Processing of submitted papers), there should be enough functionality to release it on a limited basis as a Minimum Viable Product, with the remaining sprints adding valuable capabilities while building out the robustness of the system and addressing the exceptional conditions that were omitted earlier.

4 Conclusion

Revisiting the IFIP Working Conference example after almost forty years shows how greatly information system design methodologies have changed in the interim, driven by agile methods, the Internet and the World Wide Web, as well as by huge advances in computing hardware, networking, and displays. Today's ubiquitous personal computers had just entered commercial use in 1982, and mobile "smartphone" applications were nearly two decades away. Many of today's most popular applications could barely be conceived, let alone implemented, in that earlier era.

The growth of open source software has also made a substantial contribution to rapid development of information systems and other applications. As one example, it's possible to use an off-the-shelf event management system, the open source Conference Organizing Distribution [19], built on the open source Drupal content management system [20], that comes very close to providing all of the features (plus some others) of the problem statement for the IFIP Working Conference. With access to the source code, one could consider modifying that code for the IFIP Working Conference system rather than going through the agile process shown here.

The original CRIS Conference deserves credit for bringing greater attention to the early stages of the design process. Today's methodologies for system design place even greater emphasis on meeting user requirements, as well as assuring a positive user experience with the application. Those aspects of information system design will certainly endure through future generations, even as new technologies emerge.

Appendix – Problem Definition

Here is the original problem definition that was used in the call for submissions to the CRIS conference.

1. Background

An IFIP Working Conference is an international conference intended to bring together experts from all IFIP countries to discuss some technical topic of specific interest to one or more IFIP Working Groups. The usual procedure, and that to be considered for the present purposes, is an invited conference which is not open to everyone. For such conferences, it is something of a problem to insure that members of the involved Working Group(s) and Technical Committee(s) are invited even if they do not come. Furthermore, it is important to ensure that sufficient people attend the conference so that the financial break-even point is reached without exceeding the maximum dictated by the facilities available.

IFIP Policy on Working Conferences suggest the appointment of a Program Committee to deal with the technical content of the conference and an Organising Committee to handle financial matters, local arrangements, and invitations and/or publicity. These committees clearly need to work together closely and have a need for common information and to keep their recorded information consistent and up to date.

2. Information System to be designed

The information system which is to be designed is that necessary to support the activities of both a Program Committee and an Organising Committee involved in arranging an IFIP Working Conference. The involvement of the two committees is seen as analogous to two organisational entities within a corporate structure using some common information.

The following activities of the committees should be supported.

Program Committee

1. Preparing a list to whom the call for papers is to be sent.
2. Registering the letters of intent received in response to the call.
3. Registering the contributed papers on receipt.
4. Distributing the papers among those undertaking the refereeing.
5. Collecting the referees' reports and selecting the papers for inclusion in the program.
6. Grouping selected papers into sessions for presentation and selecting chairman for each session.

Organising Committee

1. Preparing a list of people to invite to the conference.
2. Issuing priority invitations to National Representatives, Working Group members, and members of associated working groups.
3. Ensuring all authors of each selected paper receive an invitation.
4. Ensuring authors of rejected papers receive an invitation.
5. Avoiding sending duplicate invitations to any individual.
6. Registering acceptance of invitations.
7. Generating final list of attendees.

3. Boundaries of System

It should be noted that budgeting and financial aspects of the Organising Committee's work, meeting plans of both committees, hotel accommodation for attendees and the matter of preparing camera ready copy of the proceedings have been omitted from this exercise, although a submission may include some or all of these extra aspects if the authors feel so motivated.

References

1. Olle, T., Sol, H., Verrijn-Stuart, A.: Information Systems Design Methodologies: A Comparative Review. North-Holland, Amsterdam (1982)
2. Manifesto for Agile System Development. https://agilemanifesto.org. Accessed 22 Nov 2020
3. Schwaber, K.: Agile Project Management with Scrum. Microsoft Press, Redmond (2004)
4. Blank, S.: Four Steps to the Epiphany, 2nd edn. K&S Ranch, Uvalda (2013)
5. Holtzblatt, K., Wendell, J., Wood, S.: Rapid Contextual Design: A How-to Guide to Key Techniques for User-Centered Design. Morgan Kauffman, San Francisco (2004)
6. Agile/Evolutionary Data Modeling: From Domain Modeling to Physical Modeling. http://agiledata.org/essays/agileDataModeling.html. Accessed 22 Nov 2020
7. Storyboard That: The World's Best Free Online Storyboard Creator. https://www.storyboardthat.com. Accessed 22 Nov 2020
8. Jacobson, I.: Object-Oriented Software Engineering. Addison-Wesley, Reading (1992)
9. Rumbaugh, J., Jacobson, I., Booch, G.: The Unified Modeling Language Reference Manual, 2nd edn. Addison-Wesley, Reading (2004)
10. Ideal Modeling & Diagramming Tool for Agile Team Collaboration. https://www.visual-paradigm.com. Accessed 22 Nov 2020
11. Balsamiq. Rapid, effective and fun wireframing software. https://balsamiq.com. Accessed 22 Nov 2020
12. Wasserman, A.: The user software engineering methodology: an overview. In: Information Systems Design Methodologies: A Comparative Review, pp. 591–628. North-Holland, Amsterdam (1982)
13. What is a Minimum Viable Product (MVP)? | Agile Alliance. https://www.agilealliance.org/glossary/mvp. Accessed 22 Nov 2020
14. No SQL Tutorial. https://www.guru99.com/nosql-tutorial.html. Accessed 22 Nov 2020
15. Online Form Builder with Drag & Drop. https://www.123formbuilder.com. Accessed 22 Nov 2020
16. Optimizely: The World's Leading Experimentation Platform. https://optimizely.com. Accessed 22 Nov 2020
17. What is a Product Owner? https://www.scrum.org/resources/what-is-a-product-owner. Accessed 22 Nov 2020
18. What is CI/CD? | Opensource.com. https://opensource.com/article/18/8/what-cicd. Accessed 22 Nov 2020
19. UseCod.com | Open Source Event Management Software. https://usecod.com. Accessed 22 Nov 2020
20. Drupal | Open Source CMS. https://drupal.org. Accessed 22 Nov 2020

Development of a Method and a Software for Decision-Making, System Modeling and Planning of Business Processes

Anna Antonova⬥, Konstantin Aksyonov^(✉)⬥, and Polina Ziomkovskaya

Ural Federal University, Ekaterinburg 620002, Russia

Abstract. The article is devoted to the study of an actual problem of decision-making in the field of business process planning. In the decision-making process, the analyst is faced difficulties in accounting for restrictions on all types of resources, including stored and non-stored ones, and time restrictions on a period for work performing. Analysis of the existing methods for solving a problem revealed a lack of consideration in the methods of restrictions on stored resources. The article proposes a hybrid method for planning business processes based on the integration of simulation, multi-agent and evolutionary modeling. The method is implemented in the decision-making software based on the BPsim family of products using the developed genetic optimization wizard. The developed technology has been tested in solving the real problem of planning business processes.

Keywords: Decision-making · System modeling · Processes planning · Problem-oriented software

1 Introduction

Planning is one of the key tasks of organizational systems managing. The problem of developing computer systems for supporting planning processes to increase the efficiency of developed plans has a great economic importance. In connection with this, development of the planning and modeling method in a problem-oriented software that implements this method is relevant.

Complexity of the solved planning problem is associated with availability of restrictions on resources and time during works planning. We consider both limited non-stored and stored resources including the lifetime of the stored resources. Non-stored resources include resources that can be reused after release, for example, staff or mechanisms. Stored resources include resources that are completely consumed in a given volume during execution, for example, technical objects during installation.

One of the key problems that the manager faces during planning is occurrence of contradictions between deadlines and restrictions on non-stored resources. A possible solution is to attract subcontracting resources in case of inaccessibility of own resources. In view of the abovementioned, the purpose of planning in addition to meet the deadlines is to reduce the cost of attracting subcontracted non-stored resources.

© Springer Nature Switzerland AG 2021
G. Succi et al. (Eds.): ICFSE 2021, CCIS 1523, pp. 148–157, 2021.
https://doi.org/10.1007/978-3-030-93135-3_10

2   Analysis of Existing Methods for Business Processes Planning

We investigate application of the scheduling theory methods to the problem of project works planning.

Sevastyanov S.V. in [1] considers the problem of scheduling with definition of the minimum schedule length in the presence of restrictions on non-stored resources and interruptions. The authors introduce a concept of "migration delay in execution" associated with the natural time delaying of work when it is interrupted and then resumed execution on another parallel machine. A low-labor approximate algorithm is proposed for the case of two machines with an estimate of the complexity and quality of the solution. Advantage of the work is expansion of the classic scheduling problem with migration delays. The disadvantages include consideration of the restrictions only on non-stored resources and lack of the deadlines accounting.

Another close problem being studied in the framework of scheduling theory is the problem of scheduling optimization of a parallel system with identical machines with the presence of given deadlines for fulfilling works. Tanaev V.S. in [2] provides an algorithm for constructing a schedule with maintenance at specified times. The Tanaev V.S. method ensures that restrictions on the time of works and on the non-stored resources used are considered. At the same time, the method does not allow one to optimize the cost of attracted non-stored subcontracted resources and does not consider stored resources.

Let's consider application of the critical path method (CPM) – one of the network scheduling methods [3]. CPM in accordance with the logic of implementation and duration of the works allows one to calculate the earliest completion time of the project and determine the critical path, that is, identify works that have zero-time reserve. For distribution of the resources among the projects, special algorithms are used that assign priorities to the works. An important aspect of the CPM method work is presence of precedence-following relations between the works. However, there are several scheduling tasks for which precedence relationships are not required. For example, the task of documentation development for the ready-made technical solutions. In addition, network methods as shown by the authors in [4] have limitations on the description of a life cycle of stored resources: supplies, consumptions and resource lifetime.

A comparative analysis of the scheduling problems solved by the considered scheduling theory and CPM algorithms is shown in Table 1. As follows from the analysis, the CPM algorithm is the most universal from the considered ones. It includes operations of individual projects, network representation of operations, directive deadlines, priority of operations and the possibility of interruptions. In addition, this algorithm is implemented in the commercial software MS Project [5].

There are following restrictions of applying these algorithms to the considered scheduling problem:

- the algorithm doesn't have accounting for the lifetime of the stored resources (lifetime is determined, for example, by the coagulation of concrete in construction or cooling of steel in metallurgical production);

Table 1. Comparative analysis of the planning methods.

Evaluation criterion	CPM method	Algorithm of Tanaev V.S.	Algorithm of Sevastyanov S.V.
1. Operation input data			
1.1 Duration	Yes	Yes	Yes
1.2 Order delay	Yes	Yes	Yes
1.3 Early start dates	Yes	No	No
1.4 Policy deadlines	Yes	Yes	No
1.5 Priority	Yes	No	No
1.6 Interruptions	Yes	Yes	Yes
1.7 Belonging to the project	Yes	No	No
1.8 Cost	Yes	No	No
1.9. Network view	Yes	No	No
2. Resource restrictions			
2.1 Stored resources	No	No	No
2.2 Non-stored resources	Yes	Yes	Yes
3. Target function			
3.1 Makespan minimization	Yes	Compliance with the policy deadlines	Yes
3.2 Subcontracting cost minimization	No	No	No
4. Free software implementation	Commercial software	Test implementation	Test implementation

- the algorithm doesn't have accounting for the specified dates for the early start of works;
- the algorithm doesn't have searching for the optimal assignment of the non-stored resources to work in terms of minimizing the cost of subcontracted resources applied.

Presence of these restrictions indicates the need for additional methods for solving the considered planning problem, namely, application of a system modeling to consider the identified criteria.

We investigate some modeling methods including discrete-event simulation, agent-based modeling and evolutionary modeling.

3   Analysis of Simulation and Evolutionary Modeling Application to Solving the Planning Problem

The scheduling process using system modeling begins with consideration of some initial feasible plan obtained experimentally or based on the data reflecting the current situation at the enterprise. An objective function is used to determine the need to change the parameters of the resulting plan. The simulation model does not impose restrictions on the objective function structure. Agent modeling is one of the directions of computer modeling [6]. Modern approaches are widely used in supply chains [7, 8], industrial automation [9–12] and research of operations [13, 14].

A simulation model is a computer model of a system designed to carry out experiments on it. Simulation modeling is intended to obtain system characteristics, for example, performance or reliability when study ongoing processes, analyze statistical data and identify the optimal configuration and parameter values of complex systems. Simulation modeling provides the analyst with a tool for developing control actions and assessing the impact of the developed actions on the system functioning.

A multi-agent system is a system that contains agents interacting with each other to achieve their goals. Agents are models of the decision makers. The collective behavior of agents in multi-agent models presupposes the cooperation of agents in collective problem solving. During the operation of a multi-agent system, an agent can turn to other agents for help if he is not able to solve the task assigned to him on his own. The basic types of interaction between agents include the following ones: cooperation or collaboration, competition or confrontation, compromise considering the interests of other agents, conformism with giving up one's interests in favor of others and avoidance of interaction.

Multi-agent software Magenta has been used to allocate restricted non-stored resources on the works with time restrictions satisfaction in [15]. In this case, each non-stored resource and each single work is represented by an agent. The agents interact with each other and allocate the resources to the works by mean of negotiations.

As a result of the comparison of multi-agent models [16] for formalizing the scheduling and execution processes, a multi-agent resource conversion process (MRCP) model has been selected due to its full compliance with the stated requirements. The agent in the MRCP model is a manager model whose knowledge about resources allocation is formalized using production rules in the form 'If-Then'. In addition, the MRCP model includes a logistics agent that monitors the current volume and lifetime of the stored resources and monitors the fulfillment of the restrictions on the stored resources. The logistic agent generates requests for production (purchase) of the required amount of the stored resources in case if their current volume is decreased to a critical value or is exceeded resource lifetime.

Depending on the paradigm of multi-agent systems, the following system architectures are distinguished: 1) reactive architectures based on stimulus-response models; 2) deliberative or intelligent architectures based on the knowledge; 3) hybrid architectures that combine the first two. Currently, almost all multi-agent systems have a hybrid architecture that supports a multi-level view of the agent's functionality.

The hybrid architecture of the agent, simulation, expert modeling and modeling of queuing systems are implemented by the MRCP model. A reactive agent in the MPPR model has a knowledge base formalized with the help of the production rules. The agent's response is the impact on the processes, resources and claims of the MPPR model. An intelligent agent in the MRCP model searches for a solution according to the decision search diagram, which is the extension of a sequence diagram of the UML language. In the considered planning processes, agents represent a model of a decision-maker.

The advantages of using simulation multi-agent models in the decision-making process in the planning subject area include possibility of assessing alternative solutions of the problem using a computer model of the process under study, accounting the dynamic characteristics of the process, probabilistic assessment of the process parameters and considering the decision-maker's model at various decision-making levels.

The disadvantage of using simulation multi-agent models in solving the scheduling problem is the need to formulate such an experiments plan with the model that would contain an effective or optimal solution, which is impossible without application of the experimental theory methods or additional heuristic methods. Popular heuristic methods are evolutionary modeling methods.

Based on the integration of simulation, multi-agent, and evolutionary modeling, authors developed a method of multi-agent genetic optimization (MAGO) [17] intended to solve the investigated problem of the business processes scheduling. The proposed MAGO method allows to search for a decision to the scheduling problem using a modified genetic algorithm. The MRCP model is designed to assess the fitness function of decisions during the operation of the genetic algorithm. The controlled parameters (start dates of the operations) and initial parameters described during the problem statement are fed to the input of the MRCP model. The parameters formed in the decision-making process are model outputs: the cost of attracting subcontracting resources and the downtime of the own resources of each competence. In the MRCP model, agents are used to implement the distribution algorithm of the stored and non-stored resources and consider restrictions on the stored resources; simulation modeling is used to describe the performance of operations.

4 Development of a Software for System Modeling and Planning of Business Processes

In order to implement the new MAGO method, the products of the BPsim family [16, 17] have been selected as the most fully meeting the requirements of the multi-model simulation and decision support in the field of organizational systems management. Currently, the family is represented by the following products: BPsim.MAS dynamic situation modeling system, BPsim.MSN technical and economic design system, and BPsim.SD CASE-tool for designing of the information systems. Products of the BPsim family are free software designed to support decision searching and business process modeling.

The BPsim.MAS system is intended to development and application of the MRCP models of the studied processes. The BPsim.MSN system supports development of intelligent agents or wizards to manage the developed models and implement their integration while solving the user tasks.

The architecture of the developed software is based on the InteRRap architecture of a hybrid agent. This architecture is a set of vertically ordered levels linked through a common management structure and using a common knowledge base. The architecture consists of the following blocks: an interface with the external world, a reactive sub-system, a scheduling subsystem, a subsystem for cooperation with other agents and a hierarchical knowledge base. The interface with the external world determines the agent's capabilities in perceiving objects or events of the external world, influencing him and the means of communication. The reactive subsystem uses the basic capa-bilities of the agent for reactive behavior and partially uses the knowledge of the agent of a procedural nature. The scheduling component contains a scheduling engine that allows one to build local agent plans that are not related to cooperative behavior. The component that responsible for the cooperation of agents participates in the con-struction of plans for the joint behavior of agents and coalitions to achieve some common goals.

The architecture of the hybrid agent and the software developed is shown in Fig. 1.

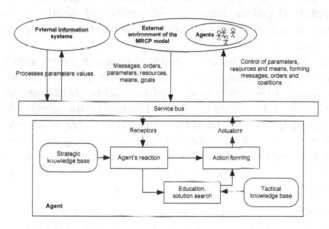

Fig. 1. Agent-based software architecture.

All components of the agent-based architecture of the software developed are linked through a common management structure and a common knowledge base. In the architecture of the MRCP model, the general knowledge base is a combination of the tactical knowledge base that stores the agent's production rules and the strategic knowledge base on frames.

A method of developing a wizard using products of the BPsim family is presented in the IDEF0 standard in Fig. 2. Functional definition, construction of a conceptual model of the subject area and design of the wizard operation algorithms are carried out via the BPsim.MSN system using the DFD diagrams, class diagrams, use cases and sequences diagrams with the conversion of some diagrams into others. In the CASE-tool BPsim.SD, the user configures interface screen settings and generates the wizard code, database and documentation structure.

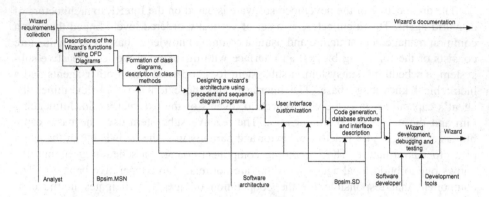

Fig. 2. Wizard development method using BPsim family products.

To solve the task of implementing the MAGO method, a genetic optimization wizard has been developed and integrated with products of the BPsim family as part of the development of a unified software for decision-making, modeling and planning of business processes.

The genetic optimization wizard is designed to search for the next population of solutions and transfer information about each solution to the BPsim.MAS modeling system. The BPsim.MAS system is intended to build the MRCP model of the work execution processes and evaluate the fitness function of the current chromosome or coded work schedule. The BPsim.MSN system is intended to encode the solution phenotype or work schedule into the genotype or bit string-chromosome. Software implementation of the basis of the BPsim family products and genetic optimization wizard was possible due to application of a single database based on MS SQL-server.

The developed software has the following features:

1. Integration of simulation, expert, multi-agent and evolutionary approaches.
2. Description of system models using graphical notations of MRCP and UML.
3. Providing users with the ability to customize the work of the evolutionary component, namely the genetic algorithm (GA), for the specific conditions of the planning task by setting the parameters of the GA: used genetic operators, probabilities of their use, population size, stopping criterion, rules for the formation of the initial population.
4. Providing users with the opportunity to correlate simulation and evolutionary scheduling models with the help of a wizard technology or interactive software assistant.
5. Support for development by users of their additional coding options for solving the alternative problem decision into genes of the GA chromosome.

The forms of the MAGO wizard user interface are shown on Fig. 3 and Fig. 4.

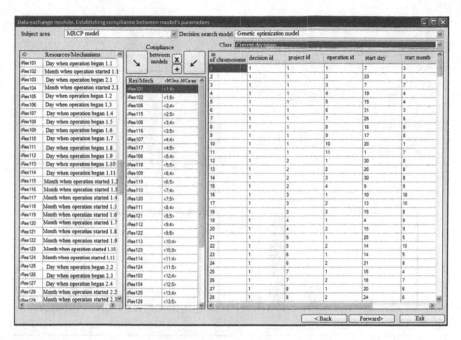

Fig. 3. Form for establishing compliance and data exchange between scheduling simulation and evolutionary models.

The agent-based architecture of the software for system modeling and planning of business processes includes three layers: 1) data storage; 2) data exchange with other information systems of the enterprise and local databases; 3) agent-based modeling and decision-making on the formation of a control impact on the process model.

The first layer of the software architecture is designed to store data in a local database and a shared knowledge base for using the data in decision making. Storage is carried out using the MS SQL Server database management system.

The second layer of the software architecture is intended for data exchange with enterprise information systems. Software agents include receptors and actuators for exchanging information with external systems. Receptors are designed to form antecedents of the rules for the reaction of agents to the influence of the external environment; actuators are designed to form a control action on the external environment based on the results of the agent's search for a solution to the problem.

The third layer of the software architecture is intended for the following actions: development of MRCP models, development and adjusting of the MAGO genetic optimization models, finding a solution to the problem based on inference from the tactical knowledge base using genetic optimization and the MRCP model.

As a result, the multi-agent genetic optimization wizard using BPsim.MAS, BPsim. MSN and BPsim.SD tools, UML language sequence diagrams, Transact-SQL database management language and Microsoft SQL Server has been developed.

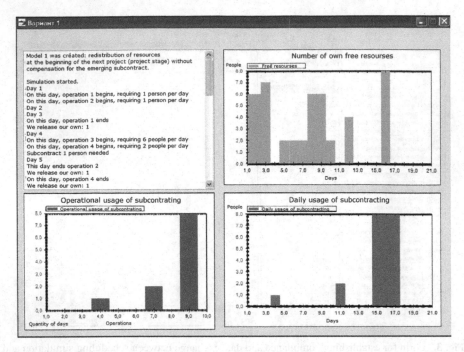

Fig. 4. Form for viewing the output characteristics of the found solution to the problem.

5   Conclusion

The aim of the study was to develop a method and a software for decision-making, modeling and planning of business processes. Analysis of the existing mathematical approaches to solving the scheduling problem has been carried out, their advantages and disadvantages have been identified, the conclusion has been drawn on the need to use simulation multi-agent modeling to consider all restrictions of the problem of business processes managing. The method of multi-agent genetic optimization of decision support that integrates simulation and evolutionary approaches to provide an optimized search for a solution has been developed. The new method has been implemented in the software for decision-making based on products of the BPsim family. This technology has been tested in solving the problems of business processes scheduling at the "Telesystems" enterprise [17].

Future work is related with the further approbation of the proposed method and software in solving real problems of planning business processes.

Acknowledgments. This research was funded by Act 211 Government of the Russian Federation, contract no. 02.A03.21.0006.

References

1. Van Bevern, R.A., Pyatkin, A.V., Sevastyanov, S.V.: An algorithm with parameterized complexity of constructing the optimal schedule for the routing open shop problem with unit execution times. Siber. Electron. Math. News **16**, 42–84 (2019)
2. Tanaev, V.S., Gordon, V.S., Shafransky, J.M.: Schedule Theory. Single Stage. The Science, Moscow (1984)
3. Moder, J.J., Elmaghraby, S.E.: Handbook of Operations Research: Models and Applications. Van Nostrand Reinhold, New York (1978)
4. Aksyonov, K.A., Antonova, A.S., Aksyonova, O.P., Kai, W.: Rules for construction of simulation models for production processes optimization. In: 3rd International Workshop on Radio Electronics and Information Technologies, vol. 2076, pp. 9–18 (2018)
5. Microsoft Project. https://www.microsoft.com/en-gb/microsoft-365/project/project-management-software. Accessed 01 Sept 2021
6. Wooldridge, M.: Intelligent agent: theory and practice. Knowl. Eng. Rev. **10**(2), 115–152 (1995)
7. Sokolov, B., Dolgui, A., Ivanov, D.: Ripple effect in the supply chain: an analysis and recent literature. Int. J. Prod. Res. **56**(1–2), 414–430 (2018)
8. Sokolov, B., Dolgui, A., Ivanov, D.: Scheduling of recovery action in supply chain with resilience analysis consideration. Int. J. Prod. Res. **56**(19), 6473–6490 (2018)
9. Cao, L., Zeng, Y., Symeonidis, A.L., Gorodetsky, V., Müller, J.P., Yu, P.S. (eds.): ADMI 2013. LNCS (LNAI), vol. 8316. Springer, Heidelberg (2014). https://doi.org/10.1007/978-3-642-55192-5
10. Gorodetsky, V.: Big data: opportunities, challenges and solutions. In: Ermolayev, V., Mayr, H., Nikitchenko, M., Spivakovsky, A., Zholtkevych, G. (eds.) Information and Communication Technologies in Education, Research, and Industrial Applications, vol. 469, pp. 3–22. Springer, Cham (2014). https://doi.org/10.1007/978-3-319-13206-8_1
11. Borodin, A., Mirvoda, S., Porshnev, S., Ponomareva, O.: Design of DSQLM language extensions. In: Ural Symposium on Biomedical Engineering, Radioelectronics and Information Technology, pp. 295–298 (2019)
12. Borodin, A., Mirvoda, S., Porshnev, S.: Intra page indexing in generalized search trees of PostgreSQL. In: CEUR Workshop Proceedings, vol. 2523, pp. 169–181 (2019)
13. Shorikov, A.F.: Solution of the two-level hierarchical minimax program control problem in a nonlinear discrete-time dynamical. In: 2th IFAC Conference on Modelling, Identification and Control of Nonlinear Systems. Book of Abstracts, p. 33 (2018)
14. Khalyasmaa, A.I., Zinovieva, E.L.: Intelligent decision support system for technical solutions efficiency assessment. In: IEEE 2nd International Conference on Control in Technical Systems (2017)
15. Skobelev, P., Zhilyaev, A., Larukhin, V., Grachev, S., Simonova, E.: Ontology-based open multi-agent systems for adaptive resource management. In: 12th International Conference on Agents and Artificial Intelligence, pp. 127–135 (2020)
16. Aksyonov, K.A., Bykov, E.A., Antonova, A.S., Aksyonova O.P., Sufrygina, E.M., Goncharova, N.V.: Tools and methodologies for business processes formalization: application to multi-agent systems. In: 5th European Symposium on Computer Modeling and Simulation, pp. 113–118 (2011)
17. Aksyonov, K.A., Antonova, A.S.: Multiagent genetic optimisation to solve the project scheduling problem. In: Eighth International Multi-Conference on Computing in the Global Information Technology, pp. 237–242 (2013)

"Extreme Development" as a Means for Learning Agile

Paolo Marzolo[1], Matteo Guazzaloca[1], and Paolo Ciancarini[1,2](✉)

[1] University of Bologna, Bologna, Italy
paolo.ciancarini@unibo.it
[2] Innopolis University, Innopolis, Russia

Abstract. During the 2020 pandemic a new modality for the capstone project in Software Engineering was introduced to our third-year students in Computer Science. They have been tasked with the development of a non trivial software product - a Twitter client capable of visual analytics - using some Agile practices, exploiting a Scrum-like process model, and using only open source tools. Due to circumstances that were either planned (in the selection of tools and requirements) or unintended (the pandemic forbade any physical meeting), the project had some interesting outcomes. The project was not easy to enact, neither for the students nor for the instructors. The main problems were two: the students were not ready to practice agile teamwork, and the open source tools they had to use were demanding and only partly suitable for the goal they were chosen for. We term this experience - where students applied an agile discipline and were required to use only open source tools - an "extreme" agile development project. This paper - written by two students together with their instructor, summarises some lessons learnt: characteristics and features of the tools and practices used, the evolution of product artifacts and some difficulties encountered, along with the solutions we adopted. An important lesson learnt is that an agile project developed by Computer Science students requires specific training in communicating correct information at the right moment, and avoiding telling "social lies" concerning the status of both the product and its development process.

1 Introduction

Agile software development has been introduced more than twenty years ago, and it is now considered mainstream in the industry.

Countless higher education institutions have adopted agile as a way of introducing students to teamwork during software development. There are several approaches to teaching agile practices, most of them including some kind of teamwork training, like pair or mob programming.

However, Computer Science students notoriously do not like and are scarcely trained to teamwork [24], so the adoption of agile process models inside undergraduate courses suffers from a number of impediments. One of the most important impediments is that students have to work in groups with scarce or zero

© Springer Nature Switzerland AG 2021
G. Succi et al. (Eds.): ICFSE 2021, CCIS 1523, pp. 158–175, 2021.
https://doi.org/10.1007/978-3-030-93135-3_11

training to build "self-organizing teams". In fact, the topic of team building is a crucial one for agile developments, and student teams are no exception [20]. Another issue is that the students are not used to self tracking their productivity, and even less to "team tracking", namely the act of measuring the effectiveness of their teamwork.

Yet another impediment derives from the necessity of face to face cooperation between a "customer", who is often the instructor of the course, and the developing teams. The agile principles highlight the importance of face to face communication and cooperation over process and tools. This kind of communication is intended to increase the trust and collaboration spirit between the product owner and the developers. However, in an educational setting there is a specific problem: the students tend to develop the project as an effort necessary to pass the exam, so it is natural for them to minimize efforts and possibly lie about the real status of their process.

This situation changed dramatically in the spring of 2020 as the pandemic compelled most teaching to be offered online. The project has been introduced to overcome the limitations connected to a traditional exam based on written exercises. Students were given specific training concerning the process and the tools to use during the development. The tools were all open source and made available online on a departmental server, in a form downloadable and deployable on a cloud using Docker.

Students were introduced to some team build activity with the serious game Scrumble[1], that is a Scrum simulation. Students were also instructed to conduct their retrospectives with the help of Essence cards [16].

In this paper we will describe a project-based course with 21 teams including each five or six students as developers, and two people (one instructor and a teaching assistant) playing the role of product owners. The teams were requested to use a set of open source tools especially tailored for agile development. This condition was especially burdensome for the students, transforming the project in a sort of "extreme development" experience, as it combined an agile discipline, that was new for the students, with the mandatory use of open source tools, which were also new for most students.

The main research questions are the following:

RQ1: Can an agile development discipline (e.g. Scrum) and open source software tools be effectively combined when training novice developers?
RQ2: How can we evaluate the teamwork and agility of a team of novice developers who use open source tools?

The first question concerns the ability of students of using only specific development tools, exiting from their comfort zone of well known IDEs and limiting or even forbidding the use of commercial tools. We call "extreme development" this combination of agile and open source, plus the requirement of self tracking their productivity. The second question concerns the evaluation of teamwork in such an agile setting.

---

[1] Available at http://scrumble.pyxis-tech.com.

After this introduction, this paper is organized in the following sections. Section 2 summarizes some related works, aiming at describing how novice students adopt agile development practices and tools. Section 3 introduces the course structure. Section 4 describes the tools and practices integrated in the development process. Section 5 analyzes how process artifacts evolved, and Sect. 6 describes some issues in the evaluation of the students and their teamwork. Finally, Sect. 7 discusses some issues and gives suggestions for future editions of the course.

2   Related Works

Recent surveys have shown how widespread the adoption of agile software engineering practices has become [8]; although some surveys report only a portion of manufacturing companies rely strongly on Agile, the majority of them rely on a combination of agile methodologies [10], and a large percentage of software developers use Agile in their work [18].

Although Agile is, at its core, a series of principles and guidelines [2], multiple frameworks provide actionable plans and activities. One of such frameworks is Scrum [19], that is reported as one of the most used process models for software development, but it is not limited to this field: its stated objective is to help "generate value through adaptive solutions for complex problems" [22]. Scrum is not the only agile framework, and each of its practices has many variants [1].

Scrum has been used with reported success in high schools [15] and in several different university settings, both as the main learning goal, in its same-site and distributed versions, or as a method for teaching [25]. In contrast to what has been possible until now, last year's pandemic has made impossible students working together in the same room or in close proximity. Moreover, in our case, relevant government regulations changed considerably the rules to enter university labs between the first and the last sprints, making quick adaptations unavoidable. Few publications have investigated the effects of the sudden move to remote working [6].

Due to its novel nature, past research on university projects during the COVID-19 pandemic are scarce; at the same time, industry has already proved that Scrum (and agile workflows in general) can still be effective in remote contexts [17,23] the same was true during the pandemic [13]. The additional challenges presented by the changing environment were exacerbated by the documented difficulty of evaluating agile processes in university [9,21]: past research propose various metrics [14] to grade students on their application of agile process, but mostly fail to capture the ability of students to be agile instead of following any given formula. In this paper, we will outline the challenges one group faced, the support given by instructors, the adaptations they implemented and why their freedom of choice helped them learn the importance of adapting. In order to better represent their viewpoints, some parts of this article will be written from the point of view of the students.

3   Course Structure and Project Description

The course in Software Engineering at the Department of Computer Science of our University was reconfigured to face the challenges offered by the 2020 pandemic caused by COVID-19. The main novelty has been the introduction of a project to be executed using a Scrum-like process, to be enacted using several open source tools supporting remote collaboration.

In the past, the course had covered agile processes and XP/Scrum like best practices in the last few years, but only from a theoretical viewpoint. The students were tested individually by a written exam and an oral presentation. Since physical interactions were strongly limited, and written exams in presence were forbidden, the instructors decided to redefine the final exam as a team project, to be performed online to avoid unnecessary personal contacts.

The product to develop was a Twitter client, enriched with features for data analytics: the product should be able to capture large sets of geolocalizable tweets and: a) put them on a map; b) create a word cloud with their contents; c) create a temporal diagram to show the distribution of collected tweets across time, and so on. The main uses case were: a) using Twitter in an emergency, like an earthquake, to collect help messages; b) using tweets to track the movements and collect the picture of a group of travelers in a city or across a region; c) using tweets for simple diachronic sentiment analysis.

In the last few years a research project has developed an open source agile development environment deployable on a private cloud, thus avoiding any external dependence for privacy and security reasons. The environment is called Compositional Agile System (CAS) [4]. The main idea behind this environment is to offer a customizable environment, including powerful albeit free services for collaborating and managing agile development activities.

Thus, having this resource, that will be described in the next Sect. 4, the students could exploit a powerful, fully open source environment to start with. The environment can be deployed either on personal workstations, or on a departmental server, or in a public cloud.

4   Tools and Practices

The CAS environment in the version we used includes the following tools:

- Taiga for project management;
- GitLab for versioning;
- bugzilla for issue tracking;
- Mattermost for team communication;
- SonarQube for software analyses;
- open source productivity dashboard.

All the tools that were given to the students (including the productivity dashboard, discussed later) are open-source and available in a self-hosted instance.

This constraint transforms the project in an experience of "extreme development", where all interactions, all artifacts, all data produced by the tools can be saved locally and later examined, without any dependency from external services, for instance on commercial clouds.

4.1 Proposed Tools

The instructors introduced us to the basics of Agile Development and Scrum, but they were confident in both our ability to pick it up as we went and the importance of practice. Because of the nature of the course, we did not approach this in the most focused or comprehensive way, but instead considered various alternatives and recent advances: a clear example of this is the use of Essence Cards. We will outline this and other tools and practices in this section.

Taiga. Taiga, as its website says, is "an open source project management software that supports teams that work Agile across both Scrum and Kanban frameworks". Clearly, this software is one of the two main tools we used, together with GitLab, to manage and organize the teamwork during the software development process. Taiga's capabilities are vast; so vast, in fact, that we found some of them useless for a project of our size, and we ignored them. They range from the basic Kanban board, to a sprint task board for each sprint, the availability of a point breakdown of each user story and task, an issue tracking system, a comment system, different roles with varying responsibilities and a lot more. For us, Taiga was a most sensible alternative to Jira, that was out of the question as fully closed-source and mostly enterprise oriented. The use of Taiga will be documented in the next section.

GitLab. GitLab needs no introduction: as the most popular open-source alternative to GitHub, it was suggested by the instructors and we quickly adopted it as our (only) version control software.

BugZilla. BugZilla was initially proposed as a complementary service to Taiga for issue tracking, thanks to its integration possibilities and historical relevancy. We decided not to use it, as our organizational overhead was already too large to include one more tool we were not likely to use.

Mattermost. Mattermost was the solution of choice by the instructors for day-to-day communication and light issue tracking (which would then be moved to either BugZilla or GitLab, integrated with Taiga). Mattermost works well: it is light, the self-hosted instance is simple to set up, it has a well-working mobile app and an appealing interface. Unfortunately, all of us had been using Telegram for the longest time (partly open-source), so even though we completed the setup we jointly agreed we would favor Telegram.

SonarQube. SonarQube was new to the students: it is a code analysis tool that runs static analysis on source code and brings vulnerabilities or possible future problems to the attention of developers. Then, it generates a report on the current position, and proposes changes to improve the code. The students used SonarQube starting from the second sprint, and it helped to find some hard to spot vulnerabilities.

Productivity Logger. The Instructors were also interested in our productivity data, for future research purposes. The environment has a logging facility which can record any keystroke pressed when using an IDE like Eclipse. This logging function was not fully set up at the start of the project. This resulted in some misunderstandings on our part and moreover raised privacy concerns that we later brought up with the Instructors. We had two main problems with the logger: its scarce availability constrained us to a single IDE we were not comfortable with and we were not given a self-hosted version to install on our own server. We will now tackle those issues and describe the steps we took to resolve them.

The plugin availability was a direct consequence of the nature of the software: this logger is the result of a mentioned research project [4]. The plugins that were made available were for the following IDEs: Atom, Eclipse, and IntelliJ. Most of our development team uses VS Code, or alternatively vim for remote development, so we were not thrilled to be requested to move to and learn a completely new (and sizable) IDE as IntelliJ WebStorm.

Some teams investigated for alternative ways to track development activity and the related productivity measures. Since the productivity data were required in the final report for documenting the process, some teams settled for using Wakatime, as described in Sect. 4.2.

Essence. Essence is an open standard for the creation, use and improvement of software engineering practices and methods. In order to classify, explain, apply and evaluate such practices, the Essence Kernel was created as part of the SEMAT initiative [12]. The Essence kernel and the Essence Language as embedded in the cards for Agile allow teams to describe, discuss, evaluate, and improve both their product and their process. Essence is now an OMG standard [16]; because of its agnostic viewpoint, independent from any software process model, it is well suited to the educational setting [3].

Essence allowed our students to avoid to study the classic Scrum documentation: they used the Essence cards for Scrum, instead. Condensing information to the size of a card is a great way to keep a reader interested and give a bird's eye view that aids understanding, without getting distracted by specific details and missing the complete picture or, on the opposite side, skipping key parts of the process. The cards themselves proved to be very useful as well, since the students used them in two "serious games" which helped us approach the Review and Retrospective activities.

The first game we learned consists of going through the seven "Alphas" - the key elements and areas of interest common to all software projects, as identified by the SEMAT Kernel - and for each of them identify which state the current product resides in. The seven Alphas are Requirements, Software System, Team, Work, Way of Working, Opportunity and Stakeholders, and their states are complemented by checklists, informal ways to move in-between states. This provides the developers with two great advantages: a clear idea of where the project sits (and which Alphas still need to be worked on), and a clear path ahead, due to the checklists. We completed this activity at the end of all sprints, since we found it extremely useful for the two uses outlined here.

Instead, in the Retrospective, we adopted a second serious game called "Practice Patience". A detailed description is available here[2], and discussion about it can be found later in this paper in Sect. 4.4.

4.2   Final Tool Configuration

Throughout the first two sprints, the tool selection varied. What we will now describe is our final usage, what we used since the end of the second sprint. We find that this selection allowed us to respect the Instructor's wishes without adding so much configuration work to go beyond a full sprint's number of hours.

We hosted all self-hosted tools on a Google Cloud machine. We picked this because of both ease of use and how generous the "first use" credit is: thanks to the initial credit and how long it lasts, we were able to use it for free. All management and system administration tasks were completed by the development team.

GitLab. We already discussed GitLab in the previous section. Git Lab was the corner stone of our tool architecture and contained the complete source code and branches. Initially, we mainly worked together on one branch, but later we moved to a feature branch approach, with new features being developed in experimental branches and merged in master once they were completed and tested. Tests were man operated.

Taiga. As we mentioned in the last section, Taiga was our management software of choice. We installed a self-hosted version of it in the same cloud as the other services, but initially used the web version while the setup was being completed. Our management of Taiga is discussed in the first Sprint Reports, but we will outline the main characteristics here. In order to include both User Stories and Development Needs, we used Taiga cards as "Backlog Items". Each Item would then go through a pipeline of stages from New to Archived. The stages were New, Wait Approval (by the POs), Wait Verify (confirm the request is within technical constraints of Twitter API and architecture), Ready, In Progress, Ready for Test, Done, Archived and Rejected. If either approval or verification failed, or if we deemed them too minor to include them at all, they were Rejected. User Stories could be moved to Done once they respected the Definition of Done; they were then Archived after the end of the Sprint. User Stories not explicitly required by the PO were marked as "optional". To distinguish between User Stories and Dev Needs, we used tags.

We used the Wiki to archive Sprint Documents, the Definition of Done and a Useful Links section. We included the Scrum Master role, but the point attribution quickly got out of hand, so we only used it partially. Each User Story had an estimated time attribute. User Stories were divided into tasks, both at the

---

[2] https://essence.ivarjacobson.com/publications/blog/better-scrum-through-essence-part-2.

start and during a Sprint. Each task has a field for recording how long it took to complete it, and the Tasks follow a similar pipeline to User Stories (but don't need to be approved or verified). Not all tasks were assigned, because we often worked in pairs or groups and Taiga does not allow multiple assignees for Tasks.

SonarQube. We used SonarQube since the second sprint. We did not include it into an automatic pipeline but ran oneoff scans. In each Sprint Report a section is dedicated to SonarQube metrics and performance. SonarQube was installed as a selfhosted service in the same Google Cloud account as the previous two.

Telegram. Because of our familiarity with Telegram, as soon as we picked our group members, we made a Telegram group and started chatting there. This made switching to a different service complicated. Telegram is partly open-source. We used basic messaging features, occasional polls, file upload and pinned messages the most.

WakaTime. WakaTime was our time tracking software of choice. Although all its plugins are open-source, the server code and front end are not. We understand this was a compromise on the Instructors' position, but it was driven by urgency and ease of use. In a more organized setting or a future installment, we suggest switching it with either Kimai, fully opensource but requiring more customization for our chosen use, or looking into other alternatives, such as Super Productivity or GitLab time tracker. We only used Wakatime to track IDE usage, but a Word plugin and a chrome extension are available.

Etherpad. This is a service we used for short-lived text, shared and collaborative documents. We decided against hosting it on Google Cloud and used an alternative provider (riseup) instead.

Discord. This is one of the two completely non-open-source tools we used. We used Discord because of our familiarity with it and the vastness of its features. We tried replacing it a few times with open-source tools such as Jitsi Meet, but its reliability made us use it more often than not. Still, we do not deem it unavoidable: there are many tools which provide similar functionality and, with some time and effort, we're sure they could be used instead.

MS Live Share. For the sake of completeness, we mention that we frequently used the Microsoft extension Live Share while pair-programming. It is not open-source.

4.3 Discussion

In this section, we will discuss our experience with two pervasive themes of software engineering: Being Agile compared to Doing Agile, and using Open Source Software for university projects. Then, we will review our use of Essence and what we achieved with it.

The implementation of the Agile process in our academic environment differs substantially from what is commonly done in a standard working environment: instead of following a specific set of Agile practices and a specific framework such as Scrum, we spent a lot of time thinking about what we really found useful and what we wished to change, both at the beginning and during the actual development.

This "Being Agile" way of thinking, i.e. continuously questioning our way of working while trying to improve it, as opposed to sticking to any pre-defined practice or tool, helped us a lot while having to work through unexpected problems without increasing product risk or unbalancing the team stability. These problems were either unexpected and external, such as the COVID-19 pandemic that forced us to shift to a remote setting, or internal and expected, such as the additional requirements proposed by the PO on every sprint or the privacy concerns about the logger that worried the team.

This is not to say that a completely disorganized course would be more beneficial than a structured course: as we mentioned in Sect. 3, this is only the first iteration of the new structure of the course, which meant a short amount of time to put it together. Add to this the unfortunate coincidence of the pandemic, and it is easy to see how hard it would have been to prepare accordingly. Moreover, the differences between teams made it complicated for the Instructors to grade such vastly different projects objectively. At the same time, we do wish to make an argument in favour of putting the students through some tough choices; after all, this is not a Scrum course, or a programming course: as a software engineering course, the skills of being able to select, learn, and adapt to new methods, tools, and best practices are fundamental and well connected to the modern practice of software development.

At the start of the project, we were instructed to prefer OSS (Open Source Software) tools to organize our work. As we mentioned in the Sect. 4.2, we opted against some of the suggested ones and proposed alternatives, such as WakaTime instead of the CAS Logger, that served similar purposes, although it is not a completely open-source solution. Additionally, the decision of self hosting the majority of our tools (except for Wakatime, which does not allow users to self-host) gave us a lot of freedom since we were not affected by some delays and issues which afflicted the departmental server, both at the beginning and during the project.

4.4 Essence and Framework Independence

We here discuss the role Essence had in the development project, both from process and product perspective. In our team, Essence received overwhelmingly positive feedback, so here we will outline the three most important advantages we found.

- **Product State.** The ability to clearly define the Product and Process allowed us to clearly communicate our self-evaluation to the Instructors; its checklists provided immediate actionable feedback, and going through the serious game did not need an excessive amount of time or specific tools.
- **Scrum Cards.** We used the Essence cards for Scrum. They were used in "Practice Patience" game, the Scrum Master printed them for quick reference

during the first Sprint. We found that Practice Patience revealed our true level of understanding and ability of applying Scrum, and how much we evolved compared to the previous instance.
- **Relative Novelty.** Although we understand this may not be true for all teams, and definitely should not be considered a strength of Essence *per se*, we found that its relative novelty allowed us to think for ourselves and "figure it out as we went along", rather than rely on predefined structures and practices.

Lastly, we mention an additional usage of Essence cards that we initially considered but later scrapped: using Essence to formalize the process of getting feedback and acting on it by the Product Owners (and possibly even the Professors); due to the universality the Essence kernel aims at, it is possible (and suggested) to include additional practices by using Essence to formalize practices from different development frameworks. We believe this would be an enlightening guided activity in following iterations, as it truly shows the power of Essence as an neutral, agnostic standard (as the authors call it) for formalizing and streamlining practices from different frameworks. At the same time, it would be unreasonable to expect student to have reached a sufficiently deep understanding of the standard to complete it on their own, which is why we need to be guided by instructors.

5 Artifacts

At the end of each sprint the students wrote a Final Sprint Report documenting some process data and the product status. Because of the data we collected this way, we were able to track progress throughout sprints; here, we report three relevant analyses.

5.1 User Story Evolution

First, we report a cross-section view of the way our Product Backlog evolved. In this case, we picked a main feature of the product - an epic - and a few of its notable derived user stories. Figure 1 shows some user stories in form of cards. In each card, the Sprint in which the US was completed is shown in the top left. We also included its description, part of the acceptance criteria, the points we assigned it, how long we estimated it would take to complete it and how long it actually took.

As we can see, our first story was in line with the minimum viable product; on the technical side, it required handling of the twitter API and a minimal user interface. In the second sprint both real-time and bulk versions were developed; the user story related to the map, completed in sprint 3, was included in the second sprint as well, but only completed later. The last user story, technically complex and initially optional, was only tackled in the fourth sprint.

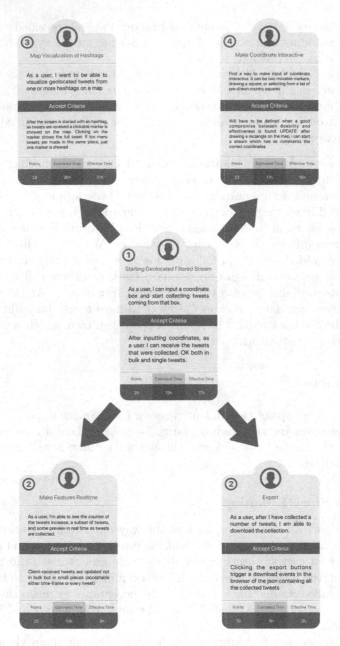

Fig. 1. User story evolution across sprints. The central card is an epic. In each card the completion sprint is shown top left in a circle

5.2   Sprint Backlog Sizes

Reporting the final state of our Backlog brought another restriction to our attention: for both sprints 2 and 3, a single User Story was delayed to the next Sprint only to be completed in the first few days of the next Sprint. In fact, a developer mentioned this in the third Sprint Review:

> "I really wish we could have had a few more days to complete our User Story. Even just one day would have meant not carrying it over to the next sprint..."

Although slight modifications to the timetable were allowed, because we had already overestimated our speed for sprint 2 we collectively decided that our mishandling should be accepted in order to avoid making the same mistake again, and moved it to the next sprint. That said, we believe both choices make sense, but giving a clear guideline at the start may clarify the process.

5.3   Review and Retrospective Evolution

As mentioned, our practices shifted considerably during the sprints: although our experience is of a single team, we believe further investigating the degree of strictness of rituals as teams mature would lead to interesting results. For what concerns our evolution, both Sprint Review and Retrospectives shifted considerably:

1. In our first Sprint Review, we first dedicated some time to recording a video showing the product, and then identified our current state using the "Alpha State" activity. We considered this part of the Sprint Review, but we acknowledge its purpose falls within the Retrospective as well. For our Retrospective, we held our first Practice Patience, and focused on giving actionable feedback to follow through on our observations.
2. The second Sprint's final activities were the same as the first, but further discussion was held based on our irregular progress on the Sprint Burndown Chart. Figure 2 shows the result of the Patience Practice game with Essence. We believe this retrospective was important to the team's feeling of growth and progress.
3. The third Sprint included a less structured activity, which we just called "Team Feedback". Although not all members were equally as vocal, a lot of useful feedback was collected: we agreed that the session was successful, and repeated it for both rituals.
4. The fourth Sprint included the Product State and Practice Patience serious games as well, but they only took on a *communicative* role to record our state and inform the PO of where we stood. The Team Feedback section became the main focus of both rituals.

As was outlined in the progression, our reliance on structured games and activities decreased steadily, as did our perceived gain from them. About this, we report our Scrum Master's thoughts as reported in the Fourth Sprint Report:

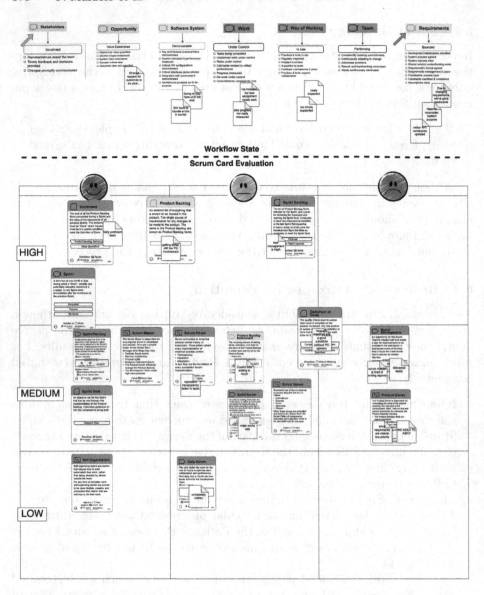

Fig. 2. The result of the retrospective of the second sprint. The top row of cards includes the seven alpha states of Essence, which represent the auto-evaluation by the team of the state of the project. The bottom part titled "Scrum card evaluation" represents the judgement on the sprint using the technique "Mad, Sad, Glad" [7]

"During this review, we all agreed that sharing the team's feedback was in fact a better way to voice our opinions than most serious games or guided activities. In my opinion, though, this was not always the case: although the developing team was very open about their doubts and trophies in this fourth review, this was not the case in some of the earlier ones."

6   Evaluation

The teams produced the following artifacts: a demo video of the final product release, its source code in gitlab, a SonarQube report of the final release, the team diary, the Essence cards arrangement produced during each sprint retrospective, some UML diagrams, personal questionnaire about team interactions. The evaluation of teams and their teamwork was conducted discussing the product in a final review and using two different quality models analyzing the main artifacts produced.

We used a teamwork quality model and an Agile maturity model. The teamwork quality model is inspired from [11], thus we name it the *Hoegl-Gemuenden model*. It is based on the assumption that any human behaviour in a team can be summarized in two major areas: activities and interactions.

The evaluation constructs are the following:

- interaction analysis;
- effectiveness analysis about software quality;
- work efficiency, which only considers schedule efficiency, because there was no budget;
- satisfaction analysis, which considers team satisfaction about learning, product, and process of Hoegl-Gemuenden's.

Since the data collection involved different evaluation metrics (1 to 5 Likert scale for students' opinions from a questionnaire about team interactions, decimal scale for instructors' evaluation of process and product, marks of Sonar-Qube for the product internal quality ratings, and percentages of completing user stories and tasks), in the data processing they were all converted in percentages.

The Agile maturity model we used is inspired by the Yin model presented in [26]. It includes five maturity levels and explores seven inner categories of analyses.

The radar graphs in Fig. 3 show the percentages obtained in each category of quality and maturity model, respectively.

The evaluations have be discussed in a companion paper [5]. We here summarize the results as follows.

The teams who performed best showed good balance of personal contribution and strong mutual support. The teams which performed worst were characterized by low quality of internal communication, scarce perception of effort spent in the project, unbalance of members' contribution to the project.

Moreover, these teams exposed often a conflict of opinions about team interactions, clearly indicating different perceptions and attitudes about teamwork.

The results of the evaluation allowed the instructor to rank the teams. However, we remark that the ranking was not used to give a grade to the students, who were evaluated in a traditional way after an oral discussion concerning the final report and a demo of the last release.

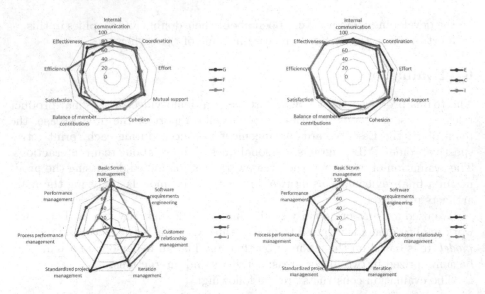

Fig. 3. Radar graphs of worst teams (left) and best teams (right) according to respectively the teamwork (top) and agile (bottom) models. From [5]

7   Conclusion

We presented the experience of one of the 21 agile teams that made up the 2020 Software Engineering Course class in our University. We aimed at reviewing the development process, in order to produce useful feedback for future work in similar contexts.

Concerning the Research Questions, we can give the following answers:

Answer To RQ1. We have asked our students to combine in a project of "Extreme Development" an Agile discipline and some Open Source tools; we believe that the combination is quite challenging and demanding for 3rd year Computer Science students of Software Engineering. All teams completed their projects, with a variety of grades.

Answer To RQ2. We have developed two quality models, one for teamwork and one for agile maturity, which have been quite effective and useful for assessing the results.

In this final section we summarize the main issues the students met throughout the sprints and what could be done in the future editions of the course.

7.1   Tools and Methods

Throughout this article, we mentioned how, in order to reach a suitable tool configuration, it was necessary to dedicate a sizable amount of time to exploratory testing and preliminary meetings. The experience was "extreme" especially because there was a strong push on using open source tools made available on a departmental server. We believe this helped push our team towards a better understanding of Agile. At the same time, we wish to reiterate that this had an effect on our productivity in our first two sprints: this is why we believe that such an activity, if deemed helpful, should be moved to the weeks preceding the start of the sprints. As part of the research behind this article, we looked into established tools selections or recent proposals, but we only found very few mentions. Some only took into account git hosting, while others expected a large infrastructure - e.g. Jira - to be supplied by Instructors. This is clearly a topic for further research.

Moreover, if the instructors wish to grade the teams on the quality of the process applied, we believe regular meetings should be held. The proposed solution of producing sprint reports was adequate for the instructors, but we believe a periodic meeting would prove more useful to both instructors and students. We understand the time instructors can dedicate to such activities is limited, so we propose that the meeting is held after Review and Retrospective have been completed, and aims at briefing the instructor on the contents of the meeting rather than participating in the rituals themselves. Alternatively, in order to include the figure of Product Owner, the instructors may only be part of the meeting for a limited amount of time.

7.2 Overlap of Learning and Applying

As outlined in the previous section, we believe less overlap between the learning and applying periods - of scrum, in our case - would have been useful to us. The Scrum Masters are also expected to have a general idea of their future duties; to these aims, we propose the following road map; although its steps may seem obvious, we found that many groups fail to complete the steps separately, and end up having difficulties during the actual coding.

1. Course and project introduction: both the course and the project should probably be introduced in the first few lessons. The introduction should make it clear that it is not possible to start early, as work will be tracked throughout the sprints, but also that listening attentively to agile practices and techniques will help make both the coding and reviewing events much easier.
2. Team building: we believe forming groups earlier would be beneficial to their ability of starting well and avoiding wasting time on simple tasks. The group will then face learning and setup as a "unit", which will help with forming interpersonal relationship that will facilitate their project development.
3. Tool setup: this is especially important if the students are expected to install their own versions of self-hosted software, as it is a time-consuming and difficult task. If some students need time to learn how to use such software, this is the correct time to do so.

7.3 Using Scrum for a Student Project

Lastly, we want to mention that in the future it should be made clear that Scrum is only a reference framework that could be modified and tailored to a specific workflow. This is because some of the requirements and practices of Scrum simply cannot be adapted to our context. As an example, we bring daily scrums: in our context of online remote education, when we have to attend several other courses beyond Software Engineering, they simply had no meaning whatsoever. They are annoying to organize, and do not allow for any further scheduling, as everyone's time constraints make it impossible to synchronize. Moreover, Scrum expects a level of involvement from the Product Owner which is simply unsustainable for an instructor alone with multiple teams.

Some teams suggested merging some of the rituals together; while we understand how useful it can be, we would advise taking into account developer exhaustion. This is because during our first two sprints, we completed review and retrospective meetings back to back; partly due to our ignorance, they both took longer than we expected, and we ended up frustrated by the amount of time they took. We also want to mention that the Retrospective - based on Essence guidance - was most definitely the most important ritual for our growth: this is supported by the final results by the teams.

As a final note, we recommend making sure to distinguish final activities and sprint planning, as they quickly collapse into one giant less-than-useful activity where it is very hard to accomplish all that's needed without growing annoyed and losing all enthusiasm.

References

1. Ashraf, S., Aftab, S.: Latest transformations in scrum: a state of the art review. Int. J. Modern Educ. Comput. Sci. **9**(7), 12–22 (2017)
2. Beedle, M., et al.: Manifesto for Agile Software Development (2001). https://agilemanifesto.org/
3. Ciancarini, P., Missiroli, M.: Teaching the essence of software development. In: Proceedings of 32nd Conference on Software Engineering Education and Training CSEE&T, pp. 1–2. IEEE (2020)
4. Ciancarini, P., Missiroli, M., Poggi, F., Russo, D.: An open source environment for an agile development model. In: Ivanov, V., Kruglov, A., Masyagin, S., Sillitti, A., Succi, G. (eds.) OSS 2020. IAICT, vol. 582, pp. 148–162. Springer, Cham (2020). https://doi.org/10.1007/978-3-030-47240-5_15
5. Ciancarini, P., Missiroli, M., Zani, S.: Empirical evaluation of agile teamwork. In: Paiva, A.C.R., Cavalli, A.R., Ventura Martins, P., Pérez-Castillo, R. (eds.) QUATIC 2021. CCIS, vol. 1439, pp. 141–155. Springer, Cham (2021). https://doi.org/10.1007/978-3-030-85347-1_11
6. Comella-Dorda, S., Garg, L., Thareja, S., Vasquez-McCall, B.: Revisiting agile teams after an abrupt shift to remote (2020)
7. Derby, E., Larsen, D., Schwaber, K.: Agile Retrospectives: Making Good Teams Great. Pragmatic Bookshelf, Raleigh (2006)
8. DigitalAI. State of agile (2021). https://stateofagile.com
9. Hanks, B.: Becoming agile using service learning in the software engineering course. In: Proceedings of Agile Development Conference, pp. 121–127 (2007)
10. Hoda, R., Salleh, N., Grundy, J.: The rise and evolution of agile software development. IEEE Softw. **35**(5), 58–63 (2018)

11. Hoegl, M., Gemuenden, H.G.: Teamwork quality and the success of innovative projects: a theoretical concept and empirical evidence. Organ. Sci. **12**(4), 435–449 (2001)
12. Jacobson, I., et al.: The Essentials of Modern Software Engineering. Association for Computing Machinery (2019)
13. Marek, K., Wińska, E., Dąbrowski, W.: The state of agile software development teams during the Covid-19 pandemic. In: Przybyłek, A., Miler, J., Poth, A., Riel, A. (eds.) LASD 2021. LNBIP, vol. 408, pp. 24–39. Springer, Cham (2021). https://doi.org/10.1007/978-3-030-67084-9_2
14. Matthies, C., Kowark, T., Uflacker, M., Plattner, H.: Agile metrics for a university software engineering course. In: Proceedings of IEEE Frontiers in Education Conference (FIE), Erie, PA, USA, pp. 1–5. IEEE, October 2016
15. Missiroli, M., Russo, D., Ciancarini, P.: Learning agile software development in high school: an investigation. In: Proceedings of 38th International Conference on Software Engineering Companion, pp. 293–302 (2016)
16. OMG. Essence Specification. https://www.omg.org/spec/Essence/1.2/PDF
17. Paasivaara, M., Durasiewicz, S., Lassenius, C.: Using scrum in distributed agile development: a multiple case study. In: Proceedings of 4th International Conference on Global Software Engineering, Limerick, Ireland, pp. 195–204. IEEE (2009)
18. PMI: Pulse of the profession 2017 - success rates rise: transforming the high cost of low performance, p. 2017. Technical report, PMI (2017)
19. Pries, K.H., Quigley, J.M.: Scrum Project Management. CRC Press, Boca Raton (2010)
20. Sahin, Y.G.: A team building model for software engineering courses term projects. Comput. Educ. **56**(3), 916–922 (2011)
21. Schneider, J.-G., Vasa, R.: Agile practices in software development - experiences from student projects. In: Proceedings of Australian Software Engineering Conference (ASWEC), pp. 10-pp. IEEE (2006)
22. Schwaber, K., Sutherland, J.: The scrum guide: the rules of the game (2020). https://scrumguides.org/docs/scrumguide/v2020/2020-Scrum-Guide-US.pdf
23. Sepulveda, C.: Agile development and remote teams: learning to love the phone. In: Proceedings of Agile Development Conference, Salt Lake City, UT, USA, pp. 140–145. IEEE (2003)
24. Waite, W.M., Jackson, M.H., Diwan, A., Leonardi, P.M.: Student culture vs group work in computer science. ACM SIGCSE Bull. **36**(1), 12–16 (2004)
25. Wedemann, G.: Scrum as a method of teaching software architecture. In: Proceedings of 3rd European Conference of Software Engineering Education, pp. 108–112. ACM (2018)
26. Yin, A., et al.: Scrum maturity model: validation for IT organizations' roadmap to develop software centered on the client role. In: The Sixth International Conference on Software Engineering Advances, ICSEA 2011 (2011)

A Meta-analytical Comparison of Energy Consumed by Two Different Programming Languages

Ikram Hamizi, Ayomide Bakare, Khadija Fraz, Gcinizwe Dlamini,
and Zamira Kholmatova[(✉)]

Innopolis University, Innopolis, Russia
{i.hamizi,a.bakare,k.fraz,g.dlamini,z.kholmatova}@innopolis.university

Abstract. Energy Consumption poses a major constraint in the battery lifetime of mobile devices, data centers and their power-hungry servers. Understanding the difference in energy consumption induced by different implementations of software and systems can equip the engineers with the necessary knowledge to make better design choices early on. Our goal is to study the impact of programming languages on energy consumption. This paper is twofold: a Rapid Review to investigate the available literature and a meta-analysis comparing Python and Java in terms of energy consumption. The review yielded 17 relevant studies and showed that Java, C, C++ are the most-widely studied languages. The meta-analysis of five eligible papers showed a non-significant difference in energy between Python and Java. We anticipate more research in this area to extend our work.

Keywords: Energy consumption · Energy efficiency · Power consumption · Programming languages · Rapid review · Meta-analysis

1 Introduction

The Information and Communications Technology (ICT) sector used up to 4.6% of the global energy consumption in 2012 [99] and is increasing to higher rates [12]. In 2018, Google alone used ten TeraWatt-hours of energy [3] - more than what is annually consumed by the state of Hawaii [3,6]. The negative environmental repercussions led to governmental interventions with policies such as the European Code of Conduct for Data Centre Energy Efficiency [12]. The European Commission included in their 2020 "Key Actions" [33] that the ICT sector, particularly Data Centers, must achieve energy-efficiency and climate-neutrality by no later than 2030.

In the ICT sector, excessive energy usage translates into high financial cost implications for companies [2] and limits the workload and productivity in Data Centers [72]. Moreover, the ICT sector is estimated to contribute to more than 2% of the global carbon emissions [33]. Thus, reducing the energy consumption of computing systems has become a major undertaking for such industries

© Springer Nature Switzerland AG 2021
G. Succi et al. (Eds.): ICFSE 2021, CCIS 1523, pp. 176–200, 2021.
https://doi.org/10.1007/978-3-030-93135-3_12

[2]. Over the last decades, ICT companies became major investors in renewable energy to compensate for their environmental footprint via Power Purchase Agreements (PPA), especially the top hyperscale Data Center operators such as Amazon, Microsoft, and Google [2]. For instance, Google's "carbon offset purchases" match 100% of the energy consumed by their offices and Data Centers by funding renewable energy projects [3]. And while such efforts are of great impact, these companies cannot themselves rely on renewable energy and still have to majorly use grid suppliers at high financial and environmental costs.

Research has been carried in this area in efforts to reduce the energy of cloud systems and servers, many of which focus on platform optimizations through energy-aware resource management and task scheduling techniques [17,39,62,71]. But since Data Centers are house to software services, what are the implications of software development approaches and frameworks on the energy consumed by such computing systems? This question has been addressed in [20,22,23,26,27,34,45,53,59,60,64,65,74,75,83,84,91], especially in mobile development [18,21], showing that Software Architecture does factor in energy consumption as discussed by Jagroep et al. [43]. Thus, understanding such implications could help the developers in making informed design choices early on. According to a study by Manotas et al. [58] that surveyed employees from Google, ABB, Microsoft, and IBM, engineers are eager to adopt energy-efficient approaches in development and are open to change programming languages, however, they lack the necessary knowledge to do so. Thus, in our paper, we study the impact of programming languages on energy consumption. For that, we conduct a review of studies carried out in this area and a meta-analytical comparison of two languages that are widely-used, especially, in Data Centers software systems.

The Stack Overflow Developer Survey [7] surveyed in 2020 nearly 65,000 developer. The results showed that the majority of respondents used JavaScript (67.7%), Python (44.1%), Java (40.2%), C# (31.4%), PHP (26.2%), C++ (23.9%), and C (21.8%). Other programming languages included Go (8.8%), Rust (5.1%), Swift (6.1%), Perl (3.1%), Ruby (7.5%), and Haskell (2.1%) were.

Accordingly, we compare Python and Java, two of the most widely-used programming languages, making their comparison a necessity in this study. The majority of the Big Data Analytics stack lives in the Java ecosystem [61,86] with Python also integrating some libraries for Big Data [61] such as Pyspark [40,94]. For instance, in 2019, the FANG giant Netflix stated that they rely on Python in Big Data Orchestration and Data Analytics [5]. Scala is another language used in Big Data. Gupta and Kumari [40] compared Scala with Python in terms of how they use Apache Spark, a framework used in processing large data, while Omar et al. [70] compared Scala with Java in terms of time performance in Apache Spark MLlib and Hadoop HDFS. Moreover, in the realm of Machine Learning (ML), Python has become a de-facto language [80]. Netflix also uses it in their Personalization ML infrastructure for marketing and recommendation systems and even in Video Encoding and Information Security [5]. Nevertheless, Java has also grown to include tools for ML and Deep Learning, beyond the ML tool

Weka, such as Deeplearning4j, RapidMiner (Deep Learning, ML, text mining), and Stanford CoreNLP libraries. Therefore, there is a need to compare these two languages, and in this study, we investigate their energy-efficiency through meta-analysis.

Meta-analysis is a statistical tool that aggregates empirical results from "combinable" primary studies. Its application in Software Engineering research is an emerging area that was adopted from Medicine and Psychology in the mid-90's according to Sheppard et al. [90]. With this paper, we aim to further popularize the application of meta-analysis in this discipline. Accordingly, the contribution of this study is:

Firstly, a Rapid Review that aims to answer the following research questions:

RQ1 *What are the existing studies on the energy consumption of programming languages?*
RQ2 *What are the widely studied programming languages with respect to energy?*
RQ3 *What are the widely used energy/power units in energy vs. language experiments?*

Secondly, to use meta-analysis in testing the hypothesis:

H_0: *There is no significant difference in Energy Consumption between Python and Java*
with the alternative one:
H_1: *There is a significant difference in Energy Consumption between Python and Java*

This paper is organized as follows: Sect. 2 provides examples of primary and secondary studies related to the impact of languages on energy consumption, Sect. 3 presents our Review and meta-analysis methodologies, Sect. 4 reports the Review results and the meta-analytical comparison of the energy consumption of Java and Python, then Sect. 5 is the discussion. The paper is concluded in Sect. 6 with possible future research directions.

2   Related Work

To the best of our knowledge, our paper is the first to apply meta-analysis to compare Python and Java in terms of energy consumption. We also believe that it is the second meta-analytical study after the work of Kholmatova [49] to compare languages or energy consumption in software. This study [49] used Google Scholar and snowballing to search for papers related to software development and energy consumption between the years 2010 and 2020. In this study, Kholmatova uses the Random Effects Model to compare Java vs C++ and Java vs C, three languages used in Android Mobile Development. The meta-analysis showed that the studies are homogeneous and no significant differences in energy consumption.

Nevertheless, there are meta-analytical studies that investigated other themes in the Software Engineering discipline. Kakarla et al. [46] compared two fault-based testing techniques: Mutation vs Data-flow, showing that Mutation is more effective while Data-Flow is more efficient. Lu et al. [56] investigated the ability of 62 Object-Oriented metrics to predict change-prone classes. They found that the Size metrics Stmts (The number of declarations and executable statements in methods of a class) and SLOC (non-commentary Source Lines of Code) had the best predictive abilities whereas Inheritance metrics had the lowest. Yi et al. [102] proposed a unique usage and technique in meta-analysis to mine hypotheses and applied it to a literature of software defect prediction. Their results showed that three out of the five generated hypotheses were indeed studied by other papers. Hosseini et al. [41] compared two defect prediction techniques which rely on using training data either from external projects or from the same project. The results showed that WPDP (within project defect prediction) outperforms CPDP (cross project defect prediction).

On the other hand, there are primary studies that compared languages, particularly Python and Java, in different environments which we identified in our review and meta-analysis. In 2017 Georgiou et al. [38] compared 14 programming languages executing nine different small tasks and reported Swift as the most energy consuming. Pereira et al. [77] compared 27 software languages running three different benchmarks. Their experiments reported Java in the fifth place while Python was second to last with considerably higher energy. In 2020, Kesrouani et al. [47] compared languages in terms of recursive vs. iterative implementations with Java and Python consuming the most energy compared to C++, C, and Ocaml. Georgiou et al. [36] compared languages in different platforms (Intel and ARM) across three Inter-Process Communication ipc technologies. Then in 2021, Pereira et al. [78] extended their benchmarks to nine in total (reported in this paper). Out of 15 languages, Java ranked 10th overall, while C and Python were the most and least energy-efficient respectively. More information on these five papers are found in our meta-analysis results (Sect. 4).

Finally, a comparative analysis between Python and Java was carried out by Khoirom et al. [48] where the interchangeability of Python and Java in areas such as Web Development and Machine Learning was compared based on code size, execution time, memory consumption, robustness, and reliability, but not energy.

3   Methodology

The review aims to bring insight to researchers and developers by synthesizing studies that answer our RQs [51]. The meta-analysis estimates the difference in energy consumed by Java and Python. Our approach is explained in detail in the next sections.

3.1 Literature Review

A Systematic Literature Review (SLR) is a rigorous means of synthesizing studies to answer a research question. In their tertiary study, Kitchenham et al. [52] add that SLRs promote the abidance of research to evidence-based guidelines, particularly, in Software Engineering.

We chose to conduct a Rapid Review due to time constraints. Cochrane defines Rapid Reviews to be "a form of knowledge synthesis that accelerates the process of conducting a traditional systematic review through streamlining or omitting specific methods to produce evidence for stakeholders in a resource-efficient manner [35]".

A review protocol is integral in SLRs to reduce *Researcher Bias* [51]. In our protocol and review methodology, we use as a guideline an abbreviated version of Kitchenham's *Procedure for Performing Systematic Reviews* [51] in the Software Engineering field.

Search Strategy. Preliminary searches, from IEEE, WOS, and ACM, among other journals, were done by the authors to investigate the existing studies related to our RQs and identify the common keywords for our search (Table 1). We define the Boolean Strings in Sect. 4 Table 4 following the PICO approach [66] to conduct the search.

Table 1. RQs and keywords

RQs	Keywords
RQ1	Energy, consumption, programming languages
RQ2	Programming languages, energy
RQ3	Energy, power, efficiency, programming languages

The search criteria is:

- Language: English
- Date Frame: 2011–2021
- Search Method: Sort by relevance

Our chosen electronic database is: Google Scholar. We further conduct a limited targeted search on IEEE and ACM Digital Library and Backward Snowballing only for papers with possibly relevant titles/keywords to the RQs. Backward Snowballing is the inspection of reference lists from relevant works to mine additional primary studies [101], which, according to Kitchenham [51], is a must in Systematic Literature Reviews.

- **Google Scholar:** 10 pages. Select all the papers appearing on the search page.
- **IEEE and ACM:** one search page per engine. Select a limited number of papers.

Inclusion and Exclusion Criteria. The Cochrane Rapid Reviews guide explains that a mandatory standard in SLRs is to define clear inclusion and exclusion criteria. According to Cochrane's recommendations, they should also be defined in the protocol of Rapid Reviews [35].

Defining pre-set criteria minimizes *Researcher Bias* [51] in reviews. Moreover, they allow to stay within the scope of the RQs and the PICO (**P**opulation, **I**ntervention, **C**omparators, and **O**utcomes) elements of the search. Sheppard et al. [90] explains that the collected literature must be scanned against these criteria to remove the irrelevant and low-quality papers because they can "contaminate" the results of the review and the meta-analyses. Following are our defined criteria that have to all be met:

1. Inclusion criteria
   - Paper describes the experiment
   - Paper reports empirical results of the energy of programming languages
   - Paper compares at least two high level programming languages
2. Exclusion criteria
   - Grey literature, non-research articles papers

Kitchenham [51] notes that *Publication Bias* can lead to a bias in the review. This occurs because the studies that reject the null hypothesis are more likely to be published compared to those that report negative results. She states that conference proceedings could address this bias, hence why we decided to include them in our review.

Quality Assessment. Quality Assessment applies narrower criteria. A quality instrument was agreed upon by the authors following some of the quality guidelines of empirical studies specified by Kitchenham et al. [50]. The questions were scored with "yes" or "no". The paper is included only if all the three questions are answered positively.

Table 2. Quality assessment questions for the review

QA	QA question
Context guidelines	Is the hypothesis clearly/implicitly stated?
Data collection guidelines	Are the software measures and their units clearly defined in the experiment? (e.g. Power (W), Energy (J), EDP, EE%..)
Presentation guidelines*	Are the quantitative results presented?

When it comes to the Study Designs, all levels of evidence, except for the Expert Opinion, were considered as this is usually the norm in Software Engineering [51]. If a primary study has more than one version, the latest is chosen.

Data Extraction. After collecting studies from the search, we extract the necessary data to scan these studies against the pre-defined criteria and the QA instrument. Moreover, Kitchenham [51] explains that designing a Data Extraction form for the review reduces the possibility of bias. The following form was piloted among the authors on a sample of studies to ensure clarity and robustness. We extract this information mainly from the abstract, experiment, and the conclusion:

- The title, year of publication, and journal
- A description of: the goal, the experiment and energy units, and the result.
- Is the experiment related to energy consumption in computing systems?
- Is the experiment is related to energy vs. programming languages?

3.2   Meta-analysis

Meta-analysis is an optional part of a systematic review [66]. While our review attempts to answer Research Questions from the literature, meta-analysis is a statistical tool with a limited focus and a specific hypothesis [90]. As Sheppard et al. [90] explain, it encompasses two purposes: (1) assessing a common Effect Size among primary studies, and (2) assessing and analyzing heterogeneity between studies with the I^2 statistic. In the following sub-sections, we explain in detail our meta-analytical methodology.

Quality Assessment. The quality assessment applies criteria that are even narrower than the review ones. In addition to the QA questions in Table 2, the Presentation Guidelines are updated in QA1 of Table 3 which was chosen from the checklist compiled by Kitchenham et al. [50].

Table 3. Quality assessment questions for the review

QA	QA question
QA1	Does the paper provide the mean and standard deviation or the necessary values to compute them? (Units limited to Joules for energy)
QA2	Does the paper report more than two experiments per language?

Due to the limited number of papers found in our search that compared Python and Java, we added two more specific search strings which are in Table 5. The search was conducted following the same protocol, but the exclusion was performed during the search rather than after the data collection.

The paper is **included** if (1) its preview on Google Scholar shows the terms "python" and "java", (2) the title is relevant, and if (3) it passes the review inclusion criteria.

The paper is **excluded** if (1) it appeared in our initial search, or if (2) it passed the review exclusion criteria.

Finally, the paper is **included to meta-analysis** if it passes the Review QA (Table 2) and the meta-analysis QA (Table 3).

Data Extraction Steps. For the review, we extract information that allow the authors to include or exclude a given paper to/from the review. In this sub-section, we define the numerical values that are a prerequisite to conducting our meta-analysis [51].

After scrutinizing the papers against the meta-analysis Quality Assessment, for each group (Python and Java) in a given study, we collect the following data:

- **n:** The number of experiments per group.
- x_i: The reported energy consumption (Joules) per experiment in a group

From this, we calculate the following for each group (Python and Java) in each study:

- **Mean:** The mean energy consumption of a group's experiments: $\bar{x} = \sum_{i=1}^{n} \frac{x_i}{n}$
- **SD:** Standard Deviation in the group: $S = \sum_{i=1}^{n} \frac{(x_i - \bar{x})^2}{(n-1)}$.

The Meta-analysis Steps. *Effect Sizes* represent the difference in energy consumption between the two languages in each study (with an independence assumption of the groups). Besides the sampling error, there is a high likelihood that co-variates exist in experiments. Therefore, we assume that each paper is estimating a different true effect, and it is generally assumed that these true effects are normally distributed [13]. Therefore, our *Summary Effect* estimates the mean μ of the distribution of the true effects Δ_i.

Hence, we use the Random Effects Model (REM) to estimate the distribution of true effects. For each study, the Effect Size is Hedge's g Standardized Mean Difference that estimates Δ_i - the study's true mean difference (true effect). Following are the calculation steps of the Effect Size g and its standard deviation SE_g [13]:

$$g - J \times d \tag{1}$$

where j is Hedge's correction factor:

$$J = 1 - \frac{3}{4df - 1} \tag{2}$$

d is Cohen's standardized difference of the sample means:

$$d = \frac{\bar{X}_1 - \bar{X}_2}{S_{\text{within}}} \tag{3}$$

and S_{within} being the pooled within-groups standard deviation (SD), with an assumption that $\sigma_1 = \sigma_2$. S_1 and S_2 are the SDs in the two groups and n_1 and n_2 are the number of experiments per group.

$$S_{\text{within}} = \sqrt{\frac{(n_1 - 1) S_1^2 + (n_2 - 1) S_2^2}{n_1 + n_2 - 2}} \tag{4}$$

The variance and standard deviation of each Effect Size g is:

$$V_g = J^2 \times V_d \tag{5}$$

$$SE_g = \sqrt{V_g} \tag{6}$$

where V_d is the variance of Cohen's d:

$$V_d = \frac{n_1 + n_2}{n_1 n_2} + \frac{d^2}{2(n_1 + n_2)} \tag{7}$$

Finally, each study's weight is calculated as:

$$W_i^* = \frac{1}{V_{g_i}^*} \tag{8}$$

$$V_{g_i}^* = V_{g_i} + T^2 \tag{9}$$

V_{g_i} is the within-study variance (Eq. 5) and T^2 is the between-studies variance (Eq. 11).

The variation in a study's observed effect g_i, as illustrated in Eq. 10, is due to: (1) ε_i: The distance of the study's observed effect from the true effect, and (2) ζ_i: The distance of the true effect from the mean of its True Distribution. ζ_i depends on τ^2 - the standard deviation of this distribution.

$$g_i = \mu + \zeta_i + \varepsilon_i \tag{10}$$

We estimate τ^2 with T^2 using the DerSimonian and Laird method:

$$T^2 = (Q - df)/C \tag{11}$$

where, given k is the number of studies, Q, df, and C are:

$$Q = \sum_{i=1}^{k} W_i g_i^2 - \frac{\left(\sum_{i=1}^{k} W_i g_i\right)^2}{\sum_{i=1}^{k} W_i} \tag{12}$$

$$df = k - 1 \tag{13}$$

$$C = \sum W_i - \frac{\sum W_i^2}{\sum W_i} \tag{14}$$

T^2 is the between-studies variance and is used in each study's weight calculation. The Summary Effect estimating μ is the Weighted Mean M^* of these weights W_i^* (Eq. 15).

$$M^* = \frac{\sum_{i=1}^{k} W_i^* g_i}{\sum_{i=1}^{k} W_i^*} \tag{15}$$

The meta-analysis reports M^* and a 95% Confidence Interval for a two-tailed test calculated from the estimated standard error of the summary effect SE_{M^*}.

$$V_{M^*} = \frac{1}{\sum_{i=1}^{k} W_i^*} \tag{16}$$

$$SE_{M^*} = \sqrt{V_{M^*}} \tag{17}$$

$$M^* \pm 1.96 \times SE_{M^*} \tag{18}$$

Table 4. Review search strings

Search string	#pages	Search engine	#papers	#unique
((energy OR power) (consumption OR efficiency)) AND "programming language"	5	Google scholars	49	27
(compare programming language) AND ((energy OR power) (consumption OR efficiency))	2	Google scholars	24	12
((energy OR power) AND (consumption OR efficiency)) AND ("programming languages")	3	Google scholars	27	10
((energy OR power) (consumption OR efficiency)) AND (programming languages)	1*	IEEEexplore	10	6
((energy consumption) OR (power consumption)) AND (programming languages)	1*	ACM digital library	6	4

4 Results

4.1 The Rapid Review

In our review, we collected 85 papers. As specified in Table 4, out of these papers, 59 were uniquely found from one string. The other 26 papers were found from more than one string. Out of the relevant papers to our RQs, we performed Backward Snowballing. We have found three papers, but they did not pass the Inclusion and QA criteria.

After applying the Review Quality Assessment (Sect. 3), 17 papers were included to the review: 16 primary studies and one meta-analysis. Figure 1 shows the distribution of languages across the primary studies, giving insight in regards to our RQ2, while Table 2 shows the most widely used energy/power units in the

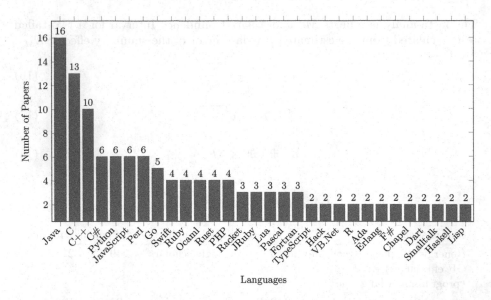

Fig. 1. Distribution of the programming languages across papers (after review QA)

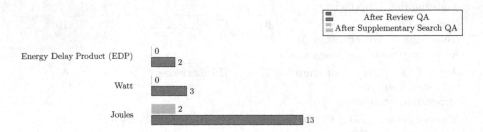

Fig. 2. Distribution of energy/power units

16 primary studies to answer RQ3. Some papers reported their results in more than one unit. The distribution of the years and journals across the 17 papers are in Figs. 3 and 4 respectively.

The literature shows that most of the papers compared Java, C, and C++ (RQ2). All the 17 studies included Java in their comparisons. To test these languages, the papers mostly relied on micro-benching for instance The Computer Language Benchmarks Game (CLBG) [1]: [24,25,28,68,69,77] and Rosetta [4]: [37,38,68,78]. Some compared the languages across different sorting algorithms [15,38,44,81]. To present insights with regards to RQ1, following are some of the papers and their results on energy consumption:

1. **Java, C, C++**
   - Corral et al. [24]: C is "more economic" than Java.
   - Corral et al. [25]: Native and Regular C consume significantly less than Java.

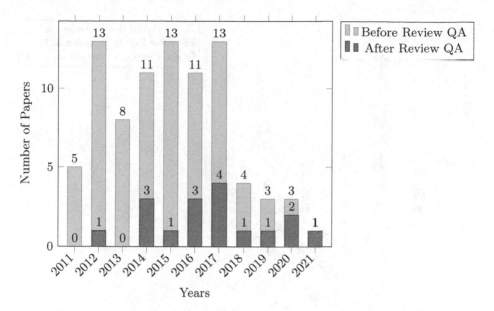

Fig. 3. Distribution of papers by publication year (before and after review QA)

- Rashid et al. [81]: C consumes significantly less than Java.
- Chen et al. [16]: C and C++ consume less than Java.
- Magalhães [57]: C consumes less than Java and C++ and is better in EDP.
- Kholmatova [49] (meta-analysis): no significant difference between Java and: C and C++

2. **Java, C, C++, C#**
   - Georgiou et al. [37]: C and C# are the best in terms of EDP.
   - Couto et al. [28]: C first, Java second, C# forth in energy efficiency.
   - Jain et al. [44]: C# first, Java second, C++ third in energy efficiency.
   - Chandra et al. [15]: Java consumes less than C#.Net.

3. **Java, C, C++, Python**
   - Abdulsalam et al. [9]: C++ and C: consume less than Java. Python consumes the most.
   - Noureddine et al. [67]: In default setting, Java consumes the least. With the GNU Compiler Collection (GCC) compiler option O3, C++ consumes the least, and C consumes less than Java. Python is the second worst in consumption.
   - Pereira et al. [77]: C consumes the least. C++ consumes less than Java. All were in the Top-5 energy-efficient languages. C# ranked 13th preceded by compiled languages (except two VM languages: Java and Lisp). Python is the second worst in consumption.

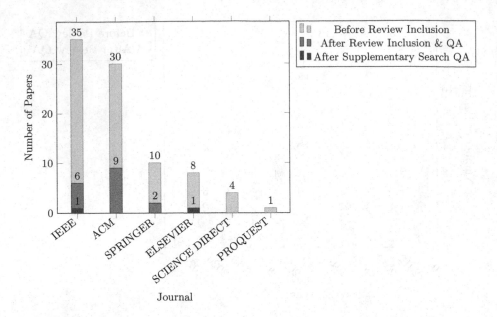

Fig. 4. Distribution of publishing journals across papers

- Pereira et al. [78]: C consumes the least. Python is the worst in consumption. C++ consumes less than Java.
- Georgiou et al. [38]: no significant results between Java and: C and C++. **Compiled:** Java and Rust consume the most, Go the least. **Interpreted:** Python, Perl, Swift consume the most, JavaScript, PhP, Ruby the least. Java consumes less than Python.

4. **Java, C, C++, JavaScript**
   - Oliveira et al. [69]: JavaScript is more EE than Java.
   - Oliveira et al. [68]: JavaScript is more EE than C++ and Java.
   - Georgiou et al. [37]: C, C#, and JavaScript are on overall the best **compiled, semi-compiled**, and **interpreted** languages in terms of energy. Python and Java were not in Top-5. Python consumed less than Java.

Chen et al. [16], Abdulsalam et al. [9], Georgiou et al. [37], and Georgiou et al. [38] categorized the compared languages to: **compiled** (e.g. C, C++) versus **interpreted** (e.g. JavaScript, Python). It should be noted that some papers consider the **semi-compiled** languages (e.g. Java, C#) as compiled ones. All these papers report that the compiled languages are the most energy efficient. Pereira et al. [77] and Couto et al. [28] also concluded that compiled languages consumed the least energy.

Pereira et al. [77] classified the languages by paradigm: **Functional, Imperative, Object-Oriented**, and **Scripting**. They found that the bottom-5 in terms of energy-efficiency are all interpreted (Perl, Python, Ruby, JRuby, and Lua). Java was the 5th most energy-efficient and the only Top-5 non-compiled language, preceded by C, Rust, C++, and Ada.

4.2 The Meta-analysis

The Eligible Papers. From our supplementary search, we found two papers, **P4** and **P5**, which we added to our meta-analytical comparison. Both of the papers were published in 2020, and their corresponding publishing journals are in the histogram Fig. 4. Backward Snowballing did not yield additional papers.

Table 5. Supplementary search strings

Search strings	#pages	#papers
energy ("consumption" or "efficiency") "python" "java"	15	1
("compare" or "comparison") ("python" and "java") AND (energy ("consumption" or "efficiency"))	10	1

The papers that are eligible for the meta-analysis are:

– **P1:** Analyzing Programming Languages' Energy Consumption: An Empirical Study (Georgiou et al. [38], 2017)
– **P2:** Energy Efficiency across Programming Languages: How Do Energy, Time, and Memory Relate? (Pereira et al. [77], 2017)
– **P3:** Ranking programming languages by energy efficiency (Pereira et al. [78], 2021)
– **P4:** Energy-Delay investigation of Remote Inter-Process communication technologies (Georgiou et al. [36], 2020)
– **P5:** A Preliminary Study of the Energy Impact of Software in Raspberry Pi devices (Kesrouani et al. [47], 2020)

In **P1** [38], nine different tasks from Rosetta Code [4] were implemented with languages including Java and Python. The languages were grouped into compiled and interpreted. The total energy consumption when using compiled languages seems to be much lower compared to that of the interpreted ones. For interpreted languages in **P1**, Python showed a considerably high average energy consumption compared to other interpreted languages in the experiments. It is noteworthy that the experiments for each task and programming language was performed in the same environment.

Similarly to **P1**, it is found in **P2** [77] that compiled languages are more energy-efficient compared to interpreted languages. Performance (including energy and speed) were measured for different programming problems using the *Computer Language Benchmarks Game* [1]. In this study, the top five energy efficient programming languages, all compiled, consumed the least amount of memory space on average, which reckons a direct relationship between energy efficiency and memory usage. Java was the only hybrid (compiled and interpreted) language in this top five list. **P3** [78] also presented that interpreted languages consume more energy compared to compiled languages, with Python at the bottom, being the least energy efficient language.

The experiments in **P4** [36] were performed on computer platforms equipped with Intel and ARM processors and based on the popular Inter-Process Communication (`ipc`) systems implemented in Go, Java, JavaScript, Python, PHP, Ruby, and C#. The study found that JavaScript and Go implementations offer the lowest energy consumption and execution time. The authors of **P4** further analysed system call traces and found that inefficient use of system calls can contribute to increased energy consumption and poor execution time.

P5 [47] presented a software-based and multi-formulas power estimation model according to CPU utilization. The experiments extracted from **P5** were on Fibonacci and Tower of Hanoi with separate recursive and iterative implementations respectively. In these experiments, Java was found to be least energy efficient of other programming languages. Second to Java was Python. The exception was in the recursive Fibonacci experiment in which Python consumed more energy.

In our meta-analysis, we separate the experiments in **P4** and **P5** by platform type and algorithm implementation respectively. **P4** performed two experiments: one on two Intel systems (client and server) and the other on two ARM systems (client and server), and they retrieved measurements from the clients and the servers separately. Therefore, we considered them as four different experimental environments in our meta-analysis. We aggregated across the three Inter-Process Communication (`ipc`) technologies studied in this paper. As for **P5**, because the languages consumed considerably more energy on average in the recursive compared to the iterative implementations and because the experiments were repeated 200 times, we decided to separate them into two experimental environments in our meta-analysis to highlight that difference.

The Forest Plot. We visualize and contextualize the meta-analysis with a Forest Plot (Fig. 5) using the `metacont` function from the R library `meta`. `Total` is the number of experiments per group (Python or Java), `Mean` is the mean energy of all the experiments for one group (Python or Java) in a given study, and `SD` is its standard deviation (with Basel's correction). `SMD` are Hedge's standardized mean differences g between each two groups (Python and Java) of a study. I^2 is the percentage of the observed difference in the true effects that is not caused by sampling error. It is a descriptive statistic and not an estimate.

- **Effect Sizes**
  - Squares: opposite to each study is a square. It reflects the contribution of the study to the Summary Effect. The bigger its size, the bigger the study's weight.
  - Horizontal Lines: represent the 95% Confidence Interval of the study. The narrower the line, the higher its precision.

- Vertical Line: represents the null line, i.e. the standardized mean difference is 0
- **The Summary Effect**
  - Diamond: represents the summary effect
  - Diamond width: represents the 95% Confidence Interval. The narrower the width, the higher the precision.

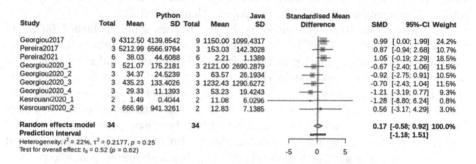

Study	Total	Python Mean	SD	Total	Java Mean	SD	Standardised Mean Difference	SMD	95%-CI	Weight
Georgiou2017	9	4312.50	4139.8542	9	1150.00	1099.4317		0.99	[0.00; 1.99]	24.2%
Pereira2017	3	5212.99	6566.9764	3	153.03	142.3028		0.87	[-0.94; 2.68]	10.7%
Pereira2021	6	38.03	44.6088	6	2.21	1.1389		1.05	[-0.19; 2.29]	18.5%
Georgiou2020_1	3	521.07	175.2181	3	2121.00	2690.2879		-0.67	[-2.40; 1.06]	11.5%
Georgiou2020_2	3	34.37	24.5239	3	63.57	26.1934		-0.92	[-2.75; 0.91]	10.5%
Georgiou2020_3	3	435.23	133.4026	3	1232.43	1290.6272		-0.70	[-2.43; 1.04]	11.5%
Georgiou2020_4	3	29.33	11.1393	3	53.23	19.4243		-1.21	[-3.19; 0.77]	9.3%
Kesrouani2020_1	2	1.49	0.4044	2	11.08	6.0296		-1.28	[-8.80; 6.24]	0.8%
Kesrouani2020_2	2	666.96	941.3261	2	12.83	7.1385		0.56	[-3.17; 4.29]	3.0%
Random effects model	**34**			**34**				0.17	[-0.58; 0.92]	100.0%
Prediction interval									[-1.18; 1.51]	

Heterogeneity: $I^2 = 22\%$, $\tau^2 = 0.2177$, $p = 0.25$
Test for overall effect: $t_8 = 0.52$ ($p = 0.62$)

Fig. 5. Meta-analysis forest plot: Python vs Java

We observe that all the studies include the null value, hence, they all report statistically non-significant results. The summary effect crosses the null line and has a $p - value = 0.62$, therefore, **we do not reject our null hypothesis that there is no difference in energy consumption between Python and Java**. I^2 reflects the amount of overlap between the studies' confidence intervals. Our value is less than 25% indicating a low heterogeneity [14].

5   Discussion

In this section, we discuss our findings from the review of the studies that passed Quality Assessment and the results obtained from meta-analysis.

5.1   Discussion of the Review

The programming languages found in the reviewed studies were compared in different aspects including energy consumption, speed, memory usage, CPU usage, and execution time. The languages and programming tasks were also categorized into: compiled and interpreted, functional and object oriented, native vs cross-platform frameworks, recursive vs iterative algorithms, etc.

A total of 85 unique papers were collected using the search strings in Table 4. Out of these, 17 passed the review Quality Assessment: 16 primary studies and 1 meta-analysis. 52.94% of the papers were published by ACM followed by IEEE (35.29%) after QA. To answer our RQ1, the papers gathered in this study benchmark programming languages in isolation (as a standalone tool) without taking into account the various fields of application of these languages. None of the papers reviewed used heavy data processing tasks or ML algorithms as benchmarks to compare languages such as Python, Scala, R, Java, C++. It could be opined that performing such benchmarks requires some expertise in the area. Therefore, more research should be carried out to compare or determine the energy efficiency of programming languages using real applications as benchmarks. In these benchmarks, different units of measurements were used including EDP, Watt, and Joules. To answer our RQ3, Joules was the most-widely used unit of measurement (81.25%) in the papers that passed QA.

To answer our RQ2, the majority of the papers studied Java (100%), C (81.25%), and C++ (62.50%), with respect to energy consumption. This can be attributed to their popularity in the software development industry [7,8]. The languages that were reported in these papers to be the most energy-efficient, such as C++, have not yet gained a large adoption by the community for Machine Learning (ML) or Big Data tasks in which Python and Java are popular [103]. This is due to the relative difficulties in language presentation (syntax and semantics), learning curve, maintainability (bulkiness and readability), and language level (low-level or high-level) [10]. Python's simple syntax allows for a more natural and intuitive ETL (Extract, Transform, Load) process and means that it is faster for development when compared to C++. The State of the Developer Nation Q3 2020 report by Developer Economics [8] surveyed more than 17,000 developers from 159 countries and reported that Python is the most popular language in Data Science (DS) and ML among developers. According to this survey, 77% of ML developers and Data Scientists use Python and only 22% use R. Moreover, while Java was reported to be the next overall popular language after Python, the survey showed that it is most popular in cloud systems and one of the least popular in DS and ML. This could be due to its structure complexity compared to Python [48]. Thus, the popularity of Python in ML is, again, attributed to its simplicity and readability. It is noteworthy to point out that popular Python libraries like Numpy, Scipy, Sklearn, and Cython used in ML have bindings to other languages like C, C++, and Fortran. It is clear that the inter-operability between C or C++ and other high-level Languages commonly used in ML or data processing makes it an interesting topic for further investigation [82].

Other programming languages like Scala, which is widely compared with Java and Python, would have been a good additional subject in our meta-analysis but proved impossible due to the limited research carried out on them.

5.2   Discussion of the Meta-analysis

The meta-analysis resulted in a non-rejection of our null hypothesis, showing no significant difference in the energy consumed due to using Python or Java. The weights of the studies rely on the within-study standard deviation. The lower the variance, the higher the precision and the higher the weight. Therefore, a higher number of experiments (Total) also contributes positively to the weight. We notice, nevertheless, that all of the studies confidence intervals cross the null line, and therefore, none of them report significant differences. Moreover, the I^2 statistic is less than 25% indicating that the studies are homogeneous, and therefore, the variability between them is non-significant.

It is also worth noting that all of these five papers relied on testing on micro-benchmarks rather than real applications, which according to Sahin et al. [87], leads to different results. Therefore, it is unclear whether or not these results generalize to large scale inputs and intensive computations commonly used in Data Centers such as Big Data tasks.

6 Conclusion

In this paper, we reviewed the impact of programming languages on energy consumption and used meta-analysis to compare it between Python and Java. We found no significant difference between them.

Because we did not conduct a Systematic Literature Review, our study is limited by the number of pages per search string investigated. Hence, we only found 17 relevant studies for the review. We also only found five papers for the meta-analysis which could be due to Python being a newly adopted language. Moreover, Rapid Reviews are known to bring about *Selection Bias*. We aim to having addressed the *Publication Bias* by considering Conference Papers in the inclusion criteria, which is, according to Kitchenham [51], a means to tackle it. By using a Review Protocol, we aim to also having reduced the possibility of a *Researcher Bias* [51]. In spite of these possible limitations, we believe that our results are of value. With this paper, we also encourage the usage of meta-analysis in Software Engineering and shed the light on a serious problem in software and system engineering, that of excessive energy dissipation [30,55].

For future research, we look forward to more comparative primary studies between these two languages to extend our meta-analysis. In a similar vein, Scala is a widely-used language in Big Data, yet we did not find studies in our review that compared it in terms of energy efficiency. Thus, we encourage research on it [19,29,54,63,73,76,79,85,88,89,92,93,95–98,100]. We also anticipate that studies do not only rely on micro-benchmarks for testing and to extend the research by using real applications [11,31,32,42] or long and intensive computations to simulate large scale data processing and analytics and Deep Learning tasks. Finally, since energy consumption is also a concern in mobile devices, we anticipate more research that compare the languages and frameworks used within iOS (e.g. Swift, Objective-C, cross-platform) and Android development (Java, Kotlin, cross-platform).

Acknowledgements. This research was funded by Russian Science Foundation grant number № 19-19-00623.

References

1. The computer language benchmarks game. https://benchmarksgame-team.pages. debian.net/benchmarksgame/index.html. Accessed 16 Mar 2021

2. Data centres and data transmission networks. https://www.iea.org/reports/data-centres-and-data-transmission-networks. Accessed 17 Mar 2021
3. Google environmental report 2019. https://sustainability.google/reports/environmental-report-2019. Accessed 17 Mar 2021
4. Rosetta code. https://rosettacode.org/wiki/Rosetta_Code. Accessed 16 Mar 2021
5. Python at netflix, April 2019. https://netflixtechblog.com/python-at-netflix-bba45dae649e
6. State electricity profiles, U.S. energy information administration (2019). http://www.eia.gov/electricity/state. Accessed 17 Mar 2021
7. Stack overflow developer survey (2020). https://insights.stackoverflow.com/survey/2020/
8. State of the developer nation 19th edition - Q3 2020, slashdata - developer economics (2020). https://www.developereconomics.com/resources/reports/state-of-the-developer-nation-q3-20201. Accessed 14 Mar 2021
9. Abdulsalam, S., Lakomski, D., Gu, Q., Jin, T., Zong, Z.: Program energy efficiency: the impact of language, compiler and implementation choices. In: International Green Computing Conference, pp. 1–6 (2014). https://doi.org/10.1109/IGCC.2014.7039169
10. Ateeq, M., Habib, H., Umer, A., Rehman, M.U.: C++ or Python? Which one to begin with: a learners perspective. In: International Conference on Teaching and Learning in Computing and Engineering (2014)
11. Atonge, D., et al.: The Development of Data Collectors in Open-Source System for Energy Efficiency Assessment, pp. 14–24. Springer, Heidelberg (2020)
12. Avgerinou, M., Bertoldi, P., Castellazzi, L.: Trends in data centre energy consumption under the European code of conduct for data centre energy efficiency. Energies **10**(10) (2017). https://www.mdpi.com/1996-1073/10/10/1470
13. Borenstein, M., Hedges, L.V., Higgins, J.P.T., Rothstein, H.R.: Random-Effects Model, chap. 12, pp. 69–75. Wiley (2009). https://doi.org/10.1002/9780470743386.ch12. https://onlinelibrary.wiley.com/doi/abs/10.1002/9780470743386.ch12
14. Borenstein, M., Hedges, L.V., Higgins, J.P., Rothstein, H.R.: Identifying and Quantifying Heterogeneity, chap. 16, pp. 107–125. Wiley (2009). https://doi.org/10.1002/9780470743386.ch16. https://onlinelibrary.wiley.com/doi/abs/10.1002/9780470743386.ch16
15. Chandra, T.B., Verma, P., Dwivedi, A.K.: Impact of programming languages on energy consumption for sorting algorithms. In: Hoda, M.N., Chauhan, N., Quadri, S.M.K., Srivastava, P.R. (eds.) Software Engineering. AISC, vol. 731, pp. 93–101. Springer, Singapore (2019). https://doi.org/10.1007/978-981-10-8848-3_9
16. Chen, X., Zong, Z.: Android app energy efficiency: the impact of language, runtime, compiler, and implementation. In: 2016 IEEE International Conferences on Big Data and Cloud Computing (BDCloud), Social Computing and Networking (SocialCom), Sustainable Computing and Communications (SustainCom) (BDCloud-SocialCom-SustainCom), pp. 485–492 (2016). https://doi.org/10.1109/BDCloud-SocialCom-SustainCom.2016.77
17. Ciancarini, P., et al.: Analysis of energy consumption of software development process entities. Electronics **9**(10), 1678 (2020)
18. Ciancarini, P., Kruglov, A., Sadovykh, A., Succi, G., Zuev, E.: Elaborating validation scenarios based on the context analysis and combinatorial method: example of the power-efficiency framework innomterics. Electronics **9**(12), 2111 (2020)
19. Clark, J., et al.: Selecting components in large cots repositories. J. Syst. Softw. **73**(2), 323–331 (2004)

20. Coman, I.D., Robillard, P.N., Sillitti, A., Succi, G.: Cooperation, collaboration and pair-programming: field studies on backup behavior. J. Syst. Softw. **91**, 124–134 (2014)
21. Corbalan, L., et al.: Development frameworks for mobile devices: a comparative study about energy consumption. In: 2018 IEEE/ACM 5th International Conference on Mobile Software Engineering and Systems (MOBILESoft), pp. 191–201 (2018)
22. Corral, L., Georgiev, A.B., Sillitti, A., Succi, G.: A method for characterizing energy consumption in Android smartphones. In: 2nd International Workshop on Green and Sustainable Software (GREENS 2013), pp. 38–45. IEEE, May 2013
23. Corral, L., Georgiev, A.B., Sillitti, A., Succi, G.: Can execution time describe accurately the energy consumption of mobile apps? An experiment in Android. In: Proceedings of the 3rd International Workshop on Green and Sustainable Software, pp. 31–37. ACM (2014)
24. Corral, L., Georgiev, A.B., Sillitti, A., Succi, G.: Can execution time describe accurately the energy consumption of mobile apps? An experiment in android. In: Proceedings of the 3rd International Workshop on Green and Sustainable Software, GREENS 2014, pp. 31–37. Association for Computing Machinery, New York (2014). https://doi.org/10.1145/2593743.2593748
25. Corral, L., Georgiev, A.B., Sillitti, A., Succi, G.: Method reallocation to reduce energy consumption: an implementation in android OS. In: Proceedings of the 29th Annual ACM Symposium on Applied Computing, SAC 2014, pp. 1213–1218. Association for Computing Machinery, New York (2014). https://doi.org/10.1145/2554850.2555064
26. Corral, L., Sillitti, A., Succi, G.: Software assurance practices for mobile applications. Computing **97**(10), 1001–1022 (2015)
27. Corral, L., Sillitti, A., Succi, G., Garibbo, A., Ramella, P.: Evolution of mobile software development from platform-specific to web-based multiplatform paradigm. In: Proceedings of the 10th SIGPLAN Symposium on New Ideas, New Paradigms, and Reflections on Programming and Software. Onward! 2011, pp. 181–183. ACM, New York (2011)
28. Couto, M., Pereira, R., Ribeiro, F., Rua, R., Saraiva, J.A.: Towards a green ranking for programming languages. In: Proceedings of the 21st Brazilian Symposium on Programming Languages, SBLP 2017. Association for Computing Machinery, New York (2017)
29. Di Bella, E., Sillitti, A., Succi, G.: A multivariate classification of open source developers. Inf. Sci. **221**, 72–83 (2013)
30. Ergasheva, S., Ivanov, V., Khomyakov, I., Kruglov, A., Strugar, D., Succi, G.: InnoMetrics dashboard: the design, and implementation of the adaptable dashboard for energy-efficient applications using open source tools. In: Ivanov, V., Kruglov, A., Masyagin, S., Sillitti, A., Succi, G. (eds.) OSS 2020. IAICT, vol. 582, pp. 163–176. Springer, Cham (2020). https://doi.org/10.1007/978-3-030-47240-5_16
31. Ergasheva, S., Kruglov, A., Shulhan, I.: Development and evaluation of GQM method to improve adaptive systems. In: ITTCS (2019)
32. Ergasheva, S., Strugar, D., Kruglov, A., Succi, G.: Energy efficient software development process evaluation for MacOS devices. In: Ivanov, V., Kruglov, A., Masyagin, S., Sillitti, A., Succi, G. (eds.) OSS 2020. IAICT, vol. 582, pp. 196–206. Springer, Cham (2020). https://doi.org/10.1007/978-3-030-47240-5_20

33. European Commission Directorate General for Communications Networks Content and Technology: Shaping Europe's Digital Future. Publications Office (2020). https://doi.org/10.2759/091014. https://data.europa.eu/doi/10.2759/091014

34. Fitzgerald, B., Kesan, J.P., Russo, B., Shaikh, M., Succi, G.: Adopting Open Source Software: A Practical Guide. The MIT Press, Cambridge (2011)

35. Garritty, C., et al.: Cochrane rapid reviews. interim guidance from the cochrane rapid reviews methods group, March 2020. https://methods.cochrane.org/rapidreviews/sites/methods.cochrane.org.rapidreviews/files/public/uploads/cochrane_rr_-_guidance-23mar2020-v1.pdf

36. Georgiou, S., Spinellis, D.: Energy-delay investigation of remote inter-process communication technologies. J. Syst. Softw. (2020). https://www.elsevier.com/locate/jss

37. Georgiou, S., Kechagia, M., Louridas, P., Spinellis, D.: What are your programming language's energy-delay implications? In: Proceedings of the 15th International Conference on Mining Software Repositories, MSR 2018, pp. 303–313. Association for Computing Machinery, New York (2018). https://doi.org/10.1145/3196398.3196414

38. Georgiou, S., Kechagia, M., Spinellis, D.: Analyzing programming languages' energy consumption: an empirical study. In: Proceedings of the 21st Pan-Hellenic Conference on Informatics, PCI 2017, Association for Computing Machinery, New York (2017). https://doi.org/10.1145/3139367.3139418

39. Gourisaria, M.K., Patra, S.S., Khilar, P.M.: Energy saving task consolidation technique in cloud centers with resource utilization threshold. In: Saeed, K., Chaki, N., Pati, B., Bakshi, S., Mohapatra, D.P. (eds.) Progress in Advanced Computing and Intelligent Engineering. AISC, vol. 563, pp. 655–666. Springer, Singapore (2018). https://doi.org/10.1007/978-981-10-6872-0_63

40. Gupta, Y.K., Kumari, S.: A study of big data analytics using apache spark with Python and Scala. In: 2020 3rd International Conference on Intelligent Sustainable Systems (ICISS), pp. 471–478 (2020). https://doi.org/10.1109/ICISS49785.2020.9315863

41. Hosseini, S., Turhan, B., Gunarathna, D.: A systematic literature review and meta-analysis on cross project defect prediction. IEEE Trans. Softw. Eng. **45**(2), 111–147 (2019). https://doi.org/10.1109/TSE.2017.2770124

42. Ivanov, V., Kruglov, A., Sadovykh, A., Succi, G.: Scenarios for the evaluation of the energy efficiency of mobile applications. In: 2019 IEEE 10th Annual Information Technology, Electronics and Mobile Communication Conference (IEMCON), pp. 0595–0601 (2019)

43. Jagroep, E., van der Werf, J.M., Brinkkemper, S., Blom, L., van Vliet, R.: Extending software architecture views with an energy consumption perspective. Computing **99**(6), 553–573 (2016). https://doi.org/10.1007/s00607-016-0502-0

44. Jain, D., Shukla, R.K., Tomar, M.S., Sharma, P.: A study of the impact of programming language selection on CO2 emission - a green IT initiative. In: 2nd International Conference on Data, Engineering and Applications (IDEA), pp. 1–5 (2020). https://doi.org/10.1109/IDEA49133.2020.9170668

45. Janes, A., Succi, G.: Lean Software Development in Action. Springer, Heidelberg (2014). https://doi.org/10.1007/978-3-642-00503-9

46. Kakarla, S., Momotaz, S., Namin, A.S.: An evaluation of mutation and data-flow testing: a meta-analysis. In: 2011 IEEE Fourth International Conference on Software Testing, Verification and Validation Workshops, pp. 366–375 (2011). https://doi.org/10.1109/ICSTW.2011.51

47. Kesrouani, K., Kanso, H., Noureddine, A.: A preliminary study of the energy impact of software in raspberry pi devices. In: 29th IEEE International Conference on Enabling Technologies: Infrastructure for Collaborative Enterprises, Bayonne, France (2020). https://hal.archives-ouvertes.fr/hal-02936861
48. Khoirom, S., Sonia, M., Laikhuram, B., Laishram, J., Singh, T.: Comparative analysis of Python and Java for beginners. Int. Res. J. Eng. Technol. **7**, 4384–4407 (2020)
49. Kholmatova, Z.: Impact of programming languages on energy consumption for mobile devices. In: Proceedings of the 28th ACM Joint Meeting on European Software Engineering Conference and Symposium on the Foundations of Software Engineering, pp. 1693–1695 (2020)
50. Kitchenham, B.A., et al.: Preliminary guidelines for empirical research in software engineering. IEEE Trans. Softw. Eng. **28**(8), 721–734 (2002). https://doi.org/10.1109/TSE.2002.1027796
51. Kitchenham, B.: Procedures for performing systematic reviews. Keele UK Keele Univ. **33**(2004), 1–26 (2004)
52. Kitchenham, B., Pearl Brereton, O., Budgen, D., Turner, M., Bailey, J., Linkman, S.: Systematic literature reviews in software engineering - a systematic literature review. Inf. Softw. Technol. **51**(1), 7–15 (2009). https://doi.org/10.1016/j.infsof.2008.09.009. https://www.sciencedirect.com/science/article/pii/S0950584908001390. Special Section - Most Cited Articles in 2002 and Regular Research Papers
53. Kivi, J., Haydon, D., Hayes, J., Schneider, R., Succi, G.: Extreme programming: a university team design experience. In: 2000 Canadian Conference on Electrical and Computer Engineering. Conference Proceedings. Navigating to a New Era (Cat. No.00TH8492), vol. 2, pp. 816–820, May 2000
54. Kovács, G.L., Drozdik, S., Zuliani, P., Succi, G.: Open source software for the public administration. In: Proceedings of the 6th International Workshop on Computer Science and Information Technologies, October 2004
55. Kruglov, A., Strugar, D., Succi, G.: Tailored performance dashboards-an evaluation of the state of the art. PeerJ **7**, e625 (2021)
56. Lu, H., Zhou, Y., Xu, B., Leung, H., Chen, L.: The ability of object-oriented metrics to predict change-proneness: a meta-analysis. Empir. Softw. Eng. **17**, 200–242 (2012). https://doi.org/10.1007/s10664-011-9170-z
57. Magalhães, G.G., Sartor, A.L., Lorenzon, A.F., Navaux, P.O.A., Schneider Beck, A.C.: How programming languages and paradigms affect performance and energy in multithreaded applications. In: 2016 VI Brazilian Symposium on Computing Systems Engineering (SBESC), pp. 71–78 (2016). https://doi.org/10.1109/SBESC.2016.019
58. Manotas, I., et al.: An empirical study of practitioners' perspectives on green software engineering. In: Proceedings of the 38th International Conference on Software Engineering, ICSE 2016, pp. 237–248. Association for Computing Machinery, New York (2016). https://doi.org/10.1145/2884781.2884810
59. Marino, G., Succi, G.: Data structures for parallel execution of functional languages. In: Odijk, E., Rem, M., Syre, J.-C. (eds.) PARLE 1989. LNCS, vol. 366, pp. 346–356. Springer, Heidelberg (1989). https://doi.org/10.1007/3-540-51285-3_51
60. Maurer, F., Succi, G., Holz, H., Kötting, B., Goldmann, S., Dellen, B.: Software process support over the internet. In: Proceedings of the 21st International Conference on Software Engineering, ICSE 1999, pp. 642–645. ACM, May 1999

61. Mehta, R.: Big Data Analytics with Java. Packt Publishing Ltd. (2017)
62. Mishra, S.K., Mishra, S., Bharti, S.K., Sahoo, B., Puthal, D., Kumar, M.: VM selection using DVFS technique to minimize energy consumption in cloud system. In: 2018 International Conference on Information Technology (ICIT), pp. 284–289. IEEE (2018)
63. Moser, R., Pedrycz, W., Succi, G.: A comparative analysis of the efficiency of change metrics and static code attributes for defect prediction. In: Proceedings of the 30th International Conference on Software Engineering, ICSE 2008, pp. 181–190. ACM (2008)
64. Moser, R., Pedrycz, W., Succi, G.: Analysis of the reliability of a subset of change metrics for defect prediction. In: Proceedings of the Second ACM-IEEE International Symposium on Empirical Software Engineering and Measurement, ESEM 2008, pp. 309–311. ACM (2008)
65. Musílek, P., Pedrycz, W., Sun, N., Succi, G.: On the sensitivity of COCOMO II software cost estimation model. In: Proceedings of the 8th International Symposium on Software Metrics, METRICS 2002, pp. 13–20. IEEE Computer Society, June 2002
66. Needleman, I.G.: A guide to systematic reviews. J. Clin. Periodontol. **29**(s3), 6–9 (2002). https://doi.org/10.1034/j.1600-051X.29.s3.15.x. https://onlinelibrary. wiley.com/doi/abs/10.1034/j.1600-051X.29.s3.15.x
67. Noureddine, A., Bourdon, A., Rouvoy, R., Seinturier, L.: A preliminary study of the impact of software engineering on GreenIt. In: 2012 First International Workshop on Green and Sustainable Software (GREENS), pp. 21–27 (2012). https:// doi.org/10.1109/GREENS.2012.6224251
68. Oliveira, W., Oliveira, R., Castor, F.: A study on the energy consumption of android app development approaches. In: 2017 IEEE/ACM 14th International Conference on Mining Software Repositories (MSR), pp. 42–52 (2017). https:// doi.org/10.1109/MSR.2017.66
69. Oliveira, W., Torres, W., Castor, F., Ximenes, B.H.: Native or web? A preliminary study on the energy consumption of android development models. In: 2016 IEEE 23rd International Conference on Software Analysis, Evolution, and Reengineering (SANER), vol. 1, pp. 589–593 (2016). https://doi.org/10.1109/SANER.2016. 93
70. Omar, H.K., Jumaa, A.K.: Big data analysis using apache spark MLlib and Hadoop HDFS with Scala and Java. Kurdistan J. Appl. Res. **4**(1), 7–14 (2019)
71. Panda, S.K., Jana, P.K.: An energy-efficient task scheduling algorithm for heterogeneous cloud computing systems. Clust. Comput. **22**(2), 509–527 (2018). https://doi.org/10.1007/s10586-018-2858-8
72. Pang, C., Hindle, A., Adams, B., Hassan, A.E.: What do programmers know about the energy consumption of software? IEEE Softw. (2015). https://doi.org/ 10.7287/PEERJ.PREPRINTS.886
73. Paulson, J.W., Succi, G., Eberlein, A.: An empirical study of open-source and closed-source software products. IEEE Trans. Softw. Eng. **30**(4), 246–256 (2004)
74. Pedrycz, W., Russo, B., Succi, G.: A model of job satisfaction for collaborative development processes. J. Syst. Softw. **84**(5), 739–752 (2011)
75. Pedrycz, W., Russo, B., Succi, G.: Knowledge transfer in system modeling and its realization through an optimal allocation of information granularity. Appl. Soft Comput. **12**(8), 1985–1995 (2012)
76. Pedrycz, W., Succi, G.: Genetic granular classifiers in modeling software quality. J. Syst. Softw. **76**(3), 277–285 (2005)

77. Pereira, R., et al.: Energy efficiency across programming languages: how do energy, time, and memory relate? In: Proceedings of the 10th ACM SIGPLAN International Conference on Software Language Engineering, SLE 2017, pp. 256–267. Association for Computing Machinery, New York (2017)

78. Pereira, R., et al.: Ranking programming languages by energy efficiency. Sci. Comput. Program. **205**, 102609 (2021). https://doi.org/10.1016/j.scico.2021.102609. https://www.sciencedirect.com/science/article/pii/S0167642321000022

79. Petrinja, E., Sillitti, A., Succi, G.: Comparing OpenBRR, QSOS, and OMM assessment models. In: Ågerfalk, P., Boldyreff, C., González-Barahona, J.M., Madey, G.R., Noll, J. (eds.) OSS 2010. IAICT, vol. 319, pp. 224–238. Springer, Heidelberg (2010). https://doi.org/10.1007/978-3-642-13244-5_18

80. Raschka, S., Patterson, J., Nolet, C.: Machine learning in Python: main developments and technology trends in data science, machine learning, and artificial intelligence. Information **11**(4) (2020). https://doi.org/10.3390/info11040193. https://www.mdpi.com/2078-2489/11/4/193

81. Rashid, M., Ardito, L., Torchiano, M.: Energy consumption analysis of algorithms implementations. In: 2015 ACM/IEEE International Symposium on Empirical Software Engineering and Measurement (ESEM), pp. 1–4 (2015). https://doi.org/10.1109/ESEM.2015.7321198

82. Rassokhin, D.: The C++ programming language in cheminformatics and computational chemistry. J. Cheminf. (2020). https://doi.org/10.1186/s13321-020-0415-y

83. Ronchetti, M., Succi, G., Pedrycz, W., Russo, B.: Early estimation of software size in object-oriented environments a case study in a CMM level 3 software firm. Inf. Sci. **176**(5), 475–489 (2006)

84. Rossi, B., Russo, B., Succi, G.: Modelling failures occurrences of open source software with reliability growth. In: Ågerfalk, P., Boldyreff, C., González-Barahona, J.M., Madey, G.R., Noll, J. (eds.) OSS 2010. IAICT, vol. 319, pp. 268–280. Springer, Heidelberg (2010). https://doi.org/10.1007/978-3-642-13244-5_21

85. Rossi, B., Russo, B., Succi, G.: Adoption of free/libre open source software in public organizations: factors of impact. Inf. Technol. People **25**(2), 156–187 (2012)

86. S., Z., Rozeva, A.: Data analytics and machine learning with Java. In: AIP Conference Proceedings, vol. 2048, pp. 1–8 (2018). https://doi.org/10.1063/1.5082135

87. Sahin, C., Pollock, L., Clause, J.: From benchmarks to real apps: exploring the energy impacts of performance-directed changes. J. Syst. Softw. **117**, 307–316 (2016). https://doi.org/10.1016/j.jss.2016.03.031. https://www.sciencedirect.com/science/article/pii/S0164121216000893

88. Scotto, M., Sillitti, A., Succi, G., Vernazza, T.: A relational approach to software metrics. In: Proceedings of the 2004 ACM Symposium on Applied Computing, SAC 2004, pp. 1536–1540. ACM (2004)

89. Scotto, M., Sillitti, A., Succi, G., Vernazza, T.: A non-invasive approach to product metrics collection. J. Syst. Architect. **52**(11), 668–675 (2006)

90. Shepperd, M.: Combining evidence and meta-analysis in software engineering. In: De Lucia, A., Ferrucci, F. (eds.) ISSSE 2009-2011. LNCS, vol. 7171, pp. 46–70. Springer, Heidelberg (2013). https://doi.org/10.1007/978-3-642-36054-1_2

91. Sillitti, A., Janes, A., Succi, G., Vernazza, T.: Measures for mobile users: an architecture. J. Syst. Architect. **50**(7), 393–405 (2004)

92. Sillitti, A., Succi, G., Vlasenko, J.: Understanding the impact of pair programming on developers attention: a case study on a large industrial experimentation. In: Proceedings of the 34th International Conference on Software Engineering, ICSE 2012, pp. 1094–1101. IEEE Press, Piscataway, June 2012

93. Sillitti, A., Vernazza, T., Succi, G.: Service oriented programming: a new paradigm of software reuse. In: Gacek, C. (ed.) ICSR 2002. LNCS, vol. 2319, pp. 269–280. Springer, Heidelberg (2002). https://doi.org/10.1007/3-540-46020-9_19

94. Stančin, I., Jović, A.: An overview and comparison of free python libraries for data mining and big data analysis. In: 2019 42nd International Convention on Information and Communication Technology, Electronics and Microelectronics (MIPRO), pp. 977–982 (2019). https://doi.org/10.23919/MIPRO.2019.8757088

95. Succi, G., Benedicenti, L., Vernazza, T.: Analysis of the effects of software reuse on customer satisfaction in an RPG environment. IEEE Trans. Softw. Eng. **27**(5), 473–479 (2001)

96. Succi, G., Paulson, J., Eberlein, A.: Preliminary results from an empirical study on the growth of open source and commercial software products. In: EDSER-3 Workshop, pp. 14–15 (2001)

97. Succi, G., Pedrycz, W., Marchesi, M., Williams, L.: Preliminary analysis of the effects of pair programming on job satisfaction. In: Proceedings of the 3rd International Conference on Extreme Programming (XP), pp. 212–215, May 2002

98. Valerio, A., Succi, G., Fenaroli, M.: Domain analysis and framework-based software development. SIGAPP Appl. Comput. Rev. **5**(2), 4–15 (1997)

99. Van Heddeghem, W., Lambert, S., Lannoo, B., Colle, D., Pickavet, M., Demeester, P.: Trends in worldwide ICT electricity consumption from 2007 to 2012. Comput. Commun. **50**, 64–76 (2014). https://doi.org/10.1016/j.comcom.2014.02.008. https://www.sciencedirect.com/science/article/pii/S0140366414000619. Green Networking

100. Vernazza, T., Granatella, G., Succi, G., Benedicenti, L., Mintchev, M.: Defining metrics for software components. In: Proceedings of the World Multiconference on Systemics, Cybernetics and Informatics, vol. XI, pp. 16–23, July 2000

101. Wohlin, C.: Guidelines for snowballing in systematic literature studies and a replication in software engineering. In: Proceedings of the 18th International Conference on Evaluation and Assessment in Software Engineering, pp. 1–10 (2014)

102. Yi, J., Ivanov, V., Succi, G.: Mining plausible hypotheses from the literature via meta-analysis. In: 2019 IEEE/ACM 41st International Conference on Software Engineering: New Ideas and Emerging Results (ICSE-NIER), pp. 33–36 (2019). https://doi.org/10.1109/ICSE-NIER.2019.00017

103. Zehra, F., Khan, D., Javed, M., Pasha, M.: Comparative analysis of C++ and python in terms of memory and time. Preprints 2020, 2020120516 (2020). https://doi.org/10.20944/preprints202012.0516.v1

Toward Inclusion of Children as Software Engineering Stakeholders

Letizia Jaccheri[1]([✉])(iD) and Sandro Morasca[2](iD)

[1] Norwegian University of Science and Technology (NTNU), Trondheim, Norway
letizia.jaccheri@ntnu.no
[2] Università degli Studi dell'Insubria, Varese, Italy
Sandro.Morasca@uninsubria.it

Abstract. Background: A growing amount of software is available to
children today. Children use both software that has been explicitly developed for them and software for general users. While they obtain clear
benefits from software, such as access to creativity tools and learning
resources, children are also exposed to several risks and disadvantages,
such as privacy violation, inactivity, or safety risks that can even lead
to death. The research and development community is addressing and
investigating positive and negative impacts of software for children one
by one, but no comprehensive model exists that relates software engineering and children as stakeholders in their own right. Aims: The final
objective of this line of research is to propose effective ways in which
children can be involved in Software Engineering activities as stakeholders. Specifically, in this paper, we investigate the quality aspects that
are of interest for children, as quality is a crucial aspect in the development of any kind of software, especially for stakeholders like children.
Method: Our contribution is based mainly on an analysis of studies at the
intersection between Software Engineering (especially software quality)
and Child Computer Interaction. Results: We identify a set of qualities
and a preliminary set of guidelines that can be used by researchers and
practitioners in understanding the complex interrelations between Software Engineering and children. Based on the qualities and the guidelines,
researchers can design empirical investigations to obtain deeper insights
into the phenomenon and propose new Software Engineering knowledge
specific for this type of stakeholders. Conclusions: This conceptualization
is a first step towards a framework to support children as stakeholders
in software engineering.

1 Introduction

A massive and ever growing amount of software intensive technologies is available
today to children of younger and younger age through sites such as Facebook
and Instagram, apps, games, and Internet of Things (IoT) devices embedded in,
for example, cars and toys. In some cases, the software is specifically made for
children, but, in other cases, it is made for the general users, like Facebook and

© Springer Nature Switzerland AG 2021
G. Succi et al. (Eds.): ICFSE 2021, CCIS 1523, pp. 201–213, 2021.
https://doi.org/10.1007/978-3-030-93135-3_13

Instagram, and also used by children. In some cases, the software aims at solving a problem, like helping children with reading difficulties to learn how to read [1] or children with obesity to exercise [2]. In other cases, the software's goal is to enhance children creativity [3], like Scratch [4]. In most cases, software is made for commercial and entertainment purposes, like war games.

With the advancement of technology and the development of new IoT applications, games, and social media sites, it is getting increasingly difficult to keep up with the associated threats and vulnerabilities for all stakeholders, and especially for children. The increasing presence of robotics, automated systems, and AI makes software more and more pervasive at all levels and for all ages. This has ethical and social implications for software engineers and users, especially for a particularly vulnerable category of users like children [5]. In the last few years, we have witnessed a series of problems generated in the digital ecosystem populated by software and children. Children can fall victim to cybersecurity threats like social engineering, cyber bullying, hacking, viruses, and damaging malware, cyber stalking, etc. through search engines, online advertisements and social networking websites such as Facebook, Twitter and lots of other websites [6]. The US National Safety Council, which tracks hot car deaths across the United States, reports than an average of 38 children under 15 die each year of heatstroke related to being trapped in a hot car—whether due to caregiver error or a child climbing into a vehicle and being unable to escape. Children's safety apps like "Kars 4 Kids" have been developed and are available to parents who want to eliminate these risks. Solutions that have been not specifically been designed for children, like airbags, pose serious risks for children. Available data indicate that, on average, children under the age of 13 are more likely to be harmed by an airbag than to be helped by it [7]. Mental health issues and even suicide are been caused by interaction with software. Instagram removed nearly 10,000 images related to suicide and self-harm every day in the months following the Molly Russell scandal (according to the Telegraph newspaper). Physical health issues, like obesity [8] and diabetes have been linked to the excessive use of videogames.

Given the greater exposure of children to digital technologies, the interaction design research community take into account children's abilities, interests, and developmental needs [9] when designing interfaces of software for children. International organizations that focus on Child's Rights, such as UNICEF [5] have recently started to examine the emerging ethical considerations regarding software development for children.

We observe that the community is producing new software for children to address the problems generated by software without considering the problems that the new software will produce. For example, [2] reports about development and evaluation of an exergame based on a shooting game, to improve physical well-being without considering how the other qualities (for example mental well-being, or privacy) will be impacted by this new game. This is a classical trade-off in software engineering: when optimizing one quality attribute, for example performance, one needs to be careful not to compromise other qualities, like for example readability and maintainability.

The final research objective of the line of research of our paper is the development of new knowledge which will enable to recognize children as competent stakeholders in Software Engineering.

Existing quality models, e.g., [10] already deal with some of the qualities that are important for children, e.g., security. However, it is not straightforward to figure out whether and to what extent they also deal with qualities like creativity or well-being. It is therefore necessary to build a comprehensive quality model for software development when children are stakeholders. This quality model should be used for several purposes: (1) assess the overall quality of the final software product; (2) assess the quality of the various artifacts produced during software development; (3) allow software stakeholders to make informed decisions about the inevitable trade-offs between all of the relevant qualities during the development of a software product for children; (4) allocate resources in an effective way to reach quality objectives with the available budget.

In this paper, we introduce an initial set of qualities that are relevant to children as Software Engineering stakeholders. The main qualities that we propose are: Security, Well-being, Fun, and Creativity. We also provide a preliminary set of guidelines for researchers and practitioners that can help them understand the complex interrelations between Software Engineering and children. Starting from the qualities and the guidelines, researchers can design empirical investigations to obtain deeper insights into the phenomenon and propose new software engineering knowledge specific for this type of stakeholders. Practitioners can use the provided knowledge to better understand children as stakeholders of their software products.

The remainder of this paper is organized as follows. Section 2 presents the relevant background on software quality and quality models. In Sect. 3, we propose a set of qualities that form a preliminary software quality model when children are primary stakeholders. In Sect. 4, we propose preliminary guidelines for research and practice. Section 5 provides conclusions and an outline for further work.

2   Software Quality Models

A number of different process and product qualities have been identified as relevant for SE practice and research and a large number of measures have been proposed in the literature for their assessment.

Qualities are traditionally divided into *internal* qualities, such as software size, structural complexity, cohesion, and coupling, and *external* qualities, such as reliability, usability, and performance [11]. Internal software qualities refer to a software product or process *per se*. External software qualities refer to a software product or process and to its users/stakeholders. For instance, the size of some software product depends only on the product itself, while its reliability depends on the product itself *and* the way the product is used.

The distinction between internal and external qualities has practical consequences. Internal qualities have no practical interest *per se*, while external qualities are the relevant ones from a practical point of view. The number of lines of code of a software product is simply a statistic, while an assessment of its reliability (e.g., how often it fails) is useful to developers and users/stakeholders.

However, this is not to say that internal measures are useless. An internal measure has practical value if a model exists that relates it to an external quality, i.e., if a model exists that can be used to quantify/estimate/predict an external quality of practical interest [12]. For instance, the number of lines of code is an useful size measure because it is used in several models for various external qualities, such as reliability, fault-proneness, and reusability.

Software quality models (e.g., those of the SQUARE 25000 series [10]) provide an organized view of a number of qualities that are believed to be important in the evaluation of software products (and processes). Quality models are usually general-purpose, in that their objective is to take into account the needs and goals of many and diverse software users and developers. However, to be practically used, quality models need to be "instantiated" for specific sectors, or companies, or even projects.

The fact that it was promoted from being a subcharacteristic of functionality in the ISO/IEC 9126-1:2001 standard to being a full-fledged characteristic in the ISO/IEC 25010:2011 standard shows that Security has become a fundamental quality for all types of software over the years. Security has five subcharacteristics in the ISO/IEC 25010:2011 standard: 1) confidentiality, i.e., allowing only authorized actors to access data; 2) integrity of software or its data; 3) non-repudiation, i.e., proof of the occurrence of actions or events that have taken place; 4) accountability, e.g., traceability of actions, such as transactions; 5) authenticity, i.e., identifiability of the actors interacting with software.

The ISO/IEC 25010:2011 standard also includes a "Quality in Use" model, which includes five characteristics, which are about how a software product interacts with its stakeholders, namely, 1) Effectiveness, 2) Efficiency, 3) Satisfaction, 4) Freedom from Risk, and 5) Context Coverage. Satisfaction is refined into Usefulness, Trust, Pleasure, and Comfort. Freedom from Risk encompasses: Economic Risk Mitigation, Health and Safety Risk Mitigation, and Environmental Risk Mitigation. Subcharacteristic Health and Safety Risk Mitigation is the one that is most related to safety, but it is quite generic, in that it is related to potential risk to people in the context of use. We can envision physical and mental risks related to the use of software.

To the best of our knowledge, no quality models have been proposed or specifically tailored for software for children, which also balance security, the various dimensions of well-being, fun and creativity.

3   Relevant Product Qualities for Children

It is therefore necessary to build a comprehensive quality model for software development when children are stakeholders To this end, in addition to being functionally correct, software products must have adequate levels of a number of qualities that are specifically relevant for children.

It is certainly too early to identify the quality levels (i.e., the thresholds and constraints) that need to be satisfied by software products for children. However, as a necessary preliminary step, we need to identify the qualities themselves that are of interest when children are stakeholders.

Quality models were generally introduced in such a way that they could be customized for specific application domains, for specific users, and for specific goals and needs. However, they were all probably conceived with grown-ups as stakeholders, and there is no indication that children were included in the set of stakeholders even as an afterthought. However, given the ever-increasing pervasiveness of software, children are a set of stakeholders that is becoming more and more important, since software is already affecting children's lives and will affect them more and more in the years to come.

We here propose a preliminary set of qualities that are specifically relevant for children, in several classes of applications, both those explicitly developed for children (e.g., games, etc.) and those developed for the general users (e.g., social media, etc.), but with children as stakeholders. Some qualities have already been addressed in existing quality models, but others may be missing or they may not have received sufficient emphasis.

The relation between the software and the child is bidirectional. On the one hand, it is important that the software exhibit some specified characteristics, but on the other hand is important that the child be empowered with knowledge necessary to interact with the software so that this characteristic is achieved. For example, for security, on one hand, the software must be designed and developed so that it does not have security traps. On the other hand, each child must be empowered with knowledge and awareness about security. The same holds for fun, creativity, and well-being.

3.1 Security

Security is an important characteristics of all software products and gets even more importance when it comes to software for children.

Ensuring secure interaction between children and a software system entails several different sub-challenges. The two most important subcharacteristic are:

- **Cybersecurity** is related to all those threats that may affect teenagers and countermeasures to support teens and their parents and the awareness that teenagers have on the various cybersecurity threats. For example, [6] reports an investigation about teen agers and cybersecurity awareness. A mobile app called CyberAware, destined to cybersecurity education and awareness is reported in [13].
- Privacy is related to how to ensure that private information about the children is not made public (**privacy**). Privacy is a characteristics of the software system, that has to be carefully addressed by the software engineers. How to deal with own information and how to share online, is a skill that children and teenagers have to acquire. [14] reports about the role of parents of influencing children's willingness to disclose information online (Fig. 1).

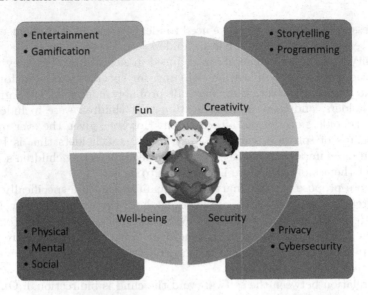

Fig. 1. Preliminary quality model for children software. Uses picture designed by user10320847/Freepik.

In this respect, education plays a fundamental role. It is of paramount importance to ensure that children are fully aware of the importance of protecting public data (cybersecurity) and own data (privacy).

The ISO/IEC 25010:2011 standard's subcharacteristic that is most closely related to the above issues is Confidentiality.

3.2   Well-Being

Well-being has physical, mental, and social aspects that need to be identified and addressed, as follows.

- **Physical** well-being is addressed for example by the studies about exergames which show how children who suffer from game addiction and obesity [8] may become physically active [2].
  In [15], the authors have studied how healthcare games and applications for toddlers who suffer from respiratory issues. Physical well-being can also be related to safety, like for example, addressing the question of how to ensure that cyber physical systems (like robots, cars, and even digital toys) do not physically harm children safety.
- Concerning the **mental** dimension, [16] reports about how to develop software for motivating adolescents with Intellectual Disabilities to become active.
- We define **social** well-being as the ability to establish and maintain healthy relations to other people. [17] introduces a digital story tool that facilitates the process of connecting human beings and increase empathy as a function of their relation.

There is a SQUARE 25010 subcategory of the Satisfaction characteristic of Quality in Use called "comfort": degree to which the user is satisfied with physical comfort.

3.3 Fun

One of the main qualities of software for children is that it should be fun. We define "fun" as the degree to which children enjoy interacting with a software product. Fun can be divided into two main subcharacteristics:

- Digital **Entertainment** is mainly associated with teenagers playing video games online. The interactivity of the medium allows a player to choose settings or the unfolding of a narrative, to participate in the narrative, pursue goals, accept challenges, and experience. The study of the relation between software and children has been dominated by computer games research [18].
- **Gamification** is defined "As a way to use game elements to learn" [19]. Gamification uses game-like features including points and various levels in a way that is not meant to be mere entertainment, but to provide solutions to problems and/or to provide training, practice, and interactions that are engaging while utilizing real-world objects" [20]. Gamification has been defined as a process of enhancing services with (motivational) affordances in order to invoke gameful experiences and further behavioral outcomes. The role of gamification in general software is to add a layer that provides the same psychological experiences as games do.
  Since the invention of the digital computer, games have been developed for education in various subjects, like mathematics and foreign languages, by adding a layer of gamification to subject learning, and according to [21], educational games were already popular in elementary and secondary schools in the 70's. Key influences on the successful use of games to support struggling readers (repetition, feedback, motivation, self-efficacy, parental beliefs) are reported in [1]

Overall, Fun can be seen as related to the Pleasure subcategory of the Satisfaction characteristic of Quality in Use, which also includes the pleasure to use a product to satisfy such as acquiring new knowledge and skills.

3.4 Creativity

Digital creativity for children is characterized by creativity support tools and activity designs to assist users engaged in creative work. Examples of creativity measures can be found in [22].

Digital creativity is defined as the creativity manifested in all forms that are driven by digital technologies. Digital creativity can be divided into two subcharacteristics.

- Creativity for **Storytelling**. Digital storytelling tools enable children to develop multimedia stories. As observed by [23], digital storytelling creativity cannot be achieved only by digital device to support the creative process. The software has to be introduced into already existing practices, including the interaction between the child, the teachers, and educational processes.
- Creativity for **Programming**. Since the public launch in May 2007, the Scratch Web site functions as a platform and online community for digital creativity for children, with people sharing, discussing, and remixing one another's coding projects [4]. Paper [24] explores digital creativity for children and proposes activities that combine art and programming for children.

4   Guidelines

We now provide two sets of preliminary guidelines, one for developers (in Sect. 4.1) and the other for researchers (in Sect. 4.2).

Common to both research and development is attention to Ethical issues. When developing for children and with children and when researching children as subjects, parents or guardians must grant practitioners and researchers consent to collect and store data. Procedures must be established in accordance with the national authorities for data. When health data are collected, one needs to be even more careful and requests for extra permissions must be addressed to health authorities. In general, data have to be anonymized and there must exist a precise plan for when to delete the data after the analysis. Special attention has to be given to ethical issues when children are subjects of empirical investigations for software development. More refined guidelines must be defined specifically addressing the involvement of children, similarly to existing guidelines for using university students as subjects in SE research while balancing research and educational goals [25].

The EU General Data Protection Regulation (GDPR) brought new rights for European residents to have control over their online personal data. In addition, online data controllers and processors must also take new steps for ensuring personal data is secured. GDPR[1] devotes one of its 178 recitals (Recital 38 Special protection of children's personal data). In the United States, Children's Online Privacy Protection Rule ("COPPA")[2] imposes certain requirements on operators of websites or online services directed to children under 13 years of age, and on operators of other websites or online services that have actual knowledge that they are collecting personal information online from a child under 13 years of age.

4.1   Guidelines for Development

Based on previous studies carried out about single qualities, like well-being [16] [15], we propose a preliminary set of guidelines that we outline next.

---

[1] https://gdpr-info.eu/.

[2] https://www.ftc.gov/enforcement/rules/rulemaking-regulatory-reform-proceedings/childrens-online-privacy-protection-rule.

1. The **child and the caregivers** should be included as much as possible in the software development process, including testing. It is not uncommon nowadays that children are invited to universities and to industries to participate in coding workshops. The ideas developed by the children should be incorporated as much as possible into the software developed by the companies, especially when the companies develop software for children.
2. **Each of the qualities** (and subqualities) should be considered **in each phase of the software development process.** If a quality is regarded as not to be of primary importance for a specific software development project, the software development team should discuss and document why it is not important. Consider for example fun. It cannot be intuitive to consider fun when developing a system for safety, but studies, see for example [26], reveal the importance of understanding and measuring fun in software systems that are devoted to children, which should be fun to use.

4.2 Guidelines for Research

Software engineering is a multi-disciplinary field, crossing many social and technological boundaries. Software engineering processes are studied by interdisciplinary efforts that combine technical, business, and social perspectives [27].

Thus, research should be carried out in the context of a general research question that should guide future research in Software Engineering with children:

– How can Software Engineering knowledge be extended to incorporate knowledge about children as stakeholders?

This general question can be refined in several ways. For instance, if the focus in on software development, a relevant research question may be

How to design processes for involving children in Software Engineering development?

As an example, when it comes to software quality, this general question can be refined as:

– What are the relevant qualities of software aimed at children?

We now introduce a few guidelines with the long term **aim** to develop validated interdisciplinary knowledge about **software quality and children** to help answer these research questions (and other related ones).

1. The building of software, whether especially conceived for children or not, must be studied from the point of view of various stakeholders, such as:
   – children of various ages, skills, and different social and cultural contexts and their caregivers.
   – software engineers who work in software projects that develop software for children.

- software engineers who work in software projects that develop software for all, since, as observed before, children use both specific software and software made for general users.

2. Researchers must be aware of the fact that technical aspects, although necessary, represent only a part of the set of problems that need to be addressed. To understand processes that develop and evolve software systems with children as stakeholders, researchers need to investigate tools and also the social and cognitive processes surrounding them. Research must draw from several different sources and disciplines.

3. Research in this field cannot be purely theoretical or speculative, but it must be carried out via empirical studies. It will be necessary to carry out systematic collections and analyses of empirical data to develop validated knowledge about why and how organizations, teams, and individual software engineers develop software [28] when children are, or should be considered, relevant stakeholders.

4. Data collection should be carried out for specific goals and in the framework of a quality model like the one we proposed in Sect. 3. For each quality, carefully designed templates should be used to gather information from each stakeholder about:
   - characteristics of the software under development;
   - characteristics of the software process in use, like agile, extreme programming, etc.;
   - the intention of children to participate in Software Engineering activities;
   - the intention of software engineers to integrate children in the Software Engineering activities;
   - relations between qualities and software development phases (Like for example, "in which phase do you work with mental well-being issues?")
   - the reciprocal relations between the network of qualities and their sub qualities
   - the relative importance of the qualities, like fun can be perceived as more important by small children, than by adolescents, or software developers.
   It will be important to translate these questions into a language that is understandable for children, see for example [26] for tools to elicit information from young children. Study [15] reports about data collection about the interaction of toddlers and their care givers with researchers and medical personnel. They have used Affinity diagram to structure the elicited knowledge.

5. More generally, it will be important to define what type of Software Engineering knowledge and education children need to be able to effectively participate in Software Engineering processes.

5 Conclusions and Future Work

We have proposed a model that puts children goals and well-being as an integral part of the software engineering processes, so that the children who use software systems will be offered new possibilities to influence the future of software systems and they will be made aware of threads that can be caused by software systems.

There is no common definition about how to characterize an individual as a child, given her age. Age-related development periods and examples of defined intervals include (according to [29]): newborn (ages 0–4 weeks); infant (ages 4 weeks - 1 year); toddler (ages 12 months-24 months); preschooler (ages 2–5 years); school-aged child (ages 6–12 years); adolescent (ages 13–19). In this work, we have studied children from the perspective of their relation to technology and we have presented related work and background that spans from research about toddlers and technology, like in [30] to research with adolescents, like in [16]. A limitation of our work is that we have not gone in depth into the different age categories and this distinction by age has to be addressed by further work.

We have reviewed studies devoted to understand single qualities, like creativity and guidelines to develop for one quality, but the qualities and the guidelines have not been evaluated in its wholeness yet. The proposed characteristics and sub-characteristics have to be validated by setting up systematic investigations of the literature and of the practice. We have proposed a road map to set up empirical investigations to grasp the perspective of the different stakeholders, including software engineers, children, care givers. The proposed road map (four main qualities and guidelines for practice and research) will enable researchers to set up the empirical investigations interventions in SE with children.

There is consensus in the SE literature about the distinction between qualities and the respective activities to achieve the given quality, like "maintenance" is an activity, but "maintainability" is the corresponding quality. On the contrary, in existing literature about software for children, Gamification is used for both the quality of the software and the activity of gamifying the software. The same applies to creativity. Further work will refine our model and propose increased understanding and better definitions of the qualities and the respective activities. We will also explore the relationships between existing quality models and the qualities of interest for children. For instance, while the Confidentiality of Security in the SQUARE 25010 standard can be somewhat mapped into our preliminary quality model, the role and relevance (if any) of the other subcharacteristics, i.e., integrity, non-repudiation, accountability, and authenticity, still need to be investigated. In general, further work will establish Software Engineering with children as a sub discipline of Software Engineering with a specific terminology, models, techniques, and methods.

References

1. Holmes, W.: Using game-based learning to support struggling readers at home. Learn. Media Technol. **36**(1), 5–19 (2011)
2. Hagen, K., Chorianopoulos, K., Wang, A.I., Jaccheri, L., Weie, S.: Gameplay as exercise. In: Proceedings of the 2016 CHI Conference Extended Abstracts on Human Factors in Computing Systems, pp. 1872–1878 (2016)

3. Papavlasopoulou, S., Giannakos, M.N., Jaccheri, L.: Empirical studies on the Maker Movement, a promising approach to learning: a literature review. Entertain. Comput. **18**, 57–78 (2017)
4. Resnick, M., et al.: Scratch: programming for all. Commun. ACM **52**(11), 60–67 (2009)
5. Office of Global Insight and Policy. Workshop report: AI and child rights policy. Technical report, United Nations Children Fund (2019)
6. Hamdan, Z., Obaid, I., Ali, A., Hussain, H., Rajan, A.V., Ahamed, J.: Protecting teenagers from potential internet security threats. In: 2013 International Conference on Current Trends in Information Technology (CTIT), pp. 143–152. IEEE (2013)
7. Peden, M., et al.: World report on child injury prevention. Technical report, World Health Organization (2008)
8. Vandewater, E.A., Shim, M., Caplovitz, A.G.: Linking obesity and activity level with children's television and video game use. J. Adolesc. **27**(1), 71–85 (2004)
9. Hourcade, J.P., et al.: Interaction design and children. Found. Trends® Hum.-Comput. Interact. **1**(4), 277–392 (2008)
10. ISO/IEC 25010. ISO/IEC 25010:2011, Systems and software engineering - Systems and software Quality Requirements and Evaluation (SQuaRE) - System and software quality models. ISO/IEC (2011)
11. Fenton, N.E., Bieman, J.M.: Software Metrics: A Rigorous and Practical Approach. Chapman & Hall/CRC Innovations in Software Engineering and Software Development Series. 3rd edn. Taylor & Francis (2014)
12. Morasca, S.: A probability-based approach for measuring external attributes of software artifacts. In: Proceedings of the 2009 3rd International Symposium on Empirical Software Engineering and Measurement, ESEM 2009, Lake Buena Vista, FL, USA, 15–16 October 2009, pp. 44–55. IEEE Computer Society, Washington (2009)
13. Giannakas, F., Kambourakis, G., Papasalouros, A., Gritzalis, S.: Security education and awareness for K-6 going mobile. Int. J. Interact. Mob. Technol. (iJIM) **10**(2), 41–48 (2016)
14. Lwin, M.O., Stanaland, A.J.S., Miyazaki, A.D.: Protecting children's privacy online: How parental mediation strategies affect website safeguard effectiveness. J. Retail. **84**(2), 205–217 (2008)
15. Høiseth, M., Giannakos, M.N., Alsos, O.A., Jaccheri, L., Asheim, J.: Designing healthcare games and applications for toddlers. In: Proceedings of the 12th International Conference on Interaction Design and Children, IDC 2013, pp. 137–146. Association for Computing Machinery, New York (2013)
16. Michalsen, H., Wangberg, S.C., Anke, A., Hartvigsen, G., Jaccheri, L., Arntzen, C.: Family members and health care workers' perspectives on motivational factors of participation in physical activity for people with intellectual disability: a qualitative study. J. Intellect. Disabil. Res. **64**(4), 259–270 (2020)
17. Escribano, J.G., Jaccheri, M.L., Maragoudakis, M., Sharma, K.: Digital storytelling for good with Tappetina game. Entertain. Comput. J. **30**, 100297 (2019)
18. Mayer, R.E.: Computer games in education. Ann. Rev. Psychol. **70**, 531–549 (2019)
19. Hamari, J., Koivisto, J., Sarsa, H.: Does gamification work?-a literature review of empirical studies on gamification. In: 2014 47th Hawaii International Conference on System Sciences, pp. 3025–3034. IEEE (2014)
20. De Byl, P.: Factors at play in tertiary curriculum gamification. Int. J. Game-Based Learn. (IJGBL) **3**(2), 1–21 (2013)

21. McLean, H.W.: Are simulations and games really legitimate? Audiov. Instr. **23**(7), 12–13 (1978)
22. Cherry, E., Latulipe, C.: Quantifying the creativity support of digital tools through the creativity support index. ACM Trans. Comput.-Hum. Interact. (TOCHI) **21**(4), 1–25 (2014)
23. Rubegni, E., Landoni, M.: Fiabot! Design and evaluation of a mobile storytelling application for schools. In: Proceedings of the 2014 Conference on Interaction Design and Children, pp. 165–174 (2014)
24. Papavlasopoulou, S., Giannakos, M.N., Jaccheri, L.: Exploring children's learning experience in constructionism-based coding activities through design-based research. Comput. Hum. Behav. **99**, 415–427 (2019)
25. Carver, J.C., Jaccheri, L., Morasca, S., Shull, F.: A checklist for integrating student empirical studies with research and teaching goals. Empir. Softw. Eng. **15**(1), 35–59 (2010)
26. Read, J.C., MacFarlane, S., Casey, C.: Endurability, engagement and expectations: measuring children's fun. In: Interaction Design and Children, vol. 2, pp. 1–23. Shaker Publishing Eindhoven (2002)
27. Fitzgerald, B., Stol, K.-J.: Continuous software engineering: a roadmap and agenda. J. Syst. Softw. **123**, 176–189 (2017)
28. Easterbrook, S., Singer, J., Storey, M.-A., Damian, D.: Selecting empirical methods for software engineering research. In: Shull, F., Singer, J., Sjøberg, D.I.K. (eds.) Guide to advanced empirical software engineering, pp. 285–311. Springer, London (2008). https://doi.org/10.1007/978-1-84800-044-5_11
29. Sein, M.K., Henfridsson, O., Purao, S., Rossi, M., Lindgren, R.: Action design research. MIS Q. **35**(1), 37–56 (2011)
30. Marques, M.R., Quispe, A., Ochoa, S.F.: A systematic mapping study on practical approaches to teaching software engineering. In: 2014 IEEE Frontiers in Education Conference (FIE) Proceedings, pp. 1–8. IEEE (2014)

Author Index

Printed in the United States
by Baker & Taylor Publisher Services